Consider the Earth

CONSIDER THE EARTH

Environmental Activities for Grades 4–8

Second Edition

Julie M. Gates

1999
TEACHER IDEAS PRESS
A Division of
Libraries Unlimited, Inc.
Englewood, Colorado

To Randy, whose encouragement
and belief in me keeps me going.

TEACHER IDEAS PRESS
A Division of
Libraries Unlimited, Inc.
P.O. Box 6633
Englewood, CO 80155-6633
1-800-237-6124
www.lu.com/tip

Library of Congress Cataloging-in-Publication Data

Gates, Julie M., 1949-
    Consider the earth : environmental activities for grades 4-8 /
Julie M. Gates. -- 2nd ed.
    xi, 246 p. 22x28 cm.
    Includes bibliographical references and index.
    ISBN 1-56308-725-1 (softcover)
    1. Environmental education--Activity programs.   2. Environmental
education--Experiments.   I. Title.
GE77.G38   1999
372.3'57044--dc21
                                                    99-11611
                                                       CIP

CONTENTS

INTRODUCTION

Environmental education is a combination of learning through self-discovery and learning from those who are more knowledgeable. Children cannot develop rich inquisitive minds simply by listening to others or by assimilating what a teacher expounds. Students must discover for themselves through a process of gathering data, interpreting data, and drawing conclusions for what it is they want to know. Children are fed from the minute they are born and later learn to feed themselves. Similarly, those children must learn to feed on knowledge and not accept constantly being fed by others. Life takes on more meaning if discovered experientially. In this learning process, a teacher, being a parent, sibling, friend, or classroom teacher, cannot be omitted. Knowledge is gained slowly, and nobody is as essential in that process as a teacher. A good teacher will guide and provide explanations and incentive, and not dictate or presume righteousness. A teacher helps awaken creativity and curiosity in young minds, an essential quality in a knowledgeable person.

In an era when so much emphasis is placed on the environment, it is imperative that young children learn about that environment in a beneficial way. Children should grow up feeling an affinity with their environment rather than taking it for granted. If children do not actively learn about their environment as they grow, they may be deprived of those experiences when they are grown. Then what can they do? How can they learn to love something that no longer exists in a pleasurable form? Our environment will always be with us. The question is, in what state? Do we want our children to only experience an urban environment, or do we want them to know of the beauty and opulence of the natural environment as well? Cities will exist forever, but the natural environment will not unless we all take pains, every day, to preserve it. Preserving our natural environment means learning about its every facet, knowing it, understanding it, appreciating it, and having a rapport with it. One cannot preserve something unless one understands it and knows its importance.

Children are curious about and sensitive to their environment. Consequently, they need to explore all the different facets of their environment, learn how it is assembled, and how one element invariably affects another. Everything on Earth works for the benefit of all others. Without nutrients, plants cannot grow. Without plants, people cannot live. Yet, over the years humans have adversely affected the natural world. We make it difficult for the natural world to live and grow in harmony with the human population. The Earth changes naturally, but people accelerate those changes, and so much so sometimes, that the Earth's natural balances are upset.

Nature works in cycles. These cycles are part of an interwoven, interrelated whole called an *ecosystem*, or ecological system. Ecosystems are interrelated and independent communities of plants and animals interacting with their total surroundings. There are many individual ecosystems on Earth, but the world as a whole is one vast ecosystem. People have a direct influence and effect upon this great ecosystem, and only by understanding its intricacies can we correct our ecological mistakes of the past and prevent new ones from occurring in the future.

There is a great discrepancy between our unlimited needs and nature's limited resources. Children must learn to understand this concept and how to deal with it. Otherwise, our unlimited needs are going to deplete nature's limited resources completely. Forests are a prime example. Hundreds of years ago, trees were chopped down for fuel and materials. As an area was consumed, people moved to other areas. This scenario is no longer possible. The greater the number of people, the faster resources are consumed. In this case, it is not just the trees that are wasted. Forests provide homes for birds, insects, and other animals. Trees hold water, and the roots keep the soil from eroding and washing away. By cutting down trees, people upset the balance between different living things and the Earth itself.

The interconnection of living things is called *ecology*. When changes are introduced quickly, the ecology is upset. People must decide whether these changes are worth the accomplishments they are trying to implement. People must also realize that if one nation upsets the ecology, the effect spreads around the world. If resources are used wastefully in one country, the rest of the world is also deprived.

Environmental education's main aim is to produce knowledgeable citizens concerning the interrelationships of the environment and the problems associated with it. People must be made aware of these problems and how to solve them.

Major objectives to keep in mind while studying environmental education are to help children acquire a succinct understanding of our inseparable part in the ecosystem and that we are able to alter the balance of these interrelationships quickly and drastically. Environmental education studies will give children a better understanding of the biophysical environment and a better understanding of natural resources and their characteristics, distribution, interrelationships, and uses. Children will also develop an understanding of the problems facing people concerning their biophysical environment.

Our ecosystem consists of people, their cultures, and the biophysical environment. The biophysical environment is composed of two groups: physical things, or nonliving things such as sunlight, water, air, and rock, and living things, things that live in the physical environment and help build up that environment but also help change it. Because people are able to alter things, either by strengthening, weakening, or maintaining the interrelationships in this system, they must develop a quality system interacting through civilization with their biophysical environment. In order to be able to develop a quality environment and maintain it, people must first understand how to plan conscientiously to preserve what we now possess and avoid its destruction in the future.

Children should have an awareness and an understanding of their community and its myriad problems, such as inadequate environmental planning; air, water, and noise pollution; community blight; and inadequate arrangements dealing with such environmental problems. The citizens within a community need to be more actively involved in helping to make decisions that affect their environment. Conservation education not only pertains to natural resources but encompasses a wider span of different environments, including cities and their associated problems.

This book is divided into eight categories representing eight aspects of the environment specifically because each aspect of the environment is important unto itself. Each part must be viewed in a different way, then assimilated into a whole. If one part is eliminated, the others are meaningless. Discover each part separately, then combine them to see how each fits together like a puzzle to produce our irreplaceable Earth. This book provides activity-oriented experiences to enable anyone to discover and learn about the different aspects of the environment. The activities are not always easy or quick, but they are always fun and enlightening.

Children living in an urban environment have a completely different viewpoint on life than do children living in a rural environment. This book is designed so that both urban and rural children may profit from it. Of course, there are certain experiments that are suited more to urban children than rural children and vice versa, but as a rule all children can learn from the activities if they do them and use all of their senses.

After going through the activities in this book, children will have gained certain understandings—humans are animals and are living organisms; animals differ from plants in their ability to move from place to place and in their inability to make their own food; and humans have five senses that help them to enjoy and to understand their world.

The level referred to for each activity is designated as lower or upper. Lower refers to grade levels four through six, and upper refers to grade levels six through eight. Many activities are overlapping or suitable for both levels. Use your discretion in determining the activities' suitability for your students. Vocabulary words are introduced in each new activity and are defined at the end of each section. Projects, instruments, or constructions made in earlier activities may be used subsequently in later activities, so save them. In addition, materials and directions for building or producing items in an activity are certainly only offered as guides or suggestions; please use your imagination.

Every child is an individual, determined in part by his or her genes. Most important, a child's environment is crucial to his or her mental development. People have highly developed brains, which means they can control, change, preserve, or destroy their environment. People are the only animals who destroy their environment, either deliberately or unconsciously. Because humans have a conscience, they are capable of moral judgment and are able to change their behavior concerning preservation of the environment.

1

SOIL

Soil is one of the main supporters of life. Without it, plants could not grow. Without plants, people could not live. Soil appears lifeless and useless, but it is teeming with life and is always changing. These changes are brought about because of regional conditions in which soil is situated, because of the materials of which it is composed, and because of the live organisms within it. Soil is composed of living, or *biotic*, and nonliving, or *abiotic*, materials, from gophers and ants to microscopic plants and animals to decomposed material and detritus feeders. The parent material of soil, or the basic ingredient of which it is composed, is rock or minerals, which is entirely inorganic. *Inorganic* means that none of the component parts were derived from living matter. Parent materials may be derived from wind and weather, freezing and thawing, the pull of gravity, or the movement of streams. Without organic matter, parent material will remain infertile and therefore inhospitable to plant and animal life. Parent material is made fertile by the addition of organic matter—plants that have died and decayed, thereby enriching the soil. The most primitive plant, providing enriched organic matter to the soil, is the lichen. *Lichens* are a combination of fungi, which are parasitic, and algae, which is the food-producing part. These tiny plants can obtain moisture from the air and from the dew that condenses on rock surfaces. Their roots penetrate into the rock and cause it to disintegrate. Lichens help break down the rock and add organic matter to the soil. In time, this process allows other plants to take hold as the soil becomes richer. Other living organisms are also in the soil, such as one-celled protozoa, ants, worms, and burrowing animals. All these add organic matter to the soil.

Life in the soil is dependent upon water content, minerals, and gases, which fill the open spaces between the solid particles. All of these things determine the fertility, texture, and physical properties of the soil. Decomposed materials greatly enhance the fertility of the soil. Therefore, there is a great need in our ecosystems for both living and nonliving organisms. The balance of nature would be greatly offset if this were not true. Soil is valuable yet carelessly wasted. It must be conserved in order to support the many life forms on Earth.

Soil is a complex of rock particles of different sizes, plant roots, microorganisms, and decaying organic matter. Soil is layered, graduating from fine topsoil particles to the subsoil and coarser particles below to the parent rock.

A soil profile is an analysis of the composition of the soil in an area. A vertical cut is made into the soil, exposing a profile of various layers. These layers are called *horizons*. The surface layer is made of either wholly or partially decomposed material. The next layer is still predominantly organic and contains minerals derived from the parent material. The next horizon is mainly composed of parent material in a state of disintegration. The last layer is only rock unchanged by weathering. Horizon depths and the number of horizons found within an area vary from one place to another.

The top layer of soil is rather dark because of the accumulation of molds and decayed organic matter. Below this are lighter layers, which have been changed by plant activity, and through which run the roots of trees, absorbing minerals. Minerals from the lower layers are brought up to the upper layer through the roots of plants.

Water, temperature, air, and other climatic factors affect soil formation. Soil forms more slowly in areas of low rainfall and low temperatures. In areas of high rainfall and high temperatures, the vegetation is greater, adding larger amounts of organic matter to the soil. Hot desert conditions produce soil with sparse vegetation. In colder areas, the organic matter accumulates but does not decompose as readily.

Natural forces break down rock into soil with tremendous energy. Temperature changes are also effective in breaking down rocks. Materials expand when their temperature increases, and they contract when it decreases. Temperature changes are limited to thin surface layers, causing these layers to pull apart from the rock below. *Exfoliation* is when the layers peel off in sheets. When water freezes, it expands, subjecting the rock to enormous pressure.

Rock materials must be broken into fragments before soil can be formed. Weathering, breakage, freezing, thawing, wind, and water erosion take place upon the bare rock. Plants also aid in breaking up rocks. Lichens are the primary plants that help break down rocks. Lichens cling to rocks, breaking them down in one of two ways—they either secrete acids that dissolve substances in the rock, or they loosen particles from the rock's surface by shrinking and swelling in dry and wet weather. The tiny particles that flake off are washed or blown into depressions or cracks. They are accompanied by tiny plants and small invertebrates. Larger plants anchor their roots in crevices and loosen rock fragments. In time, what once was hard rock is now an accumulation of weathered materials in which vegetation has begun to grow. To put it simply, that is how soil is formed.

Fungi and bacteria bring about the decay of plant and animal remains. Decay returns minerals to the soil and produces humus. Bacteria also enrich the soil by bringing nitrogen to the soil from the air. These nitrogen-fixers get their energy from humus. *Saprophytic fungi* are the primary organisms of decomposition. They secrete enzymes that break down organic molecules in dead organisms.

Most living things require air to function properly. The only exceptions are anaerobic bacteria, living without air deep in the soil and at the bottom of lakes. Living bacteria in the soil use up the oxygen and leave an excess of carbon dioxide. Therefore, cultivation of the soil is necessary to provide a fresh supply of oxygen. This cultivation can be achieved by burrowing animals, by plant roots, or by people with the use of plows and hoes. Earthworms' tunnels comprise a network of air passages through the soil. Plant roots perforate the soil, also creating air passageways.

Air provides oxygen for oxidizing minerals before plants can absorb this mineral matter. The minerals also must be dissolved in water because plant roots can absorb only water-soluble materials. The quantity of water the soil is able to hold is dependent upon the makeup of the soil and the size of the particles in the soil.

There are many cyclic processes taking place within the soil, producing materials to be absorbed by plant roots. There are organic and inorganic cycles, constantly moving and enmeshing with each other. There are two major cycles referred to as *biogeochemical cycles*. Chemical elements involve biological organisms and their geologic environment.

One of these cycles is the carbon cycle. Carbon is returned to the environment almost as quickly as it is removed and involves carbon dioxide from the atmosphere. Plants manufacture the carbon compounds used by other living things. Animals release carbon dioxide back into the air as waste products. Plants use carbon dioxide and release oxygen during photosynthesis. The decomposers break down the waste products and release carbon dioxide into the atmosphere. Simply put, the basic movement of carbon is from the air to producers to consumers to decomposers and back to the air.

The other major cycle is the nitrogen cycle. Atmospheric nitrogen must be converted to nitrogen salts, or *nitrates*, before living things can use it. This conversion is accomplished by the nitrogen-fixing bacteria in the soil. The nitrates may then be used by plant roots. When an organism dies, the decomposers break them down and release nitrogen in the form of ammonia. These nitrifying bacteria use the ammonia and convert it into nitrites and nitrates to be taken up once again by the roots of plants. Denitrifying bacteria also release nitrogen into the atmosphere. These organisms use nitrites and produce nitrogen, which is released into the atmosphere.

Soil was originally built by erosion, but erosion can also destroy soil. Soil is made over a countless span of time, but soil can be depleted in only a few years through erosion.

- *Wind erosion* occurs where there is little rainfall or where inadequate amounts of vegetation cover the soil. Wind erosion is enhanced where land has been plowed and left bare, especially in areas of very dry soil.

Overgrazed land is subject to wind erosion. Overcultivation of land increases the soil's susceptibility to wind erosion.

- *Water erosion* occurs wherever there is a greater amount of rainfall and runoff. It also is most severe in areas devoid of good vegetative ground cover.
- *Sheet erosion* is a form of soil washing. On areas that are not adequately covered with vegetation, sheet wash wears the soil away in layers. It is a consequence of the soil's inability to absorb and hold water.
- *Rill erosion* cuts away the topsoil. One heavy rain can cut deep channels in freshly tilled soil on a slope. Rills, or very small brooks, lead to gully erosion. Gullies will eventually cut through the mantle into the underlying bedrock.

The slope of the land and the length of the slope determine the strength of the water's attack on the soil. After soil erodes, it fills our lakes and water supplies with sediment. Sediment may kill fish and animals and contaminate our waters. Sediments are an obvious indication of valuable topsoil washed away through careless use of the land.

The following are some examples of soil conservation measures:

- *Contour plowing* is farming on the contour by going around the hillsides with curving furrows. The furrows retain runoff and allow rain to percolate into the soil. This technique reduces the amount of soil that is washed away.
- *Terracing* consists of building low ridges on the contour to retain runoff water. Greater absorption is achieved, and the runoff is guided to the sides of fields.
- *Strip cropping* is planting rows of close-growing plants between the rows of crops. These rows retain soil that washes from the cultivated rows.
- *Crop rotation* consists of the rotation of soil-depleting crops with crops that help build the soil.
- *Mulching* involves leaving the residue from the harvested crops on top of the soil. This technique reduces soil erosion and water runoff and evaporation. It also aids in beneficial bacterial growth in the soil.
- *Cover crops* are plants that grow closely together. They are planted when the field is not being used for crop cultivation, and they help protect the soil from wind and water erosion.
- *Shelter belts and windbreaks* help reduce wind erosion and snow drifts. They are strips of shrubs and trees planted near the cultivated fields.

The following are several generalizations about soil to keep in mind while studying soil:

1. Soil is composed of decomposed rock particles and plant and animal materials.

2. There is air in the soil, important for living organisms.

3. The soil is made up of three layers: the topsoil, the subsoil, and crumbly rock that rests on solid rock.

4. Soil is a water reservoir for plants.

5. Rocks break up in many different ways. They break up by:

   heating and cooling

   the force of the wind

   the cutting action of sand

   moving water—carrying sand, gravel, and rocks

   the oxidation of certain minerals

   weak acids formed from CO_2 in the air and organic acids released from plant roots

   freezing water formed in cracks that expands

   the weight and movement of glaciers wearing down parent rock and grinding it into soil

6. Microorganisms hasten the decay of organic matter. Bacteria and molds break down dead plant and animal remains into fine particles called humus.

 ## Activity 1: Soil Formation

OBJECTIVE:	To develop an understanding of how soil is formed
MATERIALS:	Rock samples, hot plate, ice, water, thermometer, plastic jug with a lid, limestone/sandstone, vinegar
RESOURCES:	Soil conservation officer, rock and mineral identification books
LEVEL:	Lower to upper
SETTING:	Classroom
TIME:	30–45 minutes
VOCABULARY:	Contraction, expansion, natural resources, renewable

LESSON DESIGN

Some parts of this activity may be optional, depending on the type of parent material available in your area, or a certain kind of rock may need to be purchased or borrowed from the geology department of a local college.

Rub two pieces of limestone or sandstone together (bricks or concrete can be substituted). Observe how long it takes to accumulate a big pile. This activity demonstrates soil formation by rubbing and grinding like the action of glaciers millions of years ago.

Heat a small piece of limestone on a hot plate, then drop it quickly into a pan of ice water. The rock should crack or break. This demonstrates soil formation by contraction and expansion.

Fill a plastic container with water, cover it with a lid, and freeze it. As the water expands, the sides will bulge out or lift off the lid. Another example of freezing and thawing is when water freezes in the cracks of rocks and pavement.

Put small pieces of limestone in a little vinegar and heat the vinegar on a hot plate. Notice the bubbles forming on the limestone. The bubbles are carbon dioxide gas made from carbon and oxygen released from the limestone through a chemical change in the rock, which was caused by the acidic effects of the vinegar. All the limestone would break down eventually if you continued with this process. This demonstrates soil formation through chemical action.

Soil is formed slowly from rocks by the action of glaciers, changes in temperature by contracting and expanding, weathering processes from water and wind, and chemical factors such as that which is done by plants. Carbon dioxide, which is given off by plants, dissolves in soil moisture and forms a weak carbonic acid. This acid reacts with limestone and will help decompose it. Lichens are also instrumental forces in breaking down rock into soil through the same process.

Supplementary Activities

See if you can devise a different way for creating soil.

Dampen a soapless steel wool pad with water and lay it on a saucer. Let it sit for three or four days. At the end of this time period, pick up the steel wool pad and examine it. Oxygen combines with the iron in the steel wool pad to form iron oxide or rust. Iron in the surface of rocks forms iron oxide when exposed to damp air. It eventually crumbles away and helps form soil.

Questions

1. Is soil a renewable natural resource? How do you know?

2. Is soil formation an ongoing activity, or is the soil on Earth today all that we will ever have? Explain.

Activity 2: Soil Particle Size

OBJECTIVE:	To find out if soil particles are all the same size or kind
MATERIALS:	Various soil samples, water, newspaper, jar, scale, marbles
LEVEL:	Lower to upper
SETTING:	Classroom
TIME:	20–30 minutes

LESSON DESIGN

Fill a jar with water to within about two inches of the top. Pour in enough soil so that the jar is almost full. Cover the jar and shake it hard. Place the jar on a table to allow the soil to settle, which may require several hours. After the soil has settled, place a piece of cardboard next to the jar and draw a diagram of the different layers showing depth and particle size, and label each layer as best as possible (clay, silt, fine sand, coarse sand, and so forth). Repeat the process with several different soil samples from different places and compare the diagrams.

Fill a jar about three-fourths full with marbles. Put the sand in a measuring cup and pour it on top of the marbles until all of the marbles are covered. Tap the jar several times to help settle the sand. This activity demonstrates that coarse soils have pore spaces that can be filled by finer soils.

Soil particles vary greatly in size, from large (like the marbles) to minute (like sand). The large particles settle to the bottom first, and the finest settle in layers on top of each other more slowly. Soil is classified into three categories: sand, silt, and clay. Clay particles are the finest, followed by silt, then sand. Particles larger than sand are classified as gravel or stones. Most soils are a combination of all three in varying proportions. Pore space in coarser soils is larger and can be filled with finer soil, resulting in a dense soil. Sandy soils with no clay or silt particles filling these pore spaces cannot hold as much water because there is less surface area for the water to cling to, and the weight of the water causes it to run off. If soil particles fill the large pores, the soil can hold more water because there is more surface area for the water to cling to.

Activity 3: Soil Composition

OBJECTIVE:	To demonstrate that soil contains water, air, minerals and living things
MATERIALS:	Various soil samples, water, newspaper, paper cup, scale, jar
LEVEL:	Lower to upper
SETTING:	Classroom or outdoors
TIME:	30 minutes
PRE-ACTIVITIES:	Discussion of soil

LESSON DESIGN

Examine various soil samples by crumbling them between your fingers and spreading them out on newspapers. Separate and categorize the different parts: plant material, animal material, minerals, unknown materials, and the like. Analyze and describe the parts.

Put some soil in a jar. Quickly fill the jar with water and put on a lid. You should be able to observe bubbles rising from the soil. These bubbles are indicators of the presence of air in the soil. The size of the bubbles and how long they last helps determine the amount of air in the soil. Repeat the process with as many different kinds of soil as possible to see if all soils have the same amount of air.

Place some freshly dug soil in a paper cup and weigh it. Let the soil sit for a week and reweigh it. The second weighing should be lighter than the first because water from the soil has evaporated.

Supplementary Activities

Collect soil samples from the top of a hill, from a slope, and from the bottom of a valley. Compare them for moisture content and organic matter.

Find evidence of living things in the soil outdoors, such as tracks, holes, humps, diggings, and so forth.

Activity 4: Soil Types

OBJECTIVE:	To develop an understanding of different types of soil
MATERIALS:	4 soil samples, paper, pencils, water spray bottle, copies of charts (one for each group of 4 or 5 students; see Figures 1.2 and 1.3), rulers, glue, cardboard, yardsticks, shovel (pH paper and soil thermometers are optional)
LEVEL:	Lower to upper
SETTING:	Classroom and natural areas
TIME:	30 minutes for discussion, 30 minutes for the indoors activity, and 1-2 hours for the outdoors activity
VOCABULARY:	Duff, horizon, humus, litter, structure, subsoil, texture, topsoil
PRE-ACTIVITIES:	Class discussion of soil, types of soil, and vocabulary. Discuss the following aspects of soil:

Soil layers or horizons. Be able to mark where soil changes color and appearance in order to differentiate between the layers.

Texture (how the soil feels). Rub a moistened soil sample between thumb and finger. If it feels smooth or sticky, it is clayey. If it feels somewhat gritty and the particles cling to one another, it is loamy. If it feels gritty, it is sandy.

Structure (how the soil is put together geometrically). Break apart a lump of soil and match its characteristics with one of the following:

columnar

blocky

granular

platey

Fig. 1.1.

LESSON DESIGN

The class discussion can be held either the same day or a day prior to the activity, whatever is suitable time wise.

Activities A and B are best suited to the outdoors. Part A (Figure 1.2) can be done either inside or outside, but Part B (Figure 1.3) has to be done outside. If Part A is done inside, the teacher must collect soil samples from four different places. The students can either analyze the soil in the field or take the soil samples to the classroom.

Part A: Have four soil samples ready to analyze. Begin by observing them to see what they look like, feel like, and smell like. Observe their color, texture (what they feel like), and structure (how they are put together), then fill in Figure 1.2.

Sample No.	Color	Texture	Structure
1			
2			
3			
4			

Fig. 1.2.

Part B: Part B has to be done in four fairly different areas. Repeat the process for each area. Concentrate on two areas if four are impossible to find close to school.

Dig a hole 3 to 4 feet deep. Mark where the soil changes color and what it looks like (pH and temperature measurements are optional, depending on whether litmus paper and soil thermometers are available). Determine and record the information for each layer as shown in Figure 1.3.

When Figure 1.3 has been completed, construct a soil micromonolith.

Attach soil samples to the cardboard using appropriate labels to show a soil profile similar to Figure 1.4.

Litter (if existing)_____   Composition _____

Duff (if existing)_____   Composition _____

Humus (if existing) _____   Composition _____

Topsoil: Depth _____   Color _____

    Texture _____   Temperature _____

    Structure _____   pH _____

Subsoil: Depth _____   Color _____

    Texture _____   Temperature _____

    Structure _____   pH _____

Parent Material: Depth _____   Color _____

    Texture _____   Temperature _____

    Structure _____   pH _____

Fig. 1.3.

LITTER
HORIZON A
HORIZON B
HORIZON C

Fig. 1.4.

Supplementary Activities

Study a soil profile in a highway cut or excavation site. Identify the surface soil, subsoil, and parent material. Describe the differences in color and texture of the three layers.

Questions

1. Are all soil samples the same—the same texture, the same color, and the same structure?

2. How are soils different? How are they similar?

 ### *Activity 5: Comparison of Soils*

OBJECTIVE:	To be able to compare soils by growing plants in them
MATERIALS:	One sample of each of the following: topsoil, subsoil, eroded soil; 3 clay pots; bean seeds; water
RESOURCES:	Soil conservationist
LEVEL:	Upper
SETTING:	Classroom and outdoors
TIME:	30 minutes to set up, several weeks for observation
VOCABULARY:	Erosion, germination, subsoil, topsoil
PRE-ACTIVITIES:	Optional: talk by a soil conservationist about soil

LESSON DESIGN

Fill three clay pots with the following kinds of soils: topsoil from an unplowed field or a flower bed, subsoil from an area without grasses or an excavated site for a building, and soil from an eroded hillside or road bank. Plant a few bean seeds in each pot. Water each equally and place them in a warm, and preferably, sunny place. Compare the rate of germination and growth, recording how fast the beans in each pot grow as well as what each plant looks like.

Plants usually grow better in topsoil than subsoil. Plants take their nutrients from the soil. Soils that are high in organic matter are more productive than soils low in organic matter. Organic matter improves the soil by increasing its water-holding capacity, serving as a storehouse for nutrients, providing food for bacteria and other living things in the soil, and making it crumbly. These reasons are usually why topsoil is more fertile than subsoil. Eroded soil has lost almost all of its nutrients because they have either been washed or blown away.

Supplementary Activities

Plant a few seeds in soil from different parts of the community, such as an old lake bed, a wooded area, lake or river soil, or something similar. Keep track of their growth rates and compare them with the first three soil samples.

Questions

1. Which soil or soils grew and sustained the plants the best and the longest?

2. If there was no difference in growth rate between the soils, explain why this may be true.

3. If you were a farmer, why would it be important not only to keep your topsoil but to keep it rich in organic matter?

Activity 6: Soil Compaction and Permeability

OBJECTIVE:	To understand how compact or loose the soil is, and if this has any effect on plant growth
MATERIALS:	2 thumbtacks, a wide rubber band, thread spool with a ¼-inch hole, 12-inch length of a ¼-inch dowel, 2 #10 cans, water, pencil, 1 copy of the chart (see Figure 1.6) for each group of four to five students
LEVEL:	Upper
SETTING:	Classroom and schoolyard
TIME:	45–60 minutes
VOCABULARY:	Absorption, compaction, permeability
PRE-ACTIVITIES:	Select three or four areas around the school grounds such as lawn, field, flower bed, woods, or path.

LESSON DESIGN

Sharpen one end of the dowel. Measure and mark one inch from the sharpened point. From the other end, measure and mark 10, 1-inch lines. Number the lines from 1 to 10. Cut the rubber band and fasten it to the top of the spool with a thumbtack on each side. Put the dowel through the spool. Force the dowel into the soil by pushing on the spool until the soil reaches the line near the pointed end. Read the number at the top of the spool. This number is the soil compaction reading. Record the information on the chart in Figure 1.6.

Cut both ends from one of the cans. Shove the can into the ground approximately 2 inches. Fill the other can with one cup of water and pour it into the grounded can. Record the number of seconds it takes for the soil to absorb the water. Repeat the process at each area and record the results on the chart in Figure 1.6.

Supplementary Activities

Let the children follow the same procedure at their homes and bring in a soil sample to test.

Remove both ends of a 1-pound coffee can. Push one end of it about half way into the soil. Pour 1 cup of water into the can and begin timing how long it takes the water to soak into the soil. Repeat the same procedure in the same place several times in a row. Record your results. Repeat the same procedure in different areas where the soils are different. Record and then compare and contrast your results from each area.

Questions

1. Can soil get supersaturated with water? Explain.

2. What happens to the extra water in a supersaturated area?

3. How could you test the permeability of soil in an area with a lot of asphalt?

4. Which soil type holds water the longest? Why? Which soil type loses water the fastest? Why?

5. Which type of soil would be the best for growing plants?

6. What is the relationship between soil compaction and permeability?

7. What effect could heavily compacted soil have on plant growth? What effect could loosely compacted soil have on plant growth?

8. Which soil absorbed water the fastest? Which soil absorbed water the slowest? What do you think the reason for this is?

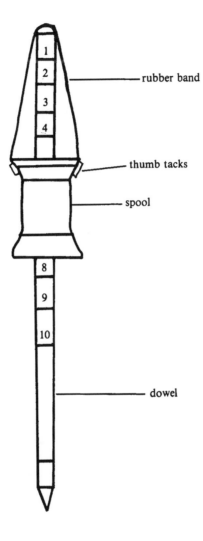

Fig. 1.5.

SOIL COMPACTION/ABSORPTION GUIDE

Site Description	Depth	Absorption Rate/Second	Soil Description	Conclusions

Fig. 1.6.

Activity 7: Capillary Action

OBJECTIVE:	To see how water moves through coarse, medium, and fine soil particles by capillary action
MATERIALS:	3 lamp chimneys, 3 wide-mouthed jars, coffee filters, rubber bands or string, ruler, clock, paper and pencil
LEVEL:	Lower to upper
SETTING:	Classroom
TIME:	30 minutes
VOCABULARY:	Capillary action
PRE-ACTIVITIES:	Discuss the concept capillary action

LESSON DESIGN

Secure the filters over the ends of each lamp chimney with string or a rubber band. Turn them upside down and fill each three-fourths full with a different kind of *dry* soil (sand, clay, soil with organic matter). Place the chimneys in the jars and pour water into the jars. Be sure *not* to pour water in the chimneys. Record how long it takes for the water to move up 1 inch, 2 inches, 3 inches, 4 inches, and to the top, if ever (see Figure 1.7). Moisture moves through soil against gravity, by capillary action, which is caused by the attraction between water molecules and soil particles. Capillary water depends on the size of the soil particles and the condition of the soil. If spaces are large between soil particles, the attraction between water molecules and soil particles will not be enough to overcome the weight of the water, and it will not rise very much, but the movement will be rapid because of little friction. This behavior is indicative of sandy areas. In fine-textured soils, like clay, because the particles are closer together, the attraction is greater, so water will rise more slowly but higher. In soil with organic matter, moisture will move from wetter soil to drier soil. Capillary water will move slowly and not very far. However, enough moisture moves to the roots of plants to sustain them.

Soil Type	Capillary Time				
	1"	2"	3"	4"	top
Sand					
Clay					
Soil with Humus					

Fig. 1.7.

Supplementary Activities

To observe capillary action in plants, place a stalk of celery with leaves intact in a jar of water with red food coloring. After several hours, the celery stalk and leaves should be tinged a light red. Experiment with other plants or flowers (white daisies work well) and different colors of dye. Place a flower in one color for a day, then switch it to another color to see what happens. Try pouring colored water on a potted plant and a plant in a jar of water. See if both change, and if so, which one changes first.

Questions

1. What determines how far and how fast capillary water will move in soil?

2. What is capillary action?

3. What happens to soil moisture when capillary water moves to the surface?

4. How can surface water evaporation be reduced?

Activity 8: Soil Absorption and Water-Holding Capacity

OBJECTIVE:	To be able to differentiate among soils with good and bad absorption rates, and explain why one is more favorable than the others
MATERIALS:	2 lamp chimneys, 2 jars, rubber bands or string, coffee filters, clock with a second hand, chart, soil sample without grasses, soil sample sample with grasses
LEVEL:	Upper
SETTING:	Classroom
TIME:	20 minutes
VOCABULARY:	Absorption, permeability, water-holding capacity

LESSON DESIGN

Secure the cloths or filters over one end of each lamp chimney. Turn each chimney upside down and fill about three-fourths full with the two different types of soil. Both should be very dry. Put each chimney in small mouthed jars so that the filters do not touch the bottom of the jars. Pour equal amounts of water (about 2 cups) into each chimney. Time how long it takes the water to *begin* to drip into the jars. Then time how long the water continues to drip and record how much water comes from each soil sample.

Soil devoid of organic matter tends to pack together and have fewer spaces. Soil with organic matter can absorb water faster and retain it longer. Because humus has a water-holding capacity of several hundred percent, it acts like a sponge. Water is also held in the pores between soil particles. The increased water-holding capacity of soils high in organic matter means there will be less erosion, fewer severe floods, and more stored water for plants.

	Time Began	Total Time	Amount of Water
Soil A w/o humus			
Soil B w/humus			

Fig. 1.8.

Supplementary Activities

Test different kinds of soils to see which ones have the best water-holding capacity and make a chart to record the observations.

Create a land usage chart to demonstrate which soils would be most useful for different kinds of activities.

Fill two jars with water to within 1 inch of the top. Collect two soil samples, one with organic matter and one without. Place the soil samples on pieces of hardware cloth (medium-meshed screen) and lower them into the jars of water. Make note of what happens to each sample. The soil with humus should hold its shape because it has a greater water-holding capacity and decreases the amount of water that runs off.

Collect as many samples of different kinds of soil as possible. Put a cup of each kind of soil in quart jars. Pour a half-cup of water in each jar. Watch as the water percolates down through the soil. After one minute, pour the water from each jar into measuring cups. Compare the amount of unabsorbed water from each sample.

Questions

1. Which soil held water the best? Why?

2. What would your results be if you repeated the procedure with the same soils?

3. In nature what happens to the water that sinks into the soil?

4. Does soil with humus have a higher or a lower absorption rate and water-holding capacity? Explain your answer.

5. Which kind of soil would erode the fastest? Why?

6. Why would it be important to manage soil well so that it doesn't erode?

 ## Activity 9: Erosion and Soil Loss

OBJECTIVE:	To demonstrate the effect of grasses on soil in protecting against erosion and soil loss
MATERIALS:	2 stream table boxes (or the following materials to make them: ¼-inch to ½-inch thick plywood. Make boxes 16 inches long by 12 inches wide and 4 inches deep), plastic sheeting, water, 2 coffee cans, 2 plant sprayers, sod, soil
LEVEL:	Upper
SETTING:	Classroom
TIME:	1 hour for table construction, 10-20 minutes for the demonstration.
VOCABULARY:	Erosion, stream table

LESSON DESIGN

Buy two stream tables or make two according to the specifications. At one end of each table, cut a V-notch 1- to 1½-inches deep and fit them with tin spouts, or plastic, to draw run-off water. Obtain a piece of sod to fit one of the boxes. Fill the other box with soil without grass or plants of any sort. Place the stream tables on a table, elevated at the back to give them slope and having the spouts extend over the table edge. Place the coffee cans under the spouts. Pour water on both boxes at the same time, at the same rate, and from the same height. Observe the rate at which the water runs off both samples and the condition of the water in the coffee cans after runoff. Grass breaks the force of raindrops and slows down running water so as not to disturb the soil as dramatically as soil with grass cover.

Supplementary Activities

Perform the same activity with different kinds and amounts of soil cover or vegetation, such as vegetable crops (radishes, beans) and flowers, or soil without vegetative cover but with a lot of internal organic matter.

As precipitation mixes with soil, some of the nutrients in the soil dissolve and run off, depleting the soil of nutrients necessary to plants. Mix a spoonful of powdered paint to a cup of soil and mix thoroughly. Insert a cone-shaped coffee filter into a funnel and place the funnel in a quart jar. Fill the filter-lined funnel half full with soil. Slowly pour a ¼-cup of water over the soil and observe the water that drips into the jar.

Questions

1. Why is the liquid dripping through the funnel colored?

2. What does the colored liquid represent?

3. What can farmers do to save the soil of fields that need to lie fallow for a year or two to regain essential nutrients to keep them from eroding away?

4. What happens to the soil that is washed or blown from a field? Where does it go? Where does it end up?

Activity 10: Soil Loss

OBJECTIVE:	To demonstrate the effect of mulch in preventing soil loss
MATERIALS:	Stream tables from Activity 9, water, straw or sawdust, 2 coffee cans, 2 jars, 8-penny nail, can
LEVEL:	Upper
SETTING:	Classroom
TIME:	20 minutes
VOCABULARY:	Erosion, mulch

LESSON DESIGN

Fill both boxes with the same kind of soil, without grass. Cover one box of soil with a thin layer of straw or sawdust (mulch). Sprinkle the same amount of water on both boxes, at the same rate and from the same height. Observe how much and how fast the water runs off into each coffee can.

From a short distance, drop water on unprotected soil and on soil protected with a mulch. Punch a hole with an 8-penny nail in the bottom of a can and fill the hole with cotton. Put a small layer of soil in two small jars. Place a layer of mulch on one and leave the other one bare. Place the cans about 4 feet above the jars containing soil. Put several inches of water in the can. As large drops of water form through the holes and drop on the soil, observe the amount of soil that splashes on the sides of the jars.

Supplementary Activities

Pack two cans (open on each end) three-fourths of the way full of soil, leaving one sample bare and covering one with a mulch. Place the jars under each can. Sprinkle the samples heavily with water and compare the amount of water that drips through the cans into the jars.

Questions

1. How are mulches important in conserving water?

2. How do mulches reduce evaporation from the wind and the sun?

From *Consider the Earth.* © 1999 Gates. Teacher Ideas Press. (800) 237-6124.

Activity 11: Contour Plowing

OBJECTIVE:	To see the effects of contour plowing on soil erosion
MATERIALS:	2 stream tables from Activity 9, water, 2 coffee cans, soil
LEVEL:	Upper
SETTING:	Classroom
TIME:	30 minutes
VOCABULARY:	Conservation, contours

LESSON DESIGN

Fill both boxes with the same kind of soil. Set up the tables and cans the same way as in Activity 9. Using a pencil, make furrows, or rows, across the soil in one box and up and down the soil in the other box. Water both tables slowly, at the same time and rate and from the same height. Compare the rates of runoff and the difference in the contents of the two cans.

The same activity can be done with two dishpans mounded with soil.

Contour plowing/farming is a common conservation practice that uses plowing across the slope of the land, on the contour. It conserves precipitation and helps prevent erosion.

Supplementary Activities

Research the Dust Bowl era and report on its impact on people.

VOCABULARY DEFINITIONS

Absorption—The process of taking something in through pores, or soaking up something, such as water.

Capillary Action—The force that causes a liquid to be raised against a vertical surface, as water is in a plant or in soil.

Clinometer—An instrument for measuring the angle of an incline.

Compaction—To pack together very solidly or densely.

Conservation—To preserve something from loss, waste, or harm, such as natural resources, soil, forests, or water.

Contour Interval—The distance in height from one contour line to the next one.

Contour Line—An imaginary line along which every point is the same height above sea level.

Contours—To follow the slope or curve of the land.

Contraction—The act of shrinking or drawing together.

Duff—Partially decomposed organic matter.

Erosion—The process of wearing away the land by weathering, abrasion, and corrosion.

Expansion—The process of increasing or swelling.

Germination—To begin to grow or sprout.

Horizon—A specific layer of soil in a cross section of land.

Humus—An organic substance consisting of partially to wholly decomposed vegetative matter that provides nutrients for plants and increases a soil's ability to retain water.

Litter—The uppermost layer of soil consisting mostly of decaying organic matter.

Micromonolith—A small model of a soil profile in columnar form, in which samples of each soil layer are attached to a card.

Mulch—A protective covering of organic matter, such as grasses or straw, placed on soil or around plants to prevent evaporation.

Natural Resources—Any material occurring naturally, such as forests, minerals, and soil.

Orientation—The process of finding your way outdoors with the help of landscape features, a map, a compass, or with all three.

Orienteering—The process of finding your way outdoors with a map and a compass.

Permeability—To pass through, to penetrate, to spread, as water sinking into soil.

pH—A measure of the acidity or alkalinity of a solution.

Renewable—To reestablish, to start over again.

Slope—Any inclined surface and the degree of such deviation from the horizontal.

Structure—How soil is put together geometrically.

Subsoil—The layer of earth beneath the topsoil.

Texture—What soil feels like: gritty, smooth, sticky, and so on.

Topographic Map—Maps of specific areas indicating elevation with contour lines.

Topsoil—The surface layer of soil.

Water-Holding Capacity—The ability of the soil to hold great amounts of water or negligible amounts.

2 PLANTS

Plants are an inseparable part of our ecosystem. Without plants, neither humans nor animals could survive. Plants provide us with food, oxygen, building materials, paper, and a host of other important and useful things. Plants are useful, valuable, interesting, and beautiful.

Plants are called *producers* because they are the only living things capable of producing their own food by a process called *photosynthesis*. Green plants need sunlight in order to grow. They store this energy from the sun in their leaves and stems in the form of certain substances. With the aid of sunlight, plants transform water and carbon dioxide into food (sugar, fats, and proteins), necessities for the maintenance of life. This process is called photosynthesis. *Photo* means "light," and *synthesis* means "putting together."

Plants help maintain a balance between oxygen and carbon dioxide by using carbon dioxide for food production and by giving off oxygen as a by-product. All other living things give off carbon dioxide and consume oxygen. All the oxygen in the air was originally produced by plant photosynthesis.

Plants use carbon dioxide and produce oxygen through photosynthesis. During respiration, plants use oxygen and release carbon dioxide. Plants increase the moisture content of air during transpiration. Water is transpired through stomata on the surface of plant leaves and stems. Transpiration increases the relative humidity of an area.

Plants and plant roots protect topsoil from wind and water erosion and reduce evaporation from the soil. Soil with good vegetative cover helps reduce floods and helps store and release runoff water more slowly.

Trees are also plants. Forests are essential to the maintenance of life on Earth. They provide oxygen, regulate water supplies, and help balance heat in the biosphere. Trees absorb dust and noise and serve as windbreaks.

From *Consider the Earth*. © 1999 Gates. Teacher Ideas Press. (800) 237-6124.

There are three main parts of a tree. The root system is important for anchorage, for support of the aerial parts, for absorption of water and minerals from the soil, and for the accumulation of food for winter storage. The trunk, which is the main stem of the tree, elevates the crown and moves sap up and down between the roots and the leaves. The crown is a mass of branches and leaves and is responsible for carrying on photosynthesis.

Cells developing from *meristems*, actively dividing cells at the root ends and on the twigs, increase the tree in height and diameter. A tree expands in thickness because of the developing cells from the cambium. These cells add width but not length to the roots and stems because they develop on the sides, not at the tips.

The annual growth rings that are added each year are produced by the cambium. The *cambium* is a single layer of cells between the bark and the wood. New cells that are formed from the cambium inwards become xylem. The *xylem* is composed of different kinds of cells, the most abundant being the tracheids. Water and dissolved minerals pass through the walls of these cells. The ray cells are thin walled and are aligned radially through the stem, extending across the annual rings. Water and minerals move laterally through these ray cells. The youngest xylem wood is the sapwood. This sapwood consists of the outermost few growth rings. The older xylem is the heartwood, which is usually darker in color. Because the heartwood is usually plugged up with gummy substances, the sapwood is the more important region, being actively involved in the movement of water, dissolved minerals, and food.

Phloem develops outward from the cambium. The *phloem* is also composed of different kinds of cells. The sieve cells are elongated with thin walls, allowing dissolved foods to move through them. Companion cells are smaller and occur with the sieve cells. Horizontal phloem ray cells and xylem ray cells join, becoming vascular rays. Xylem tissue usually carries water and minerals upward, whereas phloem tissue carries dissolved foods downward.

Bark is the outermost section of tree roots and stems. It is tissue formed by cork cambium and old phloem cells. As new xylem is formed, the stem increases in size. Stress is therefore put on the cambium, which produces new cells. These cells produce a new layer of phloem cells inside the old ones. Because of even more stress from the older phloem layers, the bark splits, producing various bark patterns and shapes in different varieties of trees.

Trees have different ways of resisting fire, some of which are briefly outlined below:

1. The lower the initial temperature of any region of a tree, the higher the fire temperature will need to be to raise the initial temperature of critical cells to lethal levels.

2. The presence, thickness, and character of the cortical covering helps resist fire. Trees with thick bark have more resistance to fire. Trees will increase their bark thickness with age, and therefore, their resistance to fire.

3. Trees that have high, open crowns and self-prune their branches are more fire resistant than trees with low, dense crowns and retain their dead branches.

4. Trees with shallow roots are less resistant to fire than trees with deeper roots. Roots have a thin cortical covering and are susceptible to surface fires.

5. Foliage of evergreens tends to be more flammable than deciduous hardwoods. Therefore, a dense coniferous stand will be subject to more damage than an open stand.

6. Some trees flourish after fire. Aspens send out lateral roots. Where these roots approach the surface, they send up new shoots, called suckers. Fire will destroy the part of trees above the ground, but the roots will produce more shoots.

The effect of fire on soil usually results in a loss of organic matter and an increase in runoff and erosion. Controlled burning is used to prepare a site for seeding or planting, to control competing species, or to control plant diseases. Prescribed burning is used to hold back the normal succession on a site leading to climax that is not as economically desirable as a subclimax species. Burning also helps destroy understory vegetation that competes with a desirable species for space, moisture, and nutrients. A climax forest occurs when a species is overcome by another because of conditions of sunlight. A shade-intolerant species will overcome a shade-tolerant species, thereby removing that species and creating a climax community.

Consider a grove of trees, or a forest, as similar to a group of people. It is a community composed of different sizes, shapes, ages, and colors of trees. As trees mature, their growth slows down, as do humans. They no longer photosynthesize as rapidly and no longer give off as much oxygen. Older trees, like humans, are prey to more external and internal causes of death, such as disease, parasites, droughts, fires, extremes in temperature, and high winds. Although these trees are subject to adverse conditions, they remain productive, dropping seeds and germinating if conditions are favorable.

There is so much more for children to learn about trees than mere leaf identification. They need to learn that forests are to be enjoyed and to be used, and that when they are cut down, they must be replaced. Trees, unlike metals or minerals, are a replaceable raw material. It takes time, but it is possible. New forests can be planted from seeds, or they can regenerate themselves. Because of the increased demands of forested lands, we must manage our forests wisely. Otherwise, we will not be able to reap their many benefits, and we will find ourselves poorer because of it. We will use our irreplaceable resources faster, with dire consequences for our environment.

Not only must children learn of the importance of forests today and their wise use for the future, but they also must know some forestry history. Otherwise, they will not understand the need for wise management.

Loggers once carelessly eliminated wildlife sanctuaries and seriously affected water and soil conservation. To the early settlers of the new world, forests were a nuisance. Forests were used for fuel and construction and many times cut down mercilessly. Wood from forests was exploited enterprisingly in later years. Timber supplies were thought to be inexhaustible. Logging during the 1800s shifted from one area to another as great forests were destroyed. After loggers had cut down massive areas of trees, fire took over as the major destroyer. The debris left lying on the ground after logging provided a great source of fuel for potential fire. In later years, forest conservation practices were employed by the federal government to help prevent the destruction of the forests. Their practices included sustained yield, or balanced timber harvest and growth to enable continued forest yield; multiple use, or forests serving a variety of uses; and an emphasis on achieving the greatest good over the longest period of time.

Equally important, children need to understand the roles trees play in the natural environment. Most children have a basic knowledge of the products acquired from trees: wood, paper, turpentine, and so on. Most children know little else aside from the products acquired from trees and their beauty. Trees purify our air and water and help conserve soil. Trees return oxygen to the air for us to breathe. Forests cool the air through transpiration and evaporation, or evapotranspiration. To feel this difference, walk on a hot summer's day through the streets of a city. Then take a walk in a city park. Feel the difference. For this simple reason, it is important to have trees in cities. Heat makes people more irritable. More trees help keep the temperature lower, thereby keeping people happier because they are cooler. Trees also help reduce noise. In cities or along highways this fact is especially important. Forests also are providers of water. Trees act as a canopy to reduce the impact of falling rain. They regulate water flow and help prevent soil erosion. Forests also provide food, water, and shelter for wildlife. Birds and animals abound and multiply here. Of course, forests provide recreation for humans. Trees can be planted on eroded land unable to support crops. The trees slow down the process of erosion and help stabilize the soil so that natural processes can slowly renew surface fertility. Soil fertility can be lost because of erosion in areas unwisely cared for as well as in areas where soil practices are good. Fertile topsoil can be covered with layers of sterile soil, either through floods or dust storms. This occurrence also renders the soil infertile. There are different layers of vegetation in a forest because plants are adapted to conduct photosynthesis at different light intensities. Because of all these things, trees need to be regrown so that we can continue to reap their benefits.

There is always a balance between plant and animal life. Animals eat the plants and use the energy from these plants. Yet animals cannot eat more plants than can be replaced by new plant growth. Otherwise, animals would die of starvation. New plant growth is about seven times the new growth of animal life. This fact is because animals lose about 85 percent of the food energy from plants. Therefore, in a food chain, the longer the chain, the smaller the animal that can be supported. Consequently, as population increases, more people must eat more plants. Land for plant growth for human consumption can support more people than an equal quantity of land used to pasture animals that are then slaughtered for consumption. These animals have stored only one-seventh the energy food value. Therefore, animal food is a luxury. Humans must be more efficient with their uses of energy. If we are not, and energy runs short, and population increases, the result will be a lower standard of living and more starvation.

Fungi also belong to the plant group. Fungi do not have chlorophyll and therefore cannot make their own food. Fungi are considered parasites because they live off other things, either alive or dead. Fungi also aid in the decaying process. Dead wood in a forest is reduced to humus by fungal activity. Decay results from the fungi digesting certain elements and leaving others. This process is successional and takes quite awhile. The fungi die when they have accrued all that they can from the dead logs or decayed leaves. Fungi learn to adapt to certain conditions just as other organisms do. Some fungi have special habitats, such as manure, decaying leaves, or special tree species. Fungi have no roots, stems, or leaves. They consist of a network of a mass of *mycelia* (small, hairlike structures serving as roots), of which there are two types. *Saprophytes* feed on dead or decaying matter; *parasites* live off another living organism. Saprophytic fungi are the primary organisms of decomposition. They secrete enzymes that break down organic molecules in dead organisms.

Fungi reproduce through spores, not seeds. Spores are microscopic, and they are distributed by the wind. Warmth and moisture are necessary for fungi to push through the soil.

Activity 1: Photosynthesis

OBJECTIVE:	To understand the chemical formula for photosynthesis
MATERIALS:	3 colors of poker chips or plastic discs, toothpicks
LEVEL:	Lower to upper
SETTING:	Classroom
TIME:	30 minutes
VOCABULARY:	Atom, glucose, molecule, photosynthesis
PRE-ACTIVITIES:	Discussion of photosynthesis and molecules

LESSON DESIGN

Through the process of photosynthesis, green plants take six carbon dioxide molecules and six water molecules and make glucose, a simple sugar. In the process of photosynthesis, not all of the oxygen taken in is used in making glucose. Some is released into the atmosphere. That is why we think of oxygen as a by-product of photosynthesis.

In groups, assemble CO_2 molecules and H_2O molecules on a table, using the poker chips as atoms and the toothpicks as bonds following the diagrams in Figures 2.1 and 2.2. Count the number of atoms of each element that you have assembled and list them on a piece of paper. Then rearrange the atoms to form the second diagram (follow Figure 2.2). The second diagram represents the end product of photosynthesis: glucose, or $C_6H_{12}O_6$.

Questions

1. How many atoms do you have left over?

2. What kinds of molecules are left over?

3. What kind of a formula can be written to represent photosynthesis?

4. What happens to the six oxygen molecules that are left over?

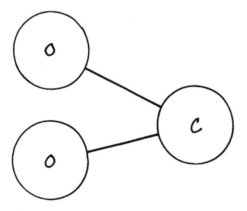

Carbon Dioxide

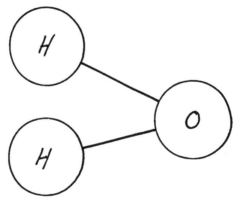

Water

Fig. 2.1.

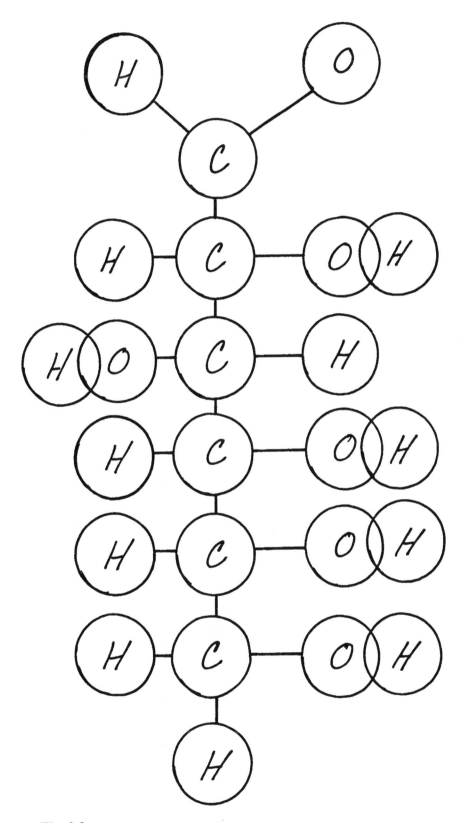

Fig. 2.2.

Activity 2: Photosynthesis and Food Storage

OBJECTIVE:	To demonstrate the presence of starch in plants
MATERIALS:	Iodine, variegated coleus plant (green and white), other plants, black paper, tape, eye dropper, different kinds of food (e.g., meat, bread, potato, butter)
LEVEL:	Lower to upper
SETTING:	Classroom
TIME:	45 minutes
PRE-ACTIVITIES:	Activity 1 (chapter 2) on photosynthesis

LESSON DESIGN

An iodine solution dropped on plants should turn them blue-black or black to show the presence of starch. Glucose is made during photosynthesis and later is converted to starch for storage.

Apply a few drops of iodine on different kinds of food and observe what happens. Record your observations.

Drop iodine on the variegated coleus leaves and observe what happens.

Cover parts of several leaves with black paper and tape. After several days, perform the starch test on the covered and uncovered parts of the leaves. Record your observations.

Supplementary Activities

A similar activity involves photosynthesis and fall leaf color. Tape a piece of black paper over part of a maple leaf in the fall, just before it turns color. Leave the paper in place during the period of color change. The maple leaf will turn red in the presence of sunlight, but the part not exposed to sunlight will be yellow. Yellow pigments appear when chlorophyll disappears. However, red pigments develop only with the aid of sunlight.

Toward the end of summer, the chloroplasts of green leaves die because their job is finished for the year. Excess food made during the summer is stored in the trunks and roots of a tree for winter use. Then the other pigments that are present in most leaves appear. These have been hidden under the chlorophyll all summer. When the green coloring matter dies, the other colors show up and create pretty fall colors. Then, as the weather turns increasingly colder, these, too, crumble and die.

Questions

1. Did all parts of the coleus leaves turn black? What is the reason for this?

2. What role does sunlight play in photosynthesis and food production?

3. Why did the iodine turn some of the food black, but not all of the food?

4. Which foods turned black? Why?

5. What substance in the foods caused them to turn black?

 ## Activity 3: Chlorophyll Extraction

OBJECTIVE:	To be able to extract chlorophyll from plant leaves and to demonstrate the presence of starch
MATERIALS:	2 pans, 2 small jars, water, alcohol, hot plate, 2 plants
LEVEL:	Upper
SETTING:	Classroom
TIME:	1 hour
VOCABULARY:	Chlorophyll, photosynthesis
PRE-ACTIVITIES:	Activity 2 (chapter 2) on photosynthesis and food storage

LESSON DESIGN

Fill two large pans one-third of the way full with water. Fill two smaller jars one-third full with alcohol. Put the smaller jars inside the larger pans and place them on the hot plate. Turn the hot plate to high. Take a few leaves from a plant that has been in the dark for two weeks and a few leaves from a plant that has been in the sunlight for two weeks. Put the leaves in the two jars of alcohol and label them WITH SUNLIGHT and WITHOUT SUNLIGHT. Boil the leaves until they lose their color or turn white, about 30 to 45 minutes. Keep adding alcohol if necessary. Remove the leaves after the chlorophyll has been extracted and place them in two bowls. Add a few drops of iodine to the leaves and observe any changes. The leaves that had been in the dark should not turn dark or as dark because they do not contain as much starch. These leaves were unable to make food in the dark. They needed to use stored food to survive, but eventually they would use all their stored food and die. The leaves that had been in the sunshine should turn dark because they contain starch.

From *Consider the Earth.* © 1999 Gates. Teacher Ideas Press. (800) 237-6124.

Supplementary Activities

Is light necessary for the maintenance of plant life? You will need two similar plants, one to place in the dark and one to place in a lighted area for two or three weeks. Water both plants the same and record what is happening to each plant. Reverse the plants for two or three weeks and record your observations again.

Questions

1. Why did the leaves kept in the dark not turn dark with the addition of iodine?

2. What did the leaves kept in the sunlight use to make food? Why did those leaves turn dark with the addition of iodine?

3. Would plants die if they never received sunlight?

4. Would plants be able to make food if they never received sunlight? Why or why not?

 ## Activity 4: Absorption of Carbon Dioxide

OBJECTIVE:	To demonstrate that plants absorb carbon dioxide in the presence of sunlight
MATERIALS:	Bromthymol blue indicator solution, elodea plants, aquarium water, straw, 3 jars, aluminum foil
LEVEL:	Lower to upper
SETTING:	Classroom
TIME:	45 minutes
VOCABULARY:	Absorption

LESSON DESIGN

Bromthymol blue indicator solution will turn blue in an alkaline substance and will turn yellow in an acidic substance. When carbon dioxide is added to water with bromthymol blue in it, the color will change from blue to yellow. When carbon dioxide is absorbed by a plant, as in photosynthesis, the yellow color is changed back to blue.

In a jar, dilute bromthymol blue with aquarium water in which an elodea plant has been growing. Blow into the solution with a straw until it turns yellow, indicating the presence of carbon dioxide.

Place the solution in the following jars:

with no plant

with an elodea plant

with an elodea plant but covered with aluminum foil

Place all three jars in the sunlight. Within 30 minutes, the jars with plants will change from yellow to blue, indicating the absorption of carbon dioxide.

Supplementary Activities

Pour equal amounts of distilled water into two drinking glasses. Label one A and one B. Add several drops of bromthymol blue to both glasses. Put a water snail in glass A. Cover both glasses with plastic wrap and let them sit over night.

Pour distilled water in a drinking glass. Add several drops of bromthymol blue. Put a water snail and an elodea plant in the glass and place in a well-lighted place.

Questions

1. Why is it important for plants to absorb carbon dioxide?

2. What will happen to the plant covered with aluminum foil if it remains covered?

3. Why did both the jars with plants turn yellow, even though one was in the light and one was in the dark?

4. What was the difference in color between glasses A and B? Why?

5. Because the water in glass A changed color, indicating the presence of carbon dioxide, is it possible to have too much carbon dioxide in the environment? How could you tell?

6. Was there a color change in the glass containing both the snail and the plant? Why or why not?

7. What happens to the carbon dioxide the snail produces? What happens to the oxygen the plant produces?

From *Consider the Earth.* © 1999 Gates. Teacher Ideas Press. (800) 237-6124.

Activity 5: Geotropism

OBJECTIVE:	To demonstrate the effect of geotropism on plant seeds
MATERIALS:	Bean seeds, plastic bags, filter paper or paper towels, tape, glass container
LEVEL:	Lower to upper
SETTING:	Classroom
TIME:	30 minutes initially, 1–2 weeks overall
VOCABULARY:	Cotyledon, embryo, geotropism, tropisms
PRE-ACTIVITIES:	Soak bean seeds for 3–4 days. Carefully remove the seed coat and separate the two halves, or cotyledons. Observe the tiny plant, or embryo, on one cotyledon. Plant several soaked seeds near the side of a glass container so you can see how the roots and stems will grow.

LESSON DESIGN

Plant bean seeds on wet filter paper or paper towels and place in the plastic bags. Tape the bags to the wall of the classroom and observe. Record when they first sprout. After the seeds sprout, observe in which direction the roots are growing. Turn the bags upside down and tape them to the wall again. Observe the roots. In time, the roots will turn downward again because of geotropism, which means they are responding to gravity.

Supplementary Activities

Research other tropisms, such as phototropism, hydrotropism, or thermotropism, and devise an experiment to show what the plant is reacting to in that particular instance.

Questions

1. If you kept turning the seeds upside down, would the roots continue to change and grow downward? Why do you think so?

2. If roots respond to gravity and grow downward, what are stems responding to by growing up? Do stems ever grow down instead of up? Explain.

Activity 6: Water Usage

OBJECTIVE:	To determine how much water is used by a plant on a daily basis
MATERIALS:	Corsage flower vials, plant cuttings
LEVEL:	Upper
SETTING:	Classroom
TIME:	30 minutes initially, several days overall

LESSON DESIGN

Insert a plant cutting in the rubber stopper of a corsage flower vial. Fill the vial with water and put the plant and the stopper in the vial. Record how much water you used to fill the vial (approximately 1 ounce). After 24 hours, measure the amount of water left in the vial to approximate the amount of water used by the plant cutting. If the water does not go down appreciably, wait until you notice a change, maybe several days, before measuring the water. Then calculate the amount used for one day by dividing by the number of days you waited before measuring. Determine water usage for the whole plant based on the amount used for the single cutting.

Supplementary Activities

Test different kinds of plants to see if they have different water needs. Research Xeriscaping as a means of conserving water.

Questions

1. How could we test for water usage for an acre of corn or grass?

2. What kinds of plants would be the smallest water consumers and the greatest water consumers? Where would each live? Why?

Activity 7: Water Requirements of Plants

OBJECTIVE:	To demonstrate the water needs of plants by building and using a moisture-gradient box
MATERIALS:	20-gallon aquarium; plants from the following groups: hydrophytes, mesophytes, and xerophytes; soil; water
RESOURCES:	Nursery
LEVEL:	Upper
SETTING:	Classroom
TIME:	1 hour to set up the moisture-gradient box and several weeks for observation
VOCABULARY:	Hydrophytes, mesophytes, xerophytes
PRE-ACTIVITIES:	Activity 6 (chapter 2) on water usage; consult a local nursery to find out what kinds of plants to use in each category.

LESSON DESIGN

Build a moisture-gradient box in the following manner: Take a 20-gallon aquarium and create a 45° slope with the soil. Plant the hydrophytes at the bottom of the slope, the mesophytes in the middle, and the xerophytes at the top of the slope. Water slope gently until a pond forms at the bottom. Do not water the plants. Just make sure the pond is full every day. When the aquarium is filled with water, a pond should be created at the bottom where the hydrophytes will grow. Through capillary action, water from the pond will work its way up the slope such that plants at the bottom will have wet soil, those in the middle will have moist soil, and those at the top will be quite dry.

Questions

1. In what kinds of environments would mesophytes generally live? In what kinds of environments would xerophytes generally live? In what kinds of environments would hydrophytes generally live?

2. How do you know that plants are water sensitive?

3. Are animals water sensitive and adapted to live in specific environments? Give examples.

Activity 8: Transpiration 1

OBJECTIVE:	To observe that plants transpire
MATERIALS:	Potted plants, plastic bags, string, glass jar
LEVEL:	Lower to upper
SETTING:	Classroom and outdoors
TIME:	20 minutes and a couple of days of observation time
VOCABULARY:	Stomata, transpiration

LESSON DESIGN

Water several potted plants well. Place a plastic bag loosely over each plant and securely tie it around the bottom of the stem with a piece of string. Observe the plant and record what it looks like. Observe every hour and record your observations.

Place plastic bags around several live branches on different trees outside and tie securely. Leave them on for several hours. Carefully remove the bags and empty the water into a measuring cup. Compare your results from the different trees. Repeat the same experiment except leave the bags on the branches overnight. Compare your results with the daytime experiment.

Place a glass jar over a potted plant and observe the water droplets that collect on the inside of the glass jar. Do the same thing with another plant but place it in a dark closet. Do the same thing with two other plants, placing one in a very cool place and one in a very warm place. Compare the amount of water transpired from all four plants.

Conduct the same experiment with two other plants. Coat one plant's leaves with Vaseline and leave the other one alone, and compare the inside of each of the glass jars. The inside of the jar with the plant's leaves coated with Vaseline should not be wet because the stomata were blocked and unable to transpire.

Supplementary Activities

Repeat the same process with a plant that has not been watered for about two weeks and see if the results are the same.

Repeat the process with different kinds of plants to see if some transpire more than others.

Questions

1. How long did it take before any changes were noticeable?

2. What changes occurred in the plastic bag over time?

3. Why were these changes happening?

4. Would there ever be a circumstance in which a plant would not transpire any water at all? Explain.

5. Where did the water in the plastic bags come from?

6. Was the water from the leaves or from the twigs?

7. Do light and temperature have any effect on the amount of water transpired? If so, what kind?

8. Would more water be collected on a dry day or a wet day? Explain your answer.

 Activity 9: Transpiration 2

OBJECTIVE:	To study the water lost by a plant through transpiration by constructing and using a potometer (an instrument to measure water lost in transpiration)
MATERIALS:	Large plant cuttings, clear plastic tubing, rubber stopper with one hole to fit the tubing, clamp, ruler, water, measuring cup
LEVEL:	Upper
SETTING:	Classroom
TIME:	1 hour to set up and several days for observation
VOCABULARY:	Evaporation, stomata, transpiration
PRE-ACTIVITIES:	Activity 8 (chapter 2) on transpiration; discussion of the differences between evaporation and transpiration.

LESSON DESIGN

Seal clear plastic tubing tightly at one end, folding the tubing over and clamping it down. Fill with water (see Figure 2.3). Record the amount of water put in the tube. Cut and assemble the plant under water in order not to get any air blockage. Cut the plant diagonally and insert it securely into the rubber stopper. The plant needs to fit the stopper tightly so that there will be no water lost through evaporation. Now, insert the rubber stopper into the open end of the tubing. Secure the apparatus on a table so that it won't fall over and tape a ruler to the side without the plant. Make daily observations and record the water level against the ruler. Calculate how much water is transpired on a daily basis, how much is transpired on a weekly basis, and how much is transpired on a monthly basis.

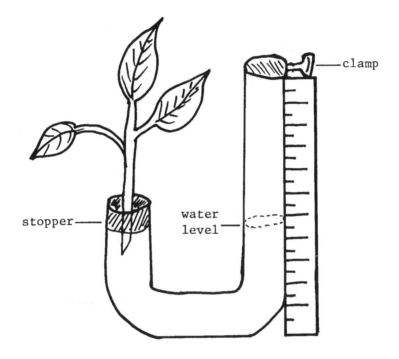

Fig. 2.3.

Supplementary Activities

Study water loss under the following conditions: cold, warm, windy, dark. Study water loss with different species of plants, keeping them all fairly consistent in size.

Questions

1. What is the effect of transpiration on our environment? Compare an urban and a rural setting to answer this question.

2. Is it possible for a plant to transpire all the water it contains and therefore dehydrate itself and die?

Activity 10: Seed Requirements

OBJECTIVE:	To experiment to see what seeds need in order to germinate and grow
MATERIALS:	6 pots, potting soil, seeds, pots
LEVEL:	Lower to upper
SETTING:	Classroom
TIME:	1 hour initial setup, several weeks of observation
VOCABULARY:	Germination, nutrients

LESSON DESIGN

Plant equal numbers of the same kinds of seeds in six different pots. Label each pot as to what each is to receive. One will get water, sunlight, and warmth. One will get no water, but it will get sun and warmth. One will get water and warmth, but no sunlight. One will get no sunlight, no water, and no warmth. One will get light and water, but no warmth. The last one will get warmth, but it will get no light and no water. Record when each pot germinates and how many seeds in each pot germinate. Keep a record of observable progress for 2 to 3 weeks.

Supplementary Activities

Perform similar experiments with tree seedlings. Obtain some seedlings from the federal or state forest service and put them in four different situations: one in a sunny area with water, one in a dark closet with water, one in a dark closet without water, and one in a sunny area without water. Make daily observations and record any changes. See if you can rescue any of the seedlings before they die, rejuvenate them with the proper nutrients, and plant them outdoors. They will need a lot of care, especially water, during the first year in order to establish themselves and grow.

Do plants need oxygen in order to grow? Place a clear jar over a small plant. What will be observed first are water droplets on the inside of the jar, which means the plant is transpiring. After all the water has transpired (several weeks), will the plant be able to continue living?

Questions

1. What do seeds need to germinate and grow?

2. Did any seeds germinate then die because they were lacking something? If so, which ones and for what reasons?

From *Consider the Earth.* © 1999 Gates. Teacher Ideas Press. (800) 237-6124.

3. Which pot germinated and grew the best? Why?

4. Do seedlings need the same things for growth as seeds?

5. Describe the importance of sunshine, water, warmth, and air to seeds and plants.

6. What are some reasons why seeds are important to most organisms?

 ## Activity 11: Tree Cross Sections

OBJECTIVE:	To be able to identify various parts of a tree using a tree cross-section
MATERIALS:	Several tree cross-sections, yarn, index cards, poster board, pins
RESOURCES:	Federal or state forest service
LEVEL:	Upper
SETTING:	Outdoors and classroom
TIME:	Two 1-hour segments
VOCABULARY:	Annual rings, cambium, dendrochronology, heartwood, phloem, xylem
PRE-ACTIVITIES:	On-site lecture outside with a forester from the local forest service about trees and dendrochronology (tree dating); a demonstration of an increment bore, which takes a core sample of a tree and is used to determine age and growth patterns.

LESSON DESIGN

After a discussion of trees, rings, growth patterns, and dendrochronology, the students should get together in groups to label their tree cross-sections. String yarn from labels to the following parts: outer bark, inner bark (phloem), cambium, annual rings, sapwood (xylem), heartwood.

Glue the tree cross-sections and the index card labels to the poster board and display them on a bulletin board or a large table.

Make labels for another tree cross-section indicating historical happenings, such as birthdays of famous people, wars, or local history.

Make labels for a third tree cross-section showing the evidence of fires, droughts, and other environmental influences. The forester may be needed for this activity.

Supplementary Activities

Form research groups to find out about the following:

How forests are used

Forestry ideas and practices—past and present

Forest management

Products from trees

Take a walk to an area where there are several trees that have been cut down. Examine as many as possible and record as many of the following observations about each one as possible in a notebook:

What kind of a tree was it? Compare the stump with nearby trees to help you. Any remaining bark will also help.

Did the tree grow from a seed, root sprouts, or root suckers? Multiple growth usually represents sprout or coppice growth, *coppice* meaning a forest originating from sprouts or root suckers rather than seeds. A single tree usually has grown from a seed.

How was the tree felled?

In what direction did the tree fall? Find the lowest cut made on the stump. The final cut usually controls the direction in which a tree falls. Look for broken limbs or crookedness in nearby trees as well as clear areas or broken branches lying on the ground.

Was the tree cut by loggers or a forester? Loggers usually cut trees lower to the ground to gain as much of the tree as possible.

How old was the tree when cut? Determine the age by counting the tree rings on the stump.

When did the tree grow most rapidly? Most annual growth is produced in the spring. These rings are usually broader and lighter.

What was the greatest amount of growth in one year? Locate the largest annual ring difference. Measure this at opposite sides of the trunk. This will determine the full annual growth.

Was the tree cut before or after it died? Usually, bark is more likely to cling to a stump for a few years if it is cut while living.

Find evidence of animals that have used the stump and write down what kinds of animals you think they were.

What plants can be found on the stump? Is there evidence of mosses or fungi?

If there were no growth rings on the stump, why is this? Trees that grow in regions with little seasonal variation grow continuously and do not develop annual rings.

Questions

1. Is there any way to tell the age of a tree without cutting it down? If so, how?

2. Why are some tree rings narrower than others and some wider than others?

3. What inferences can you make about the various cross-sections?

 ## *Activity 12: Tree Measurements*

OBJECTIVE:	To be able to measure the heights, diameters, and circumferences of trees using simple instruments and methods
MATERIALS:	2 yardsticks, hinge, string, tall stick
LEVEL:	Upper
SETTING:	Outdoors
TIME:	1–2 hours
VOCABULARY:	Circumference, diameter

LESSON DESIGN

Make a caliper for measuring tree diameter by hinging two yardsticks at one end. Take the caliper and place the ends on both sides of the tree and measure the distance between the two ends. This measurement is a rough reading of diameter.

To measure the circumference of a tree, circle the tree with a piece of string and measure the string's length. If each group measures the diameter and circumference of different trees, the students may be able to hypothesize about the relationship of circumference to diameter; in other words, that circumference is a little more than three times the diameter. If the students are old enough, the term *pi* may be introduced (pi = 3.14) and the following formula "C = pid" (circumference equals pi times the diameter).

To measure vertical distances, or heights of trees, using the inch to foot method, do the following:

Start from a tree (point A) and walk 11 steps. Mark this point "X" with a long stick. Walk one more step from point X and mark this point "B." Sight from point B, at eye level, across a point on the stick to the top of the tree, which becomes point C. Mark the point on the stick where your line of vision intersects the stick (point Y). Mark the point ("Z") on the stick where your line of sight intersects when you sight to the bottom of the tree. The distance between Y and Z in inches equals the height of the tree in feet.

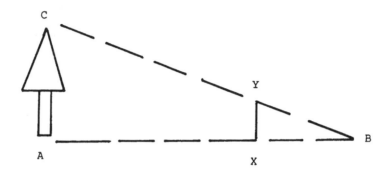

Fig. 2.4.

  Activity 13: Oxygen Production

OBJECTIVE:	To demonstrate that plants produce oxygen during photosynthesis
MATERIALS:	Aquatic plant, water, large wide-mouthed jar, test tube, funnel to fit in the jar, matches, wooden splint
LEVEL:	Lower to upper
SETTING:	Classroom
TIME:	30 minutes
VOCABULARY:	Photosynthesis, transpiration
PRE-ACTIVITIES:	Activity 1 (chapter 2) on photosynthesis; review the process of photosynthesis

LESSON DESIGN

Fill the jar with water and place the plants in the water. Cover the plants with the inverted funnel, making sure that the top of the funnel is still underwater. Fill the test tube with water, turn if over and put it on top of the inverted funnel spout, making sure no air gets into the test tube. Place the whole arrangement in a sunny place and make periodic observations. After a day, there should be a slight space in the top of the test tube that was not there the previous day, as well as little tiny bubbles, both of which indicate the plant's production of oxygen.

Carefully remove the test tube from the jar of water, still holding it upside down, and quickly place a hot, glowing wooden splint into the end of the test tube. If it bursts into flame, this demonstrates that oxygen is present.

Questions

1. With what was the space at the end of the test tube filled?

2. From where did the oxygen in the test tube come?

3. How was the oxygen produced?

4. What is produced during the process of photosynthesis aside from oxygen?

5. What happened when the glowing splint was put in the end of the test tube?

6. Why did the glowing splint burst into flame?

 ## Activity 14: Growth of Bread Mold

OBJECTIVE:	To observe the growth of bread mold, a nongreen plant
MATERIALS:	Sterilized petri dishes (or similar dishes), several slices of moldy bread, atomizer, thermometers, fresh bread, cotton swabs
LEVEL:	Lower to upper
SETTING:	Classroom
TIME:	45 minutes to set up, a week or more for observation

LESSON DESIGN

Sterilize the petri dishes. Divide the moldy bread into several small pieces and place one piece in each petri dish. Also place a small piece of fresh bread in each dish. Slightly spray each piece of fresh bread with water. Carefully graze the top of the moldy bread with a cotton swab and transfer this to the fresh bread and cover the dishes. Place your dishes in different places around the room to determine what conditions are necessary for mold growth. Place one in a sunny area, one in a warm, dark place, one in a warm but not sunny place, and one maybe in a cold, dark place, such as a refrigerator. Every day record the temperature of the area in which the molds were placed and any observations about them, such as color, smell, and shape.

Supplementary Activities

After the molds seem to be well established, examine some of them under a microscope or with a hand lens. See if you can pick out the *hyphae* or tiny thread-like structures that form a network called *mycelium*. You should also be able to see many tiny spore cases in which the spores are formed on slender stalks.

Grow molds on other kinds of foods, such various kinds of fruits. Observe them under a microscope and see if there are any differences or similarities between them and the bread molds.

Questions

1. Under what conditions did the bread molds grow the best: light and warm, cold and dark, warm and dark, or light and cool?

2. Did light or the absence of light affect the growth of the bread molds?

3. Did moisture have any effect on the growth of the bread molds? Would they have grown as well if the bread had been dry?

 ## Activity 15: Growth of Yeast Plants

OBJECTIVE:	To observe the growth of yeasts, nongreen plants
MATERIALS:	Powdered yeast, measuring cups and spoons, balloons, sugar, water, 2 jars over which the balloons will fit, cardboard, 2 glasses
LEVEL:	Lower to upper
SETTING:	Classroom
TIME:	30 minutes to set up, 1 day for observation

LESSON DESIGN

Dissolve the package of yeast in a glass of warm water and dissolve 6 tablespoons of sugar in another glass with 2 cups of water. Pour half the yeast solution and 1 cup of the sugar solution into both jars. Cover one of the jars with a piece of cardboard and fasten a balloon over the top of the other jar. Let both jars sit in a warm place for 24 hours. After 24 hours, examine the mixtures. Both jars should have bubbles and be cloudy in color. Because of the carbon dioxide gas, the balloon should be inflated. This reaction of yeast, sugar, and water produces carbon dioxide and alcohol and is called *fermentation*. If a microscope is available, examine some of the yeast mixture to see a few yeast cells that are one-celled, not green, and maybe a few buds. Yeast cells reproduce by budding, so it is possible to see one-celled yeast with buds on them.

 Activity 16: Reproduction of Fungi

OBJECTIVE:	To observe the reproductive structures of fungi and how they reproduce
MATERIALS:	Mushrooms, construction paper, jars, clear lacquer
LEVEL:	Upper
SETTING:	Classroom
TIME:	30 minutes to set up, 1 day to settle

LESSON DESIGN

Give each child a whole mushroom, stem and cap intact. Underneath the cap are tiny striations called *gills*. The gills produce the tiny spores for reproduction. Gently separate the stalk from the cap and place the cap, gill side down, on a piece of black construction paper. Cover the caps with jars so the spores won't blow away and let them remain undisturbed until the next day. Some of the spores may be white, black, or pink because different mushrooms produce different colors of spores. Gently spray the spore prints with a clear lacquer, and they will be permanently affixed to the paper; otherwise, they will rub off easily. If you know what color the spore print will be, you can decide on the color of paper ahead of time. Otherwise, it will be more of a guess. Spore prints also help experts identify fungi.

Activity 17: Phototropism

OBJECTIVE:	To demonstrate the effect light has on plants
MATERIALS:	2 plants, cardboard box in which the plants will fit, black paint
LEVEL:	Lower to upper
SETTING:	Classroom
TIME:	30 minutes to set up, several days for observation

LESSON DESIGN

Paint the inside of the box black. Cut a ¼-inch slit the length of one side of the box, level with the top of the plant. Put both plants near a window, placing the box over one and turning the slit away from the window and sealing the box shut so no light will enter except through the slit. The plant in the box is the experimental plant, and the plant out of the box is the control. Make sure both plants are well watered before covering the plant. After one week, remove the plant from the box and compare it with the control plant.

A variation on the same experiment can be accomplished using the same box with a few alterations. Tape two pieces of cardboard, half the width of the box, on alternate sides of the box—one close to the back and one closer to the front—to forma maze creating three distinct compartments. Enlarge the slit to 1½ inches. Place the plant behind the piece of cardboard farthest from the light hole and close and tape the lid shut. Turn the box so the hole faces direct sunlight. After one week, open the box and observe the plant. Keep the plant in the box long enough to observe if the plant grows all the way to the hole or not, and if so, how.

Questions

1. What were the differences and similarities between the plant in the box and the plant out of the box?

2. What did you notice about the leaves of the experimental plant in comparison to the control plant's leaves?

3. What does the experiment tell you about the response of plants to light?

4. Is light necessary for the growth of plants? How do you know?

5. Did the plant in the maze-box grow straight toward the hole, or did it curve around and turn within the compartments before it reached the hole? Why?

Activity 18: Hydrotropism

OBJECTIVE:	To demonstrate that plants grow toward water
MATERIALS:	Glass baking dish, bean seeds, water, two small clay pots, soil, clay
LEVEL:	Lower to upper
SETTING:	Classroom
TIME:	45 minutes to set up, several weeks of observation

LESSON DESIGN

Fill a glass baking dish with soil. Plug the holes in the bottom of both clay pots with clay. Sink the empty pots in opposite corners of the dish. Plant bean seeds in the dish evenly spaced throughout. Let the bean seeds germinate and establish themselves before continuing with the rest of the experiment. When the seedlings are well established, let the soil dry out somewhat, then regularly add water to only *one* pot in the glass dish. The water will seep through the sides of the pot and keep the surrounding soil moist. Observe the plants' roots through the glass dish and record your observations. After about two weeks, the plants nearest the watered pot should be taller and stronger. If you can't observe the plants through the glass, after two or three weeks, carefully uproot them and observe the direction the roots are growing. The roots should have been directed toward the watered pot.

Supplementary Activities

Fill an aquarium three-fourths of the way full with soil and plant about six bean seeds in one end of it as close to the glass as possible. Water the seeds carefully. When they have germinated, remove all but two seedlings so that they have plenty of room to grow. After this, water only the end of the aquarium opposite the seedlings. The end where the seedlings are growing will not receive any water and therefore will get dry. Observe the aquarium for a few weeks. When the roots seem to be well developed, carefully uproot the seedlings and examine them. The tiny root hairs should be obviously turned toward the source of water. The root hairs provide more surface for the diffusion of water into the root and push through air spaces in the soil to increase contact with water and dissolved minerals.

Questions

1. How does water get into a plant?

2. Why do some plants die during a drought and other plants survive?

3. How did the two plants react to the absence or presence of water?

4. How would hydrotropism be an adaptation for survival in plants?

 Activity 19: Osmosis

OBJECTIVE:	To discover how water enters a plant through the roots by the process of osmosis
MATERIALS:	Large carrot, molasses, jar, 1-hole rubber stopper, 2 feet of glass tubing, paraffin, yardstick, apple corer, test tube stand
LEVEL:	Upper
SETTING:	Classroom
TIME:	30 minutes initial setup time, several hours of observation

LESSON DESIGN

Remove a section from the middle of the carrot with the apple corer, being careful not to cut through the wall of the carrot. Insert the glass tubing into the rubber stopper. Pour molasses into the carrot and insert the stopper and tube into the carrot. Support the carrot and tube in a jar as shown in Figure 2.5. Seal the stopper to the carrot with paraffin so that there will be no leakage. Pour enough water into the jar to reach the top of the carrot. Observe for several hours to see if you notice any changes in the carrot. As the water in the jar enters the carrot, the water mixes with the molasses and rises in the tubing. This activity not only demonstrates osmosis but capillary action as well, or the transportation of water and minerals from the roots upward toward the stems and leaves. Water enters roots and passes from one cell to the next by a process called *osmosis*. Water molecules pass through a semipermeable membrane that surrounds a plant cell from an area of higher water concentration to an area of lower water concentration. Finally, the water will cease to rise in the tubing, which means that the water is entering the root with a force just great enough to hold up the weight of the water-molasses mixture in the tubing. This osmotic pressure helps explain how water enters the roots of plants and rises through the stems to the leaves.

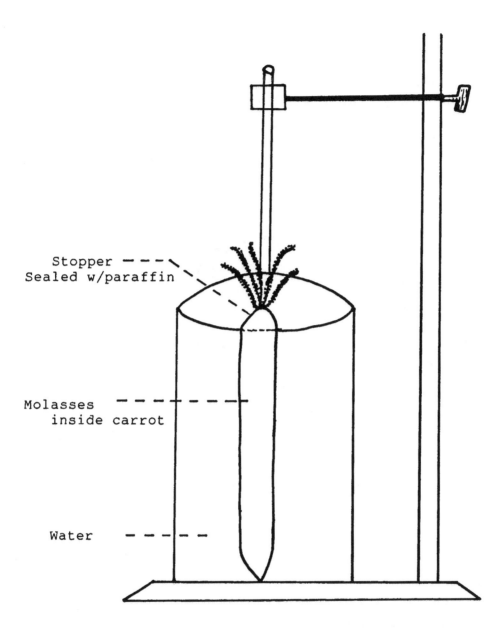

Stopper — — —
Sealed w/paraffin

Molasses
inside carrot — — — — —

Water — — — — —

Fig. 2.5.

Supplementary Activities

Carefully scrape the rounded end of an egg with a knife until you can see a thin membrane, or skin, and keep scraping until you have revealed a ¼-inch diameter of membrane. Fill a shot glass or similarly sized glass with water and place the egg in the glass so the scraped hole with the membrane intact sits in the water. Poke a tiny hole in the end of the egg sticking out of the glass, just big enough to hold a straw. Insert the straw into the egg white and seal around the edges with clay. Measure and mark with a marker the level of the water in the glass and the level of the egg white in the straw. Set the glass with the egg aside and observe the whole setup over several days. The fluid in the straw should be higher than it was the day before, and the water in the glass should be lower than it was the day before because water molecules passed through the membrane of the egg and pushed the egg white up the straw. Some egg white molecules will also pass down into the water but will be less noticeable at first because molecules move slower from a thick liquid to a thin liquid. Water moving into the egg white and egg white moving into the water is happening by a process called *osmosis*.

Supplementary Activities

Soak ¼ cup of raisins in a cup of water overnight. The raisins changed from dry and hard to soft and squishy through osmosis. Water moved from the cell membranes into the raisins through osmosis.

Place several drops of perfume or food flavoring inside a plastic bag and tie it closed. Place the bag inside a box. After approximately an hour, open the lid of the box and observe.

Questions

1. How will you be able to tell if water is entering the carrot?

2. How does osmosis help a plant to survive in times of drought?

3. Why did the raisins puff up after sitting in water overnight?

4. Why did the box smell like perfume after an hour?

 ### Activity 20: Capillary Action

OBJECTIVE:	To demonstrate the water-carrying capacity of plants from roots through stems to the leaves
MATERIALS:	Celery stalks with leaves, food coloring, water, several jars, daisies or white carnations
LEVEL:	Lower to upper
SETTING:	Classroom
TIME:	20 minutes to set up, several days for observation

LESSON DESIGN

Put enough food coloring in a glass of water to make a deep color. Cut a piece of celery diagonally across the bottom and place it in the jar of colored water. Take another stalk of celery and cut it vertically into two pieces, keeping the top and leaves intact, and place each part in a different jar of colored water. Observe the leaves of the celery and the bottom of the stems. The tubes carry water and minerals to the leaves.

Supplementary Activities

Perform the same experiment with white daisies or white carnations. The food color in the jars may depend upon the season; for instance, orange for Halloween or green for St. Patrick's Day.

Fill a shallow pan with water. Set the pan in a larger pan. Add a few drops of food coloring to the water. Stick one end of a white handkerchief in the pan of colored water, and the other end in the clear water and observe what happens.

Questions

1. Why did the leaves of the celery turn different colors?

2. Did the stem of the celery turn different colors? Why or why not?

3. What happens to the water when it reaches the leaves of the plant?

4. If you split a stalk of celery up the middle and place each half in two different colors of water, blue and yellow, for instance, would the leaves turn one blended color or two different colors on the separated parts?

 ## Activity 21: Plant Dyes

OBJECTIVE:	To obtain dyes from plants to use in dyeing yarns and cloth
MATERIALS:	Natural yarns, plant materials, water, large enamel pot, heat source, alum
LEVEL:	Lower to upper
SETTING:	Classroom
TIME:	1½–2 hours
PRE-ACTIVITIES:	Collect plant materials to use in the dyeing process or obtain enough household material to use as dye.

LESSON DESIGN

Collecting a variety of plants and using them as dyes for yarns is a fun way to experiment with plants. When boiled, plants produce different colors and shades of colors. Natural dyeing yields soft, beautiful colors. The key is experimentation because a plant in various growth stages will produce different shades, just as different parts of the plant will produce different colors and shades. Climate and soil also affect the resulting color. Keep this in mind when collecting the plant materials. Experiment with the same plant growing in different areas, and compare the resulting colors and shades. Different mordants (dye fixers) will produce different shades or even different colors from the same plant. For example, milkweed will produce a bright lemon-yellow with an alum mordant and an olive-green with a copper mordant; dandelions will produce a beige with alum and a medium olive-green with a chrome mordant; and sumac will produce a greenish-gold with alum, a chestnut-brown with chrome, and a dark charcoal-gray with an iron mordant. Household materials yield good dyes also. For instance, coffee with a chrome mordant will produce a brown-yellow dye, red onion skins with alum produce a red-brown color, yellow onion skins with alum produce a dull yellow but with tin produce a bright gold-yellow color, and black walnut hulls with alum will yield a light brown color.

The following steps are essential in dyeing yarns:

Collect at least twice as much plant material as yarn. For example, 1 pound of yarn will need approximately 2–3 pounds of plant material. To extract dye from the plant material, place the plant material in a large pot and slowly bring it to a boil and simmer just below the boiling point for approximately 1 hour. Sometimes stronger dyes will be produced if the leaves or flowers are soaked overnight before simmering them to extract the dye.

Wash the yarn in warm water before dyeing it.

Mordant the yarns for best results. This is a chemical process that helps fix the color and makes the dye permanent against washing. Different mordants result in different colors. The most common mordants are alum, chrome, tin, copper, and iron, which are available in chemical supply houses. Alum in available in drug stores and is more commonly used because it is easier and cheaper to obtain. Mordant the yarn before or at the same time as dyeing it. For instance, simmer 3–4 ounces of alum in 5 gallons of water.

An important thing to remember is to keep the yarn submerged throughout the dyeing process; otherwise, the yarn will reveal differences in shades of color or have streaks. Stir the dye bath frequently and let the yarn cool in the dye pot. Then rinse the yarn until the water runs clear.

Never boil the water, as high temperatures may destroy the dye.

The dyeing process is as follows:

Wash the yarn in lukewarm water.

Pour dye into a pot of water—approximately 4 gallons of water to 1 pound of yarn.

Put the wet yarn into the pot.

Bring the water to a simmer and simmer for 1 hour, stirring frequently.

Let the yarn and water cool in the pot.

Rinse the yarn in cool water until the water runs clear and dry it in a shady place. Never dry it in a dryer or in direct sunlight.

 ## Activity 22: Hydroponics

OBJECTIVE:	To explore the nature of hydroponics
MATERIALS:	A 2-liter soft-drink bottle, liquid house plant fertilizer, vegetable seeds, 1-gallon milk jug, aluminum pan, 1 ounce horticultural charcoal, 2 cups shredded Styrofoam
LEVEL:	Lower to upper
SETTING:	Classroom
TIME:	1 hour to set up, several weeks to observe
VOCABULARY:	Hydroponics

LESSON DESIGN

Pull the black base away from the soft-drink bottle. Place the Styrofoam and charcoal in the base, then put the base in an aluminum pan. Pour 1 teaspoon of fertilizer and 1 cup of water into the milk jug. Swirl to mix well, then pour over the Styrofoam-charcoal combination. Next scatter vegetable seeds over the top. Cut the top off the soft-drink bottle. Place the lower part of the bottle on top of the base with the seeds to form an enclosed area. Each day pour the mixture from the aluminum pan into the milk jug, then once again over the Styrofoam. In several days the seeds will begin to sprout.

VOCABULARY DEFINITIONS

Absorption—The process of taking something in through pores, such as carbon dioxide and oxygen.

Atom—The smallest particle of an element.

Annual Rings—The layer of wood produced by a single year's growth in a woody plant.

Cambium—A layer of cells in which growth of a tree's trunk and branches occur. It contains both phloem and xylem.

Chlorophyll—The green colored matter in plants that is necessary for photosynthesis.

Circumference—The distance around a circle.

Cotyledon—A leaf of a plant embryo.

Dendrochronology—The study of the growth of tree rings to determine dates and past events.

Diameter—A straight line segment that passes through the center of a circle.

Embryo—An organism in early stages of development.

Epidermis—The outermost layer of cells of a plant.

Evaporation—The process of giving off water vapor from bodies of water.

Geotropism—The response of an organism to gravity, such as plant roots growing downward.

Germination—To begin to grow or sprout.

Glucose—Sugar (food) made by green plants.

Heartwood—Older, central wood of a tree, usually darker and harder than sapwood.

Hydrophytes—Land plants growing in an environment with a moderate amount of moisture.

Hydroponics—Cultivating plants in water that contains inorganic nutrients rather than in soil.

Hydrotropism—Growth or movement of an organism in response to water.

Mesophytes—Land plants growing in an environment with a lot of water.

Molecule—The simplest structural unit of a compound.

Nutrients—Something that nourishes or has nutritive value.

Osmosis—The diffusion of a fluid through a semipermeable membrane until there is an equal concentration of fluid on either side of the membrane.

Phloem—Layer of vascular tissue that makes bark and carries food down through a tree.

Photosynthesis—The process by which green plants make food, using sunlight, carbon dioxide, and water.

Phototropism—Growth or movement of an organism in response to light.

Sapwood—Newly formed outer wood, just inside the cambium of a woody plant, and usually lighter in color than heartwood.

Starch—Naturally abundant carbohydrate found in plants. Glucose is stored in the form of starch.

Stomata—Minute pores in the epidermis of a leaf or stem, through which gas and water vapor pass.

Transpiration—The act of giving off water vapor through the stomata of plant tissue.

Tropisms—The movement of an organism in response to a specified stimulus, such as light, water, or temperature.

Vascular—Containing vessels for carrying or circulating fluids such as water, sap, or blood.

Xerophytes—Land plants growing in an environment that is deficient in moisture.

Xylem—Inner layer of vascular tissue that makes wood and carries water up through a tree.

3  *WATER*

Water is an indispensable part of our environment. All living things need water in order to live. Water occupies approximately three-fourths of the Earth's surface. It has an active part in nearly every natural process. It shapes the surface of the Earth and is essential in the functioning and existence of all living things on Earth.

Water can exist in three forms—either as a liquid, a solid, or a gas. Water is a basic compound of two atoms of hydrogen and one atom of oxygen. It freezes at 32° F (0°C) and boils at 212° F (100° C), at which time it turns to a vapor. When water freezes, its volume increases 11 percent. That is why ice floats. Water vapor is usually invisible. Sometimes this vapor is visible in the form of fog.

Approximately 97 percent of the Earth's water is in the oceans. Approximately 2 percent is in the form of glaciers and ice caps, 0.5 percent in the ground, and 0.3 percent in the atmosphere. Only approximately 0.1 percent is on the land in the form of rivers, lakes, and ponds.

Water quality is just as important as quantity, or maybe even more important because stagnant water creates problems for living things. All animals need oxygen to live, whether they are terrestrial or aquatic. Some aquatic animals had to learn to adapt to breathing underwater. Others living in the water adapted to breathing oxygen from the air.

A stream environment has fewer problems with oxygen than does a pond environment for several reasons. Rivers constantly move, adding oxygen to the water. Stream water usually is colder than pond water. Colder water contains more oxygen than warmer water. There is less decomposed material in a stream because it floats away. Oxygen is used in the decomposition process.

Oxygen is put into water through the photosynthetic activity of plants. The plants give off oxygen, which is mixed into the water to be used by the animals. Aquatic environments support a great deal of plant and animal life. Animals have learned to adapt to different aquatic environments and have developed specializations for moving in fast streams or quiet ponds.

Many things affect aquatic plant and animal life, such as changes in temperature, pH of the water, oxygen content, pollutants, and location.

The amount of water on Earth is finite. The same water is constantly being recirculated, to be used over and over again, through processes of evaporation, condensation, and precipitation. These processes have purified our water for thousands of years. Because the world's population has increased drastically since the 1900s, water usage has also increased drastically. Nature cannot purify water fast enough any more. The rivers, lakes, and other water areas of the world are now filled with dirty water.

Water pollution is defined as being any extraneous matter in water harmful to living things. The matter may be chemicals, bacteria, or heat, substances harmful to humans and aquatic life.

Water pollution becomes a more serious problem every day. Some of the pollutants that are daily dumped into our waters are sewage and wastes from cities and industries, oil, chemical compounds, silt and sand from erosion, salt from streets in the winter, and other debris. Our present waste treatment needs to be improved in order to cope with all of these pollutants. Unfortunately, many municipalities do not have adequate waste treatment methods. Therefore, much raw or poorly treated sewage is dumped into our waters daily. Phosphates hasten the deterioration of lakes and ponds by stimulating vegetative growth. Decaying vegetation uses up oxygen until water can no longer support animal life. In a lake situation, this circumstance is termed a "dead" lake.

Most public concern with water pollution is centered around municipal discharges and industrial wastes. However, other forms of pollutants are daily washing off the Earth, also into the waterways. Pollutants, such as lead from automobiles, oil drippings, fertilizers and pesticide poisons, salts, and silt, contribute to the pollution of our waters. Siltation is principally caused by land erosion through logging, farming, irrigation, and land clearing. Sediments are washed into the waters through mining and gravel washing. Consequently, water pollution must be controlled in a dual way, through conscientious soil conservation practices as well as the highest possible treatment of sewage (such as secondary or tertiary treatment).

Oil pollution is a growing environmental hazard and a new source of water pollution, both in fresh and salt waters. Oil pollution can potentially destroy the ecosystem of the water environment. Oil can be removed from the surface of waters through the use of detergents and emulsifiers. Yet a significant amount of pollution from oil eventually settles as sediment in rivers, lakes, and oceans.

Water temperature also affects aquatic life. Heat lowers the oxygen-holding capacity of water, thereby inhibiting the normal reproduction of certain species, such as trout and bass. When factories discharge millions of gallons of hot water into our waterways, they are lowering the reproductive abilities of certain aquatic species.

Activity 1: Hydrologic Cycle

OBJECTIVE:	To demonstrate the principles involved in the hydrologic cycle
MATERIALS:	20-gallon aquarium with glass or Plexiglas cover, soil, small plants, grass seed, goldfish, and elodea plant (optional)
LEVEL:	Lower to upper
SETTING:	Classroom
TIME:	1 hour to set up, several weeks for observation
VOCABULARY:	Condensation, evaporation, evapotranspiration, hydrologic cycle, precipitation, transpiration

LESSON DESIGN

Divide the aquarium into two sections, one-third for an aquatic area and two-thirds for a terrestrial area. Create a lake in one-third of the aquarium by dividing it from the rest of the aquarium with a Plexiglas divider or with a large glass bowl. Put soil in the rest of the aquarium in such a way that a hillside is created, starting high at the top and getting lower toward the lake. This will create an angle for water runoff. Plant plants and grass seed in the soil hillside and put a goldfish with an elodea plant into the bowl. When the grass has germinated and established itself, seal the aquarium with the glass cover, making sure there are no air leaks. Make careful notes over the next several days and keep a record of your observations. The grass and plants should transpire water, the lake evaporate water, and all of this water should condense on the glass cover and precipitate, creating a viable demonstration of a hydrologic cycle in action (see Figure 3.1).

Supplementary Activities

This activity is a simpler one that also demonstrates the basic principles of the water cycle. Put water in a pan and boil it on a hot plate. Water goes into the air as vapor through the process of evaporation. Put ice cubes in an aluminum pan and hold the pan over the boiling water. Drops of water will form on the bottom of the cold plate. Warm vapor touching the cold pan is condensation. As the pan gets warmer, drops on the bottom of the pan get bigger and heavier and fall. This action is precipitation.

Fill a zip-lock plastic baggie one-fourth of the way full of water. Zip the bag closed. Place the bag in the sunshine and observe for several hours. Drops of water will form on the top and sides of the baggie through the process of evaporation.

Prop up a plastic tub up at a 20-degree angle. Pour 4 ounces of water in the tub, then put a lid on it. Direct a heat lamp on the water portion of the tub. This action will create evaporation. Fill a zip-lock baggie with ice and place it on top of the lid at the opposite end from the water. This action will create condensation. After a cycle of evaporation, condensation, and precipitation has been established, add food coloring to the water in the box and observe.

Questions

1. What happens to water that evaporates?

2. What happens to precipitation?

3. To what does evapotranspiration refer?

4. Under what conditions is there only evaporation? Under what conditions is there only transpiration?

5. What factors could alter our hydrologic cycle, and what would be the effects of those alterations?

6. Why do we say we are using the same water that Abraham Lincoln and Socrates used? How is this possible?

7. What process is taking place with the heat lamp?

8. What process is taking place with the ice on top of the lid?

9. What principle is the food coloring demonstrating?

HYDROLOGICAL CYCLE

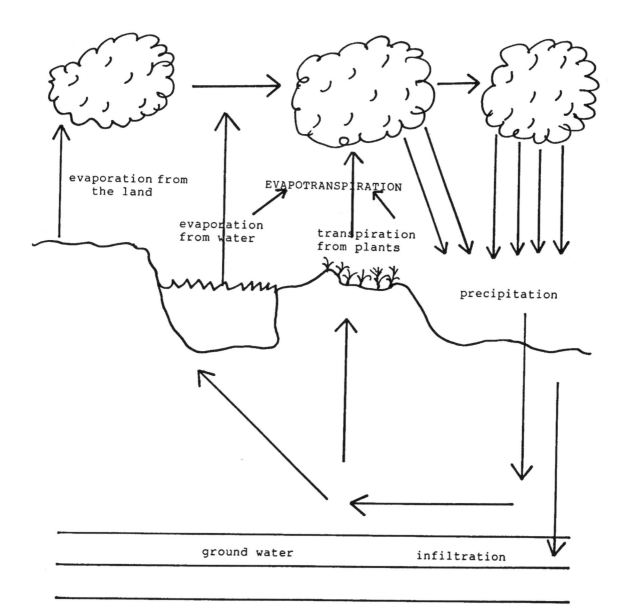

Fig. 3.1.

Activity 2: Amount of Water Flowing per Second

OBJECTIVE:	To be able to determine cubic feet of water flowing per second in a river
MATERIALS:	Paper, pencils
LEVEL:	Upper
SETTING:	Riverbank or classroom
TIME:	1–2 hours/30 minutes for calculations, but 1–2 hours if combining all at one time

LESSON DESIGN

To determine cubic feet of water per second flowing in a river, do the following calculations:

_____ feet ×_____ feet × _____ = _____ cu ft./sec.
　(width)　　　　　(depth)　　　　ft./second

Water Conversion Table:

A flow of 1 cu. ft./sec. = 448.03 gal./min.

1 cu. ft. of water = 7.48 gallons

1 cu. ft. of water = 62.4 pounds

1 acre ft. of water = 43,560 cu. ft.

A cubic foot of water is the water in a container one foot wide, one foot deep and one foot long, which equals 7.48 gallons.

Supplementary Activities

How many gallons of water are flowing in the stream each minute?

_____ × 7.48 × 60 = _____
　stream flow in　　　gal/　sec./　　gal. of water/min.
　cu. ft./sec.　　　　cu. ft.　min.

On the average, each person uses 200 gallons of water per day. How many people will the stream support?

$$\underline{\hspace{3cm}} \times \underline{\hspace{3cm}} = \underline{\hspace{3cm}}$$

| gal. per min. | no. min. per day | total gals/day |

$$\underline{\hspace{3cm}} \div \underline{\hspace{1cm}200\hspace{1cm}} = \underline{\hspace{3cm}}$$

| total gals/day | average amount used by 1 person/day | no. of people stream will support |

Make the same calculations for several rivers to determine which river would support the most people and other kinds of wildlife.

Questions

1. Which river is best suited to support the most variety and quantity of aquatic life: a slow, a fast, or an intermediate river? Give reasons for your answer.

2. What would happen to a community downstream if a fast-flowing river got dammed up upstream?

Activity 3: Dissolved Oxygen Content

OBJECTIVE:	To determine the dissolved oxygen content, an index of water quality, in a body of water
MATERIALS:	Methylene blue indicator solution, clear bottles, test tubes, measuring spoons
LEVEL:	Upper
SETTING:	Classroom and aquatic environment
TIME:	1 hour collecting samples, 1 hour to check for dissolved oxygen

LESSON DESIGN

Collect water samples in clear bottles from several different sources: ponds, lakes, rivers, and so forth. Students may also bring in samples of water from around their homes for extra samples to test or to eliminate the class going out and collecting samples. Pour about 2 ounces of water into a test tube. Add ½ ounce of methylene blue indicator solution. Record the amount of time it takes to change from dark blue to very light blue or clear. Repeat for the various samples and compare results. The faster the color changes, the less oxygen is present and the more carbon dioxide and bacteria.

Questions

1. Which sample had the highest concentration of oxygen: rivers, ponds, or lakes? Why?

2. Why is it important for an aquatic ecosystem to have a lot of dissolved oxygen?

3. What things in an aquatic ecosystem use dissolved oxygen in the water?

Activity 4: Conditions and Variants of Water

OBJECTIVE:	To determine what kind of aquatic life a river, pond, or lake is capable of sustaining
MATERIALS:	Thermometers; sounding line (snap swivel, string, lead sinker); secchi disk (10-inch circle of ¼-inch plywood, nut and bolt, cord); hydrometer (5-inch plastic straw, clay, weight, test tube, distilled water); bottom sampler (#10 can, broom handle or stick, bolt, nail or screw)
LEVEL:	Upper
SETTING:	Classroom for making the apparatus, aquatic environment for testing and using the apparatus
TIME:	2 hours assembly time, 2 hours for usage
VOCABULARY:	Specific gravity, translucent, temperature

LESSON DESIGN

Temperature, specific gravity, translucency, and rate of stream flow are a few of the important factors affecting the quantity and quality of life in an aquatic ecosystem. Aquatic organisms are adapted to living under certain conditions, and if those conditions are altered, so is the lifestyle of the aquatic organisms. The temperature of water in ponds and streams is influenced by air temperature, sunlight, depth, and water temperature of inflowing water, and temperature influences which species will be supported. The effect of water temperature on aquatic life can be severe. For example, 70° F (21° C) is the normal river temperature of a river with a lot of animals, plants, and clear water; at 80° F (27° C), almost no fish can reproduce, and many are already dead. At 90° F (32° C), most fish are killed. At 95° F (35° C), water tastes and smells unpleasant because of the increased number of microbes, and it is useless for drinking and almost useless for factory cooling. At 113° F (45° C), a river is dead except for some microbes. Specific gravity of water is increased by dissolved salts from the soil, by decreases in temperature, and by dissolved or suspended pollutants. Specific gravity is measured with a hydrometer. Quicker stream flow in the center inhibits much aquatic life. *Turbidity* refers to the amount of material suspended in the water. It affects the depth to which light can penetrate and consequently photosynthesis. Turbidity is measured with a secchi disk.

- *Sounding Line*—Tie knots at 1-foot intervals in a piece of string with a lead weight attached to one end. Lower it into the water and read the depth by counting knots. Lower a thermometer to the depth desired. Leave 3–4 minutes and record different depth temperatures.

- *Secchi Disk*—Insert a bolt in the middle of a 10-inch circle of ¼-inch plywood and secure with a nut. Paint the lid alternately black and white (see Figure 3.2) so that you end up with four sections. Attach a heavy cord, knotted at intervals of 3–6 inches. Lower the disk into the water until the black-and-white portions merge, then disappear. Raise the disk and record the depth at which you first see it reappear. The average of the two readings is the limit of visibility, or the depth of visible light penetration from the surface. The turbidity index is expressed as 100 divided by the number of feet the disk was lowered into the water. If the disk disappeared at 2 feet, then 100 divided by 2 equals 50. Water with a higher turbidity index (50) is more polluted than water with a lower turbidity index (4).

- *Hydrometer*—Plug one end of a 5-inch plastic straw with clay. Attach a nut or weight to the clay so that the straw floats partially submerged in the test tube of distilled water. Mark the straw at the water line. In salt or brackish water, the straw will float higher.

- *Bottom Sampler*—Cut a #10 can into a scoop shape. Attach this scoop to a broom handle or stick by a bolt, nail, or screw (see Figure 3.3). Scoop up sediment from the bottom of lakes and ponds to determine the contents.

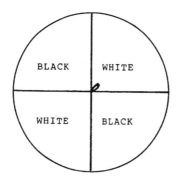

Fig. 3.2.

Fig. 3.3.

Supplementary Activities

Record temperatures of air and water around a stream and a pond. Take water temperatures at the surface and at depths of 1, 3, 6, and 9 feet (and so on) and at the bottom. Where is it the coldest? Where is it the warmest? Does the temperature change quickly? Is the air or the water colder? Sketch a thermocline of the body of water to include changes in temperature related to depth.

A trout needs approximately 1,000 cubic feet of water in which to live. How many trout could be supported in a mile of river?

Questions

1. What is the effect of each of the following factors on aquatic ecosystems: temperature, velocity, specific gravity, and translucency?

2. Is any one factor more or less important than any of the other factors?

3. What other factors could be studied to determine the viability of an aquatic ecosystem?

Activity 5: Pollution of Aquatic Ecosystems

OBJECTIVES:	To determine the effects of pollution on an aquatic ecosystem
MATERIALS:	4 or 5 1-gallon jars, 4 or 5 goldfish or many minnows, 4 or 5 aquatic plants
LEVEL:	Upper
SETTING:	Classroom
TIME:	Several weeks
VOCABULARY:	Pollutants
PRE-ACTIVITIES:	Maintenance of an aquarium under the proper conditions

LESSON DESIGN

Allow water to stand at least 24 hours to dechlorinate. Add equal numbers of fish and plants to each jar. Introduce one pollutant to each system, such as oil, detergent, pesticides, hot water, herbicides, and the like. Make careful and frequent observations of each jar and keep detailed records of your observations.

Supplementary Activities

Study the thermal effects on aquatic life by setting up an aquarium with plants and fish, an aquarium heater, and a thermometer. Maintain and stabilize the aquarium for two weeks. Raise the temperature a few degrees every couple of days until all but one organism are dead. Raise the temperature one degree each day from then on and record your observations. Did the last fish adjust or die? How were all the organisms affected (plants and animals)?

To demonstrate how far-reaching pollution can be, do the following: pour ½ cup of water into a 1-gallon jar. Add 2 drops of food coloring. Observe the pattern the food coloring makes as well as the intensity of the water's color. Now add 1 cup of water at a time and observe the water (intensity and pattern) until the water is clear. Make a chart to show additions of water and observations.

Questions

1. Were the organisms affected differently by the different pollutants? How?

2. Were any organisms not affected at all?

3. How long did it take the organisms to be affected by each pollutant?

4. Were fish more sensitive to the pollutants than the plants, or vice versa?

5. How many cups of water did it take to make the water clear again? What does this say about the effects of a pollutant on water?

6. Just because the water is clear, does that mean the pollutant is really gone? Explain.

Activity 6: Water Pollution

OBJECTIVE:	To determine the effects of phosphates on water quality
MATERIALS:	Elodea (aquatic plant), algae, daphnia (water fleas), 6 jars (2-quart or 1-gallon size), pond water, detergents, eye dropper
LEVEL:	Upper
SETTING:	Pond and classroom
TIME:	45 minutes to set up the jars and unlimited time to collect pond water and aquatic organisms
VOCABULARY:	Aquatic, eutrophication, phosphates, pollutants
PRE-ACTIVITIES:	Activity 4 (chapter 3) on conditions and variants of water

LESSON DESIGN

Detergents contain *phosphates*, which are chemicals that allow detergents to clean in all kinds of water, hard or soft. Phosphates act as fertilizers and stimulate aquatic plant growth. This stimulation makes algae multiply tremendously. They use up an amazing amount of oxygen, depleting the oxygen supply for other plants and animals and causing them to die. In this kind of a situation, the pond will slowly change into a decaying swamp. This final stage is called *eutrophication*. To see the effects of phosphates on aquatic life, find a pond out of which to collect water, some algae, daphnia, and elodea. If this is not possible, pet stores sell these aquatic organisms. While collecting the organisms, pay close attention to the pond. Does it look viable and healthy, or does it look like it is being taken over by algae and slowly dying? Fill each jar three-fourths of the way full of pond water and equal numbers of daphnia, elodea plants, and algae. Buy a detergent that is not low in phosphates. Mix a cup of detergent to a pint of water, and using an eye dropper, put 10 drops of the mixture in the first jar, 20 drops in the second jar, 30 drops in the third jar, 40 drops in the fourth jar, 50 drops in the fifth jar, and none in the sixth jar because it will be the control jar. Label each jar accordingly. Place the jars in the same sunny location and make daily observations.

Supplementary Activities

Because many plant fertilizers contain phosphates, do the same experiment using fertilizers instead of detergents. Using either liquid fertilizer or making a mixture of fertilizer and water as above, put the same number of drops of liquid fertilizer in the jars. Compare your results with those from the first experiment with detergent.

Questions

1. Did the daphnia die at equal rates in all of the jars? Explain the differences.

2. Did the algae grow equally well in all of the jars or better in some than in others? Why?

3. What happened to the elodea plants as the algae began to grow better and better?

4. What happens to an aquatic ecosystem when large amounts of detergents are added to it?

5. What were the similarities and the differences between the experiment with the detergent and the experiment with the fertilizer?

6. What happens to aquatic ecosystems when both detergents and phosphates are added to them? Does this double their chances of decaying and becoming an eutrophic ecosystem?

7. If the daphnia and the elodea were killed by the phosphates, how would this affect the other organisms in the food chain?

 ## Activity 7: Water Pollution 2

OBJECTIVE:	To determine the effects of pollutants on water supplies
MATERIALS:	Plastic soft-drink bottle, nylon stocking, sand, water, glass jar, variety of pollutants (oil, detergents, fertilizers, and the like)
LEVEL:	Lower to upper
SETTING:	Classroom
TIME:	45 minutes
VOCABULARY:	Aquifer, pollutants, toxic waste, water table

LESSON DESIGN

Make a funnel filter by cutting the bottom off the soft-drink bottle. Tape or rubber band a piece of nylon stocking over the mouth of the bottle. Insert the mouth end of the bottle into the glass jar for support and fill it three-fourths of the way full with sand. Pour clear water through the sand filter and observe. Then, one item at a time, add pollutants to the water and pour each one into the sand filter. Observe and record what happens with each item.

Questions

1. Does the sand catch any of the pollutants so that they don't end up in the water supply? Which ones?

2. How would sand and other forms of soil prevent wastes from leaking into the water table?

3. What natural things in the soil help break down organic materials in the soil?

Activity 8: Eutrophication

OBJECTIVE:	To demonstrate the oxygen depletion stage of eutrophication
MATERIALS:	Methylene blue solution, 2 one-gallon jars, soil, plants
LEVEL:	Upper
SETTING:	Classroom
TIME:	30 minutes to set up, several days for observation
VOCABULARY:	Eutrophication
PRE-ACTIVITIES:	Activity 3 (chapter 3) on dissolved oxygen

LESSON DESIGN

Fill both jars with water and add enough methylene blue solution to turn the water in both jars a pale blue. Put about 1 inch of soil on the bottom of both. Crush any kind of plant material and place in one jar. The jar without the plant material is the control jar. As bacteria decompose plant material, they also consume dissolved oxygen from the water. Methylene blue is blue in the presence of oxygen. After several days, the jar without plant material should still be blue, and the jar with plant material should be colorless, indicating the loss of oxygen.

Eutrophication is a natural process that people are accelerating by adding large amounts of sewage and organic waste to lakes and ponds. Bacteria feed on organic waste and use up the oxygen. The presence of algal growth on water is a good indication of a eutrophic lake. The algae blocks the penetration of sunlight and reduces the ability of aquatic plants to photosynthesize.

Questions

1. Why would a eutrophic lake look healthy because of all the algae but really be unhealthy?

2. What does eutrophication have to do with pollution?

3. How could people slow the eutrophication process of lakes?

 ## *Activity 9: pH Measurement of Water*

OBJECTIVE:	To determine the pH of water
MATERIALS:	pH paper and color chart, water samples, collecting jars
LEVEL:	Lower or upper
SETTING:	Outdoors, classroom
TIME:	Undetermined amount of time for collecting, 30 minutes for measuring
VOCABULARY:	pH

LESSON DESIGN

Collect several samples of water from different areas: lake, stream, pond, homes, hot springs, well, and so forth. Dip a piece of pH paper in each sample and record the source of the sample and its pH. Compare your results.

Questions

1. Were any samples extremely acidic or alkaline? What could be an explanation for this?

2. What does pH tell us about water?

3. Are aquatic organisms able to live in water with pH values ranging from 0.0 to 14.0, or do they have specific pH requirements?

 ### *Activity 10: Oil Spills*

OBJECTIVE:	To determine if oil spills have any effect on aquatic ecosystems
MATERIALS:	2 10-gallon aquariums, fish, aquatic plants, gravel, snails, used motor oil, 2 hard-boiled eggs
LEVEL:	Upper
SETTING:	Classroom
TIME:	30 minutes to set up, several weeks for observation

LESSON DESIGN

Set up two aquariums, both with aquatic plants, fish, snails, and a hard-boiled egg. Coat the water surface of one with used motor oil. Leave the other aquarium alone. Make daily observations and records to see what happens to the oil, water, live organisms, and bottom sedimentation.

Supplementary Activities

After several days or weeks, devise a variety of ways to clean up the oil spill in the aquarium. Discuss which method would be most feasible and carry it out. If it doesn't work, keep trying different methods until all the oil is cleaned up. Was it easy or difficult to clean up the oil?

Weigh a bundle of chicken or other bird feathers. Soak the feathers in oil and weigh them again. What is the difference? What happens to the birds caught in oil slicks?

Several devices are available for cleaning up oil spills. Not all of them are satisfactory or workable in all situations. Physical containment methods, such as barriers and skimmers, and chemical substances, such as detergents and solvents that break up oil, are good remedies. However, a more promising solution is *bioremediation*, or the use of organisms. Some organisms, called *petrophiles*, which include some bacteria, yeast, and fungi, actually like to eat oil and oil-based products. Research these organisms and devise an experiment with the original oil spill simulation to see how effective the organisms are in cleaning up your oil spill. Buy some petrophiles, available in scientific supply houses, and carry out your experiment to test your hypothesis.

Questions

1. What happened to the oil, water, live organisms, and bottom sedimentation in the aquarium?

2. Was the egg able to resist being permeated with oil? If so, how? If not, why not? What would happen to shore-nesting birds' eggs during an oil spill?

3. Would plants and animals be able to survive indefinitely if oil were spilled into their water and not cleaned up?

Activity 11: Testing of Water Samples

OBJECTIVES:	To see the effects of aerobic activity on sewage
MATERIALS:	2 1-liter jars with lids, manure, aquarium aerator and aerator stone, distilled water
RESOURCES:	Water and Sanitation Department
LEVEL:	Upper
SETTING:	Classroom
TIME:	30 minutes to set up, 1 week to aerate
PRE-ACTIVITIES:	Visit a sewage treatment plant; visit the water-treatment supply plant for your town.

LESSON DESIGN

Place a couple tablespoons of fresh horse or rabbit manure in each jar. Fill almost to the top with distilled water and shake. Place a lid tightly on one jar and label it Jar A. Aerate Jar B with the aquarium aerator and stone and let it bubble for one week. At the end of one week, shake both jars and inspect them for odor, sediment, and characteristics of sediment. The aerobic activity should have helped to change the organic matter in Jar B into an activated sludge that will speed up the natural bacterial oxidation process.

Questions

1. Why is oxygen necessary in the treatment of sewage?

2. What would be the problem in sewage treatment without oxygen?

3. Where does the water go after you have used it at school? What is done with it?

4. What kinds of treatments are used in the disposal of sewage and solid waste in your community?

5. What effects do present treatment methods have on underground water supplies, public health, and environmental quality? Do these methods contribute to air pollution or water pollution? If so, how?

Activity 12: Toxicity of Substances

OBJECTIVE:	To determine the toxicity of substances to aquatic life and to determine the toxic level of a pollutant
MATERIALS:	6 1-gallon jars, dechlorinated water, ammonia, eyedropper
LEVEL:	Lower to upper
SETTING:	Classroom
TIME:	45 minutes to set up, a few days for observation
VOCABULARY:	Pollutants, toxic
PRE-ACTIVITIES:	Activity 5 (chapter 3) on pollution of aquatic ecosystems

LESSON DESIGN

The number and kinds of organisms that can survive in a polluted environment are reduced from that of an unpolluted environment. The number of individual organisms capable of surviving in a polluted environment is increased because organic pollution destroys organisms associated with clean water. Consequently, the natural balance of competition and predation among organisms is destroyed.

Fill six 1-gallon jars one-fourth of the way full with dechlorinated water. Number the jars. Jar #1 will be the control and will contain no toxicant. Starting with Jar #2, add a small amount of the toxic substance (8-10 drops of ammonia, for example).

Increase the amount in each successive jar. Label each jar with the amount of toxicant used. Add two to three small fish to each jar. Observe and record actions of fish, when each one dies, and so forth.

Supplementary Activities

Make a chart listing types, sources, locations, and possible treatments of water pollution in your community.

Pollution reduces water quality. There are two basic types of water pollution: natural (acidity from decaying vegetation, silt, dissolved minerals) and people-made (trash, sewage, chemicals, thermal changes). Make a chart showing examples of both types.

Questions

1. What evidence of water pollution exists in your community?

2. What are the effects of this water pollution: odor, sight pollution, dead animals, and so on?

3. If your community does not have water pollution problems, could a water polluted community five or ten miles away affect the ecology of your area? How and why?

4. How could water pollution be avoided in the future?

Activity 13: Water Purification

OBJECTIVE:	To demonstrate different methods of purifying water to make it safe to drink
MATERIALS:	Coffee filters, 3 funnels, 4 jars in which the funnels will fit, sand, gravel, soil, clay, potassium aluminum sulfate
LEVEL:	Upper
SETTING:	Classroom
TIME:	1 hour
VOCABULARY:	Aeration, chlorination, coagulation, distillation, filtration, purification
PRE-ACTIVITIES:	Activity 4 (chapter 6) on waste production and reduction

LESSON DESIGN

Water needs to be purified before it can be consumed by people. There are several ways of doing this, each of which removes a different contaminant, such as bacteria, solid wastes, or odors. Some city water treatment plants use all of these methods, whereas other treatment plants use only one or a combination of several.

Filtration: Put coffee filters in three funnels set in three jars and fill each filter half full with either sand, gravel, or soil. Make some muddy water and pour a cup of it in each funnel. After the water has seeped through each medium and filter, compare the water samples. The gravel will be the worst filtering process, the soil will be moderately effective, and the sand will be the most effective in filtering the muddy water. After the water has been filtered through sand in settling tanks, it still needs to be purified for germs because this process only gets rid of visible particulate matter.

Coagulation: Put coffee filters in two funnels set in two jars and put 3 inches of sand in each funnel. Mix a cup of water with a few teaspoons of clay in one jar, and a cup of water with a few teaspoons of clay and a few teaspoons of potassium aluminum sulfate in another jar. Stir both mixtures well and pour one mixture in one funnel of sand and the other mixture in the other funnel of sand. After the water has settled and filtered through the sand, compare the water in the jars. The potassium aluminum sulfate should make the clay particles coagulate, or stick together, so they filter out as larger particles. The particles in the jar without the potassium aluminum sulfate should seep through the filter more easily because they are smaller. This process makes many tiny particles stick together so that they can be filtered through a settling tank. Otherwise, they would be too small to be filtered through sand or gravel.

Supplementary Activities

Fill a 1-quart pan half full of water and boil for 10 minutes. Remove the pan from the stove and let the water cool. Pour the cooled water into a clear glass and add a few drops of bleach. The water will be clearer and therefore contain fewer impurities because boiling water kills most bacteria and the bleach is a germicide that removes any color from the water.

Questions

1. What kind of water purification system does your town operate?

2. Why would the distillation of water be an expensive process for cities to use?

3. How does aerating water improve its taste and remove unpleasant odors?

Activity 14: Origin of Ponds and Streams

OBJECTIVE:	To figure out where ponds and streams form
MATERIALS:	Yard sticks, paper, carpenter's level, compass, 2 glass jars, 1 lid, masking tape, marking pen
RESOURCES:	Water sanitation personnel with a map of the local water system (and source of drinking water)
LEVEL:	Upper
SETTING:	Classroom and outdoors
TIME:	Varied time with water sanitation personnel, 1 hour outdoors, 45 minutes in classroom
VOCABULARY:	Topography
PRE-ACTIVITIES:	Visit a water treatment plant

LESSON DESIGN

During spring runoff, many ponds, streams, and puddles are formed that later dry up and disappear. This activity is one that will help students discover how small lakes, ponds, and streams form. They can adapt their information to larger situations, such as major rivers and lakes.

During a dry period, choose a site outdoors to study. Have the students draw a map of the area, locating high and low spots, landmarks, and the like. Use a carpenter's level and a compass to determine the slope of the land and the cardinal directions.

After a rainstorm, visit the site and draw on the original map the locations of puddles, streams, and ponds that have formed since the rainstorm.

Follow the paths of some of the streams to see where they go.

Supplementary Activities

Fill two jars with equal amounts of water (approximately half full). With a marking pen, place a mark on the side of each jar at the water level. Put a lid on one jar. Place both jars in an area where they won't be bothered. Every couple of days, for two weeks, check the water level in both jars.

Questions

1. Where will puddles form and streams develop? Why?

2. Where will the largest and smallest puddles form? Why?

3. Was the water in the puddles and streams clear or dirty? Why?

4. Will any of the puddles and streams last for a long time, or will they all disappear as the weather changes? Explain.

5. Why did the water level in the closed jar stay the same over the two week period?

6. Why do some lakes dry up and others stay the same?

Activity 15: Effects of Freezing on Water

OBJECTIVE:	To determine what happens when water freezes
MATERIALS:	Small jar with screw-on lid, plastic bag
LEVEL:	Lower to upper
SETTING:	Classroom
TIME:	10 minutes to set up, 24 hours to freeze, 30 minutes for discussion
VOCABULARY:	Contraction, expansion

LESSON DESIGN

Completely fill the jar with water and screw on the lid. Put the jar of water inside the plastic bag and place it in the freezer. Approximately 24 hours later, remove the jar from the freezer. Observe and discuss the results.

Supplementary Activities

Fill a small coffee can to the top with cold water and put a lid on it. Place a bottle cap on top of the lid. Put two pencils under the can and one on top of the bottle cap, facing the same direction. Wrap strong tape around the pencils at both ends to hold everything together. Place the whole contraption in the freezer for 24 hours. Remove from the freezer and discuss the results. The can's lid will be pushed up by the ice, and the pencils will have broken.

Fill a plastic drinking straw with water and seal both ends with clay. Place the straw in the freezer for several hours. Remove the straw from the freezer and observe.

Place a brick in a large bucket and cover it completely with a premeasured amount of water. Let it sit for 1 to 2 hours, then remove the brick and pour the water into a measuring cup.

Questions

1. What happened to the jar of water when it froze? Why?

2. Is the frozen water less or more dense than liquid water? Why? How do you know?

3. Why does a lake freeze from the surface down? How is this important to life in the lake?

4. Why would one of the pieces of clay be pushed out of the drinking straw?

5. What happens to water when it freezes?

6. What happens to rocks when water seeps into cracks around them?

7. How much water did the brick soak up? Why?

8. If rocks soak up a great deal of water and then freeze, what happens to them?

Activity 16: Surface Tension of Water

OBJECTIVE:	To demonstrate that water has surface tension
MATERIALS:	Aluminum foil, waxed paper, eyedropper, water, 2 1–by–4 inch pieces of wood 1 foot long
LEVEL:	Lower to upper
SETTING:	Classroom
TIME:	10–15 minutes
VOCABULARY:	Meniscus, molecules, surface tension

LESSON DESIGN

Cover one piece of wood with aluminum foil and one with waxed paper. Lean both pieces of wood against a wall at the same angle. With the eyedropper, drop a drop of water at the top of each board. Watch what happens. The drop of water on the aluminum foil-covered board will splatter, whereas the drop of water on the waxed paper-covered board will roll down the paper. Water molecules attract each other in all directions. At the surface, molecules are pulled back into the liquid, forming a tough film called surface tension. This film is what gives bubbles their spherical shape. The water molecules don't stick to the waxed paper, and the surface tension keeps the water together in a bead. Because the water molecules stick to the aluminum foil, they make the water splatter.

Supplementary Activities

Fill a small glass with water and place it in an aluminum pie pan. Working at eye level with the top of the glass, use an eyedropper to add one drop of water at a time to the glass. Observe and record how much water you can add before the water flows over the side of the glass. This extra bubble of water on the surface of the glass is called a *meniscus*.

Place a penny in the pie pan. Using an eyedropper, drop one drop of water at a time onto the penny. Observe and count how many drops the penny will hold before the water spills over the edge into the pie pan.

Questions

1. What happened to the drop of water on the aluminum foil-covered board?

2. What happened to the drop of water on the waxed paper-covered board?

3. Why did the two drops do different things?

4. Why is the glass able to hold more water above its top?

Activity 17: Water Conservation

OBJECTIVE:	To demonstrate the importance of water and the necessity to conserve it
MATERIALS:	Fresh fruit and vegetables, water
RESOURCES:	Conservation experts (forest service, fish and wildlife, and water resources personnel)
LEVEL:	Lower to upper
SETTING:	Classroom
TIME:	1 hour initially, several days of follow-through, 1 hour culmination activity
VOCABULARY:	Conservation
PRE-ACTIVITIES:	Activity 1 (chapter 3) on the hydrologic cycle, Activity 6 (chapter 2) on water usage, Activity 7 (chapter 2) on water requirements, Activity 8 (chapter 2) on transpiration, Activity 9 (chapter 2) on transpiration, talks by conservation experts

LESSON DESIGN

Find out and make a chart about water usage and percentages. For example: 3 percent of all the Earth's water is freshwater, 1 percent of the Earth's freshwater supply is available for human consumption, 75 percent of a living tree is water, 65–70 percent of an adult human body is water, 75 percent of our brains are water, approximately 48,000 gallons of water are needed to produce an average-sized Sunday newspaper, and so on.

Household Water Usage	Average Amounts of Water Consumed
toilet flushing	6–7 gallons
washing car	40–50 gallons
brushing teeth	1–10 gallons
taking a bath	25–30 gallons
taking a shower	30–50 gallons
washing hands	2 gallons
watering outside	10 gallons/minute
dishwasher/clothes washer	40–50 gallons

Approximate Percentage of Domestic Water Usage	
toilet flushing	40%
washing and bathing	40%
kitchen and drinking	12%
other (outdoors and miscellaneous)	8%

Do the following activity to spark a discussion of water. Peel a fresh apple, a potato, and various other kinds of fruits and vegetables. Weigh each piece or group separately. Record their weights. Leave the fruit and vegetables in a warm, dry place for several days, then weigh them all again. Record their weights. Compare the before and after weights. What percentage of each fruit and vegetable is water?

Time how long it takes to fill a gallon milk jug from the shower head. Time how long it takes you to take a shower, then calculate the amount of water you use to take a shower.

Number of seconds to fill milk jug _____

Divide by 60 _____ (number of minutes to use one gallon of water)

Number of minutes in shower _____

Divide minutes by seconds _____ (number of gallons per shower)

Multiply by 30 _____ (number of gallons per month)

These calculations are only for taking a shower. Try the same procedure with other forms of household water use and include the amounts in a water usage chart.

Do a water survey to find out how much water you use in a day, a week, and a month, at home and at school.

After completing the water survey, make a chart to show common household water usage.

Make a list of different ways you can conserve water. For example: take shorter showers, install water-saving shower heads, don't let the faucet run while you brush your teeth or wash vegetables, run dishwashers and washing machines only when full, check faucets and pipes for leaks, water lawns during the coolest parts of the day, mulch trees and flowers, and so forth.

Calculate the average amount of water you would use to take a bath, then compare it with the amount of water it takes to take a shower.

Questions

1. Why is it important to conserve water?

2. Which uses less/more water, a shower or a bath?

3. What are some ways you can conserve water?

VOCABULARY DEFINITIONS

Aeration—To expose to the circulation of air for purification.

Aquatic—Living or growing in or on the water.

Aquifer—A water-bearing rock formation.

Chlorination—To treat or combine with chlorine.

Coagulation—To cause a transformation of a liquid into a solid mass. To move together or condense.

Compound—A combination of two or more elements.

Condensation—The process by which moist warm air meets colder air and the moisture forms into tiny drops of water.

Conservation—To preserve something from loss, waste, harm, such as natural resources, soil, or water.

Contraction—Reduction in size by shrinking or pulling together.

Decomposition—To separate into basic elements.

Distillation—A heat-dependent process used to purify a substance.

Eutrophication—A process of increasing productivity, speeded up by pollution, that can result in the death of aquatic flora and fauna because of the depletion of oxygen. In Greek, *eutrophication* means well nourished.

Evaporation—The process of giving off water vapor from bodies of water.

Evapotranspiration—Evaporation and transpiration combined. For example, a forest ecosystem with water transpiration from trees and water evaporation from lake or river.

Expand—To be increased in size by swelling.

Filtration—To put through a filter, which is a porous substance used for removing suspended matter.

Hydrologic Cycle—The process by which water condenses, precipitates, evaporates, and cycles itself over again and again.

Meniscus—The curved upper surface of a liquid, like the extra bubble of water on the surface of a really full glass of water.

Molecule—The simplest structural unit of a compound.

pH—Potential of hydrogen. A measure of the acidity or alkalinity of a solution.

Phosphates—A chemical in detergents and fertilizers that stimulates plant growth when introduced to an aquatic system.

Pollutants—Anything that contaminates, especially gaseous, chemical, or organic wastes that contaminate the air, soil, or water.

Precipitation—Any form of rain, hail, sleet, or snow that has condensed from atmospheric water vapor and gets sufficiently heavy to fall to the Earth's surface.

Purification—The act of cleansing to get rid of impurities.

Specific Gravity—The ratio of the mass of a liquid or solid to the mass of an equal volume of distilled water at four degrees centigrade.

Surface Tension—A property of liquids, a result of which the surface tends to contract and has properties similar to a stretched elastic membrane.

Thermocline—A gradual change in temperature from one slope or area of a lake to another.

Topography—The physical features of a place or region.

Toxic—Harmful or deadly, poisonous.

Toxic Waste—Waste that is harmful or poisonous.

Translucent—Able to transmit light but having enough diffusion to eliminate perception of distinct images.

Transpiration—The act of giving off water vapor through the stomata of plant tissue.

Water Table—A permeable body of rock in a zone saturated with water.

4

WILDLIFE

A great variety of individual species exist and coexist on Earth. Each organism must use the full potential of its environment and struggle to survive because of adverse conditions in the environment. Organisms able to survive these adversities have learned to adapt. This means that an organism changes in order to survive in a particular environment. If the organism is unable to adapt, it will either move away or die. There are basically three different kinds of adaptations:

1. Structural, camouflage, for example.

2. Physiological, hibernation, for example.

3. Behavioral, migration, for example.

Each species of animal constructs its own type of home and never departs from its basic design. Thus, its construction is purely instinctive. It is not a learned ability.

The environment determines the species of wildlife in a community. The physical features of an area are the determining factors in wildlife species and populations. Wildlife populations are dynamic because of changing plant communities, microclimates, topography, or other ecological activities occurring daily within a community. Food, water, shelter, and space also regulate the kind and number of species able to inhabit a certain area.

Wildlife populations are dependent upon habitat quality. Some habitats have a higher carrying capacity than others because of an abundant food supply, more space, more accessibility to water, or a more diverse vegetative growth suitable for shelter or protection.

Wildlife species are interdependent with one another as well as with their environment. If one species is removed, the balance of the environment is upset. All animals interchange energy with each other and their environment. Plants derive their nourishment from the soil, the air, and the sun. The animals in an area derive their nourishment from these plants as well as other animals. Living requirements are different for different animals. In turn, each animal helps the other animals of an area to satisfy its specific needs. Animal droppings help fertilize the soil to stimulate plant growth to feed smaller animals, which becomes the food of larger animals. Thus, the web of life goes on and on. Because of these factors, wildlife species are kept in balance within the community in which they live. Consequently, one species usually does not run the risk of overpopulating all others. However, when environmental changes occur within an area, the organisms are affected. If the change is gradual within an area, species are more able to adapt to these changes. If change is brought about quickly, species that cannot adapt become extinct.

Animal reproduction is kept in balance by environmental factors. Heavily preyed upon animals reproduce more prolifically than others. Natural processes dispose of the surplus: predation, starvation, disease, or accident. If any of these factors are abolished, populations will increase. Sooner or later, the balance is restored because of mortality.

Activity 1: Habitat Characteristics

OBJECTIVE:	To determine the biotic and abiotic characteristics of three different habitats
MATERIALS:	1 chart for each group of 4–5 students
LEVEL:	Upper
SETTING:	3 different habitats outdoors (woods, schoolyard, park, and so on)
TIME:	45 minutes per habitat
VOCABULARY:	Biotic, abiotic, food chain, food web, habitat

LESSON DESIGN

In small groups, spend approximately 45 minutes in three different habitats. Fill in both charts, from Figures 4.1 and 4.2, for each habitat.

List under its proper heading (predator, carnivore, herbivore, or omnivore) the species of animals seen or suspected of living in each area. Use evidence found to determine the list. Then see if you can determine its food preference and list that. Write down any visible evidence used to identify a species (nests, scat, burrows, and the like).

Characteristics of Habitat	Evidence & Signs of Animals
Biotic Factors:	
Abiotic Factors:	
Human Influences:	

Fig. 4.1.

Evidence	Food	Predator	Carnivore	Herbivore	Omnivore
1.					
2.					
3.					
4.					
5.					
6.					

Fig. 4.2.

Supplementary Activities

From the evidence gathered, draw a food chain for each area. Put in arrows to show which factors affect other factors. Include plants, herbivores, carnivores, decomposers, and sunlight.

Design an imaginary animal that you think would be perfectly suited or adapted to one of the habitats you studied. Note its food requirements, its space requirements, its value and detriment to the environment, and its adaptations for seasonal change. If each group deals with a different habitat, discuss the possibilities and feasibility of each group's animal adapting to the other habitats.

Identify and describe six animal adaptations for each habitat studied.

Questions

1. What relationship exists between animals and their environment in the areas you studied?

2. What evidence might be found that animals live in these areas?

3. Were any habitats completely devoid of animal life? If so, why?

4. Which area had the greatest evidence of animal life? Why?

5. Which area had the most variety of animals?

6. What can be inferred or concluded about animals and their environments?

Activity 2: Soil Enrichment by Earthworms

OBJECTIVE:	To demonstrate the importance of earthworms to the soil
MATERIALS:	2 cardboard boxes (at least 12-by-12 inches), topsoil, 25 to 30 earthworms, 2 1-quart jars
LEVEL:	Lower to upper
SETTING:	Classroom
TIME:	30 minutes to set up, 3 weeks to stand

LESSON DESIGN

Fill two boxes with topsoil. Put 25 to 30 earthworms in one box and leave the other one empty. Cover both boxes. Moisten the soil and keep both boxes damp for about three weeks. After three weeks, crinkle one end of each box to make a spout. Pour 1 quart of water on the box without worms, 1 quart of water on the box with worms, and catch and measure the runoff from both boxes.

The box with the worms should have more water seepage into the soil than the box without worms because earthworms tunnel through the soil, making passages. Earthworms also add nutrients to the soil.

Supplementary Activities

Fill several large plastic tubs (5–6 quarts) three-fourths of the way full with peat moss. Dig three holes in the peat moss to make three indentations approximately the size of a cup. Fill each indentation with organic matter (partially decayed leaves, grass clippings, manure, food). Although each tub will have a different kind of organic matter, all three holes in each tub will hold the same kind of matter. Sprinkle each tub with water and place an equal number of earthworms in all but one tub. One tub will not have worms in it. Sprinkle each tub with a fine layer of cornmeal and put their covers on. Place the tubs away from direct sunlight and heat and observe them weekly for several months. Every couple of weeks, spoon out a sampling of organic matter from each tub and make notes of their characteristics.

Questions

1. Would plants grow better in soil with or without earthworms? Why?

2. In which soil would plants be better nourished? Why?

3. How are worms important to soil building?

4. What were the differences in organic matter in each tub?

5. What was the difference in organic matter between the tub without worms and the tub with worms? What does that tell you about the value of worms?

6. Was there any detectable odor to the tubs (other than soil)? What do you think the reason is?

Activity 3: Limiting Factors

OBJECTIVE:	To study the factors that limit growth because of too much or too little of something required to live
MATERIALS:	Brine shrimp eggs, dechlorinated water, non-iodized salt, several jars, 2 5-gallon aquariums, male and female guppies, fish food, goldfish, salt
LEVEL:	Lower to upper
SETTING:	Classroom
TIME:	1 hour to set up, several weeks for observation
VOCABULARY:	Limiting factors
PRE-ACTIVITIES:	Dechlorinate the water for the aquariums and brine shrimp by letting it sit for at least 24 hours. To prepare water for the brine shrimp, mix 32 tablespoons of non-iodized salt with 1 gallon of water.

LESSON DESIGN

Have each group of four to five students add a pinch of brine shrimp eggs to a jar of salt water and store in a moderately warm place (70–80° F). Eggs should hatch in approximately 24–48 hours. After the eggs hatch, if some brine shrimp die, the salinity of the water is low. Add more salt. Feed the shrimp in each jar a pinch of brewer's yeast every several days.

Try hatching eggs in regular water, vinegar and water, alcohol, iodized salt water, and the like.

After hatching eggs the proper way, put all the shrimp in one jar to study the effects of overcrowding.

Record observations from all experiments.

Supplementary Activities

Set up an aquarium with several male and female guppies. Do not feed them the first two days. The third day give them a pinch of food. Add more and more food until you exceed the proper amount. Record your observations.

Set up an aquarium with some goldfish. Each day add half a teaspoon of salt. Record the amount of salt added and your observations.

Discuss and make a chart of limiting factors in various ecosystems, such as ponds, lakes, deserts, and tundras, and for the human ecosystem.

Questions

1. Which medium was the most successful in hatching brine shrimp eggs? Why?

2. Of what importance are brine shrimp to a salt-water ecosystem?

3. What part do brine shrimp play in a food chain?

4. What effect did overcrowding have on the brine shrimp?

5. What effect did salt have on the goldfish?

6. What effect did food have on the guppies?

7. What are limiting factors and of what use could they be to an ecosystem? Would they always be detrimental, or could they sometimes be beneficial? Explain.

Activity 4: Oxygen–Carbon Dioxide Cycle

OBJECTIVE:	To demonstrate the oxygen–carbon dioxide cycle using a sealed aquarium and the dependence of fish on green plants and green plants on fish
MATERIALS:	1-gallon jar with a lid, 3–4 aquatic plants, sand, a snail, 2 goldfish
LEVEL:	Lower to upper
SETTING:	Classroom
TIME:	1 hour to set up, several weeks for observation
PRE-ACTIVITIES:	The aquarium from Activity 5 (chapter 3) on pollution of aquatic ecosystems could be used for this exercise

LESSON DESIGN

Place approximately 2 inches of sand in the bottom of the jar and plant the aquatic plants. Fill with water, then let it sit for about 24 hours to dechlorinate. Then add the fish and the snail. Screw on the lid and seal tightly with a rubber seal or wax. Keep the jar in the light but don't allow it to overheat. Keep records of any activity in the jar and your observations.

Supplementary Activities

Add bromthymol blue indicator solution to a jar of water. Change the color from blue to yellow by blowing into the water through a straw. Put an elodea plant into the jar of water solution and seal the jar. Put the jar in the sunlight. The water should turn blue. At night, without light, the water should turn yellow again.

Questions

1. How long will your mini-ecosystem be able to stay balanced and function like this?

2. What will upset the balance?

3. What role does each organism play in this ecosystem?

4. Why does the bromthymol blue water solution change from yellow to blue and from blue to yellow?

5. Is there any way to keep the bromthymol blue water solution always blue or always yellow? Explain.

Activity 5: Hay Infusion

OBJECTIVE:	To make a hay infusion to study protozoa
MATERIALS:	Hay, several dried leaves, jar of pond water, mud from the bottom of the pond, a few grains of rice, microscope, microscope slides and cover slips, eyedropper
LEVEL:	Lower to upper
SETTING:	Classroom and pond
TIME:	45 minutes of classroom time, whatever time is necessary to collect pond water and mud, and several days of standing time
VOCABULARY:	Protozoa

LESSON DESIGN

Either take a class trip to a pond to collect bottom mud and water, or have a student bring in the mud and water from a pond. After filling a jar half full of pond water and a little mud, add a small handful of hay and several leaves. Let the jar sit uncovered in a warm part of the classroom for several days. After several days, add a few grains of uncooked rice to the water. This combination of hay (timothy grass), leaves, and pond water is an *infusion*. The dried grass and the leaves will begin to decay, and scum will begin to appear on the surface of the water. Parts of the decayed leaves and grass will settle to the bottom, and an unpleasant odor will develop. The plant matter in the jar contains spores of decay bacteria and some one-celled animals enclosed in cases called *cysts*. With the right amount of moisture and warmth, the one-celled animals will come out of the cysts. In order to grow, the decay bacteria need food, warmth, and moisture, which they find in the remains of living plants and animals that have been buried in the water. When the conditions are right, the decay bacteria break through their protective spore coats and start to feed and grow. The dead plant and animal matter upon which the decay bacteria feed is broken down into its original compounds. The decay bacteria not only feed on the vegetative matter in the jar and cause it to decay, but they grow and multiply as well. These microscopic decay bacteria will grow and multiply as long as there is food available, but they will die as soon as the decayed matter is gone.

These simple, one-celled animals in the hay infusion are *protozoa*. Using the eyedropper, remove some water from the bottom of the jar. Place a small drop of pond water from your hay infusion on a microscope slide and carefully cover with a cover slip. View these one-celled protozoa under the microscope with low and high power. Make a second slide of pond water in exactly the same way, but collect the water from the top of the jar instead of from the bottom. Compare the two slides for differences and similarities.

 ## *Activity 6: Metamorphosis of Insects*

OBJECTIVE:	To observe the different stages through which a butterfly or moth passes
MATERIALS:	Large jar or dry aquarium, perforated cover, caterpillar, leaves on which the caterpillar was found
LEVEL:	Lower to upper
SETTING:	Classroom
TIME:	20 minutes to set up, several weeks of observation
VOCABULARY:	Chrysalis, cocoon, metamorphosis

LESSON DESIGN

Make sure when collecting caterpillars that you also collect a large amount of the vegetation on which the caterpillars were feeding. Caterpillars won't eat just any kind of vegetation. They are very selective. After collecting a caterpillar, place it in the dry aquarium or large jar and cover with cheesecloth or something else that air can pass through it. Replace dead and eaten vegetation with new vegetation as long as the caterpillar is still active. Caterpillars eat massive amounts of food to store for use during their metamorphosis into an adult moth or butterfly. After a while, the caterpillar will either spin a cocoon, if it is a moth caterpillar, or it will spin a chrysalis if it is a butterfly caterpillar. During the chrysalis/cocoon stage, the caterpillar will not eat anything. This stage of the process lasts several weeks, at which time the caterpillar will emerge from the cocoon or chrysalis as a moth or a butterfly. After emerging, a moth or butterfly must allow its wings to dry before flying away. They emerge folded up and slowly dry and unfold.

Activity 7: Metamorphosis of Amphibians

OBJECTIVE:	To observe the change of tadpoles into adult frogs
MATERIALS:	Frog eggs (either collected from ponds or purchased from biological supply stores), pond water, aquariums, plastic bags for collecting, small bowls
LEVEL:	Upper
SETTING:	Classroom and pond
TIME:	45 minutes to set up, several weeks for observation
VOCABULARY:	Metamorphosis

LESSON DESIGN

Collect several masses of frog eggs and place them in small bowls for observation. The eggs should be encased in a jelly-like substance and have dark spots on the top of the eggs, which indicate they are fertile. Underneath the black spot is a yellow area, which is the yolk sac such as the one in a chicken egg and contains food for the developing tadpole. Place the frog eggs in the aquariums with pond water collected from the same source as the eggs. Look at the eggs every day to observe any changes. The eggs will take longer to hatch in colder water, so it is a good idea to keep the water about 60–65° F. The eggs will take anywhere from eight days to a few weeks to hatch. After the eggs hatch, examine the tadpoles carefully, noting the yellow sac on the tadpole's stomach. At this point, food will need to be introduced into the aquarium, such as algae and other aquatic plants from the original pond. It will take the tadpoles almost three months to change into adult frogs. When the tadpoles start to develop tiny legs, arrange the aquarium such that there is a combination of land and water so they can climb out of the water occasionally.

Questions

1. What is the dark spot on the top of a frog's egg?

2. What purpose does the jelly-like substance serve?

3. What purpose does the yellow area, or yolk sac, serve in the egg stage and in the tadpole stage? When does it disappear?

4. What changes will tadpoles have to do through in order to become adult frogs?

5. After emerging from an egg, will a tadpole need food right away? Why or why not?

6. What is the difference between what tadpoles eat and what frogs eat?

7. What are the different stages in the life cycle of a frog?

Activity 8: Fruit Flies

OBJECTIVE:	To observe the reproduction and development of fruit flies
MATERIALS:	Very ripe fruit (bananas or apples), pint jars, hand lens, paper towels
LEVEL:	Upper
SETTING:	Classroom
TIME:	10 minutes to set up, 2–3 weeks for observation

LESSON DESIGN

Place pieces of very ripe fruit in the bottom of the jars. Keep the jars in a warm place but not in direct sunlight for a day or two. By that time, several flies should be in the jars. They either hatched from eggs in the fruit or adult flies were attracted to the ripe fruit. Place a piece of paper toweling in the jars and cover them with one as well and secure it with a rubber band around the rim. Lids may be used, but they need tiny holes poked in it to allow oxygen to get into the jars. Count the number of flies in the jars and record this on a chart. Periodically throughout the day, examine the jars to see if any eggs have been deposited on or in the fruit. The eggs that are very small, white, and oblong-shaped are difficult to see without a hand lens. After noticing the presence of eggs, keep a careful eye on them and watch for larva that will hatch from the eggs and live in the fruit. Record on the chart when the larva first appear, how many you see, and a short description of them. Examine the jars every day and record any new developments that may occur. After awhile, some brownish-looking things will appear. These are the skins being shed by the larva as they get bigger. Fruit fly larva shed their skins three times during their metamorphosis. In approximately a week, the larva will crawl out of the fruit and begin their pupal stage. During this time period, the larva turn brown and acquire a hard outer covering.

Keep a record of how many days pass between each stage. The fly should emerge from the pupal stage in approximately five to seven days. When the flies emerge, count them and record this on the chart. This entire process takes approximately two or three weeks, and because fruit flies live only about ten days, the original flies will probably be dead by the time the new flies emerge from the pupal stage. At this point, the flies can either be set free outdoors or fed to the frogs you grew in Activity 7. If the flies are kept, they will mate within twelve hours, the females will lay eggs within a day or two after mating, and the whole cycle will begin again.

FRUIT FLY STAGES

Form	Date	Number	Description
Egg			
Larva			
Pupa			
Adult			

Fig. 4.3.

Questions

1. Through how many stages does a fruit fly go?

2. Approximately how long does the fruit fly stay in each stage of its development?

3. Approximately how long does it take the fruit fly to develop from an egg to an adult?

4. What did the larva eat? What did the pupa eat?

Activity 9: Ant Colonies

OBJECTIVE:	To observe how ant colonies function
MATERIALS:	Ants, food (bread crumbs, grains), ant home, black construction paper
LEVEL:	Lower to upper
SETTING:	Classroom
TIME:	Varies depending on which home is built and how the ants are procured
PRE-ACTIVITIES:	Spend a fair amount of time before doing this project researching ants, their life cycles, and habits. Go outdoors and find an anthill to observe in its natural habitat.

LESSON DESIGN

These directions are for building two different kinds of ant homes, one more involved than the other.

The simpler version: Place a lidded 1-quart jar inside a 2-gallon jar and pour soil around the 1-quart jar, leaving the upper one-fourth exposed. Place a lid, with holes poked in it, on the 2-gallon jar. Wrap a piece of black construction paper around the jar because ants shy away from light. The paper can be temporarily removed for observation purposes.

The more involved version: Cut two pieces of wood ¾-by-¾ inches and 11¼ inches long, one piece 16 inches long, and two pieces 6 inches long. Form a frame by nailing the pieces together. The two 6-inch strips will be nailed on the bottom perpendicular to the rest of the frame to serve as a base. Tape a piece of red cellophane over a sheet of glass 12-by-16 inches. Tape the cellophaned glass to the wood frame with heavy waterproof tape. Tape a piece of clear glass the same size to the other side of the frame. Set the frame in a pan of water so that the ants won't escape. The red cellophane paper will obscure some light, allowing you to observe the ants in a more normal atmosphere than through the clear glass. Cover the whole home with black construction paper that can be lifted off easily for observation. Compare the ants' reactions near the clear glass and near the red cellophaned glass.

The third option for an ant home is to buy one from a biological supply store. They aren't too expensive and allow more time for observation rather than construction.

Buy ants from a biological supply store to insure a complete colony, or acquire them from eggs, larvae, pupae, workers to a queen, or from the anthill you observed outside. With a shovel, dig down into the anthill and scoop up workers, larvae, pupae, eggs, and a queen. The colony won't work unless a queen is present. Transfer the ants and soil to the ant home in the classroom. Sprinkle the soil with water every other day just to moisten it. Do not saturate it. Put bits and pieces of different kinds of food on top of the soil and watch to see which food the ants prefer. Keep a record of the ants' progress, their cooperative activities, their progress in building tunnels, and the like.

Questions

1. Why is it necessary for a queen to be present in an ant colony in order for it to function properly?

2. Why is it important to keep the ant colony covered with black paper when not observing their behavior?

3. What are the specialized tasks each member of the colony has to perform?

4. What would happen if an ant from a different colony were introduced into your ant colony?

5. What would happen if you removed an ant from your colony and replaced it several days later?

Activity 10: Hydra Regeneration

OBJECTIVE:	To study the reproduction and regeneration of hydra
MATERIALS:	Hydras (ordered from a biological supply store or obtained from a pond), jars, pond water, daphnia and brine shrimp (ordered from a biological supply store)
LEVEL:	Upper
SETTING:	Classroom
TIME:	Varies depending upon the method of procurement
VOCABULARY:	Asexual reproduction

LESSON DESIGN

Hydras are small (maybe one-half inch in length), fresh-water relatives of the jellyfish. They are invertebrates and consist of a saclike digestive cavity. The mouth is surrounded by stinging tentacles.

Hydras may be bought from biological supply stores or collected from ponds. If the hydras are to be collected from ponds, gather totally submerged plants and place them in jars of pond water. After a few days, the hydras will attach themselves to the side of the jar by means of a sticky substance. Hydras defend themselves with stinging tentacles, and they quickly contract to about one-twentieth their extended size and become almost inconspicuous if alarmed. Examine the hydras with hand lenses and describe what they look like, picking out the protrusions on the hydras' sides. These protrusions are one way in which hydras reproduce. It is an asexual form of reproduction called *budding*. When the new hydra has fully developed tentacles, it drops off the parent and lives independently. In asexual reproduction, the new individual (or growth) is exactly like the parent. Put some brine shrimp or daphnia into the jar with the hydras and observe how they eat. The hydras will not move toward these organisms. Instead, when a brine shrimp brushes against the hydra's tentacles, the hydra will push the food into its body cavity. Hydras are able to regenerate lost parts. Put a few hydras on a piece of glass and cut them in two or remove a tentacle. Put each part in a separate test tube to determine which parts are able to regenerate and which parts cannot. Most of the activities with the hydras need to be done with hand lenses because they are fairly minute and their parts are particularly minute. They could be placed on a projecting microscope, if available, and viewed more easily.

Supplementary Activities

To study regeneration further, collect some planaria and flatworms from a pond, or order some from a biological supply store. Perform different experiments to find out which parts of a planaria are regenerative.

Questions

1. How are hydras able to defend themselves against predators?

2. How are hydras able to attach themselves to the sides of things, such as the jars?

3. How are hydras able to defend themselves against larger animals?

4. How do hydras reproduce?

5. What is meant by asexual reproduction?

6. How would sexual reproduction be a more advantageous adaptation than asexual reproduction?

7. What are a hydra's means of locomotion?

8. Why is regeneration an advantageous adaptation?

 ## Activity 11: Symbiosis

OBJECTIVE:	To understand the symbiotic relationships that occur between some species of plants and animals
MATERIALS:	Legume seeds, clay pots, soil, legume plants
LEVEL:	Upper
SETTING:	Classroom and field outdoors
TIME:	30 minutes to set up, several weeks for observation
VOCABULARY:	Bacteria, nitrogen fixation, nodules, symbiosis

LESSON DESIGN

Find an area where you can dig up alfalfa, clover, and soybeans along with their roots. In class, carefully wash off the plants' roots and examine the swellings, or *nodules*. These nodules contain hundreds of tiny bacteria. Because bacteria do not make their own food, they must live off something else. Some bacteria, such as tuberculosis, diphtheria, and malaria, are harmful. Other bacteria, however, are helpful to their host organism. Bacteria that live in nodules take food from their hosts and provide their hosts with valuable minerals the hosts cannot obtain for themselves. In this case, the bacteria take the mineral nitrogen from the air and convert it into a form that the plants can use. Legumes can grow in nitrogen-poor soil because they have these nitrogen-fixing bacteria on their roots. Tomatoes and corn, which do not have nitrogen-fixing bacteria on their roots, cannot live in nitrogen-poor soil. Bacteria enter the cortex of the root by osmosis at the root hairs. Their presence stimulates the area to grow nodules. Therefore, two organisms, bacteria and legumes, live in a symbiotic relationship mutually beneficial to each other.

Questions

1. What is a symbiotic relationship?

2. What are nodules? Why are they useful to some plants?

3. How can some bacteria be beneficial rather than harmful to organisms?

4. Why are clover, soybeans, and alfalfa used in crop rotation?

 ## Activity 12: Earthworms' Movements and Reactions

OBJECTIVE:	To observe how earthworms move and to investigate how earthworms react to light, touch, and moisture
MATERIALS:	Earthworms, large piece of burlap, piece of glass, shallow box, small plastic tubes, 3-foot trough filled with loose soil
LEVEL:	Upper
SETTING:	Classroom
TIME:	1 hour

LESSON DESIGN

Collect some earthworms and keep them in moist soil. Select one earthworm, wash it off, and place it on a piece of burlap. After it acclimatizes itself, carefully observe its movements. It will move forward with alternate contractions and extensions of each segment. Waves of contractions passing down the worm can be observed. Listen carefully and you will be able to hear the worm making a faint scratching sound as it inches forward. It has little tiny bristles sticking out of each segment that act as anchors fixing one part of the worm to a surface while drawing the other part up to it. Next, place the worm on a piece of glass and see if it can move forward in the same manner. It should not be able to move because it cannot grip the glass with its bristles.

Place several earthworms in an open box with some small plastic tubes. The worms will probably crawl into them because they normally live in situations where their bodies are totally in touch with solid surroundings, such as soil. Earthworms continue to move until they are in a situation where they have maximum bodily contact with their environment.

The skin of earthworms is studded with light-sensitive organs that are most concentrated on the surface of their front ends. If a light beam is aimed at these regions, the worms quickly retreat, which means that they are *photo negative* and tend to avoid light and seek darkness. Cover one-half of a large box with aluminum foil (to create a light barrier) and leave the other half alone. Put several worms in the center of the box and observe their behavior. After 15–20 minutes, all the worms should be in the dark half of the box.

Earthworms must have a small amount of gaseous oxygen in contact with their moist skin. They breathe by taking oxygen in through the skin. Too much moisture will drown them, and not enough moisture will kill them by asphyxiation. Therefore, earthworms seek environments containing just the right balance of moisture and air for efficient respiration. Fill a long trough with loose soil or sawdust. Water one end until it is soggy. Water the middle so it is barely moist, and do not water the other end at all so that it is completely dry. Place several worms in various parts of the trough. After several days, locate all the worms and make a conclusion as to the optimum environment in which worms prefer to live.

Supplementary Activities

Fill several large plastic tubs (5–6 quarts) three-fourths of the way full with peat moss. Dig three holes in the peat moss to make three indentations approximately the size of a cup. Fill each indentation with organic matter (partially decayed leaves, grass clippings, manure, food). Although each tub will have a different kind of organic matter, all three holes in each tub will hold the same kind of matter. Sprinkle each tub with water and place an equal number of earthworms in all but one tub. One tub will not have worms in it. Sprinkle each tub with a fine layer of cornmeal and put their covers on. Place the tubs away from direct sunlight and heat and observe them weekly for several months. Every couple of weeks, spoon out a sampling of organic matter from each tub and make notes of their characteristics.

Questions

1. Why do we find a lot of worms on the soil's surface after a rain?

2. Why do worms die if they don't get any moisture?

3. Why are worms not able to crawl on a piece of glass as easily as on a piece of burlap?

4. Why would a worm prefer a dark area to a light area?

5. What were the differences in organic matter in each tub?

6. What was the difference in organic matter between the tub without worms and the tubs with worms? What does that tell you about the value of worms?

7. Was there any detectable odor to the tubs (other than soil)? What do you think the reason is?

Activity 13: Birds

OBJECTIVE:	To learn about birds by observing them and building various bird houses and feeding stations
MATERIALS:	Bird seed, suet, bird chart, various materials ranging from tin cans to wooden dowels and planks, to pine cones, to old trash can lids, to nylon net bags
LEVEL:	Lower to upper
SETTING:	Classroom and school grounds
TIME:	2–3 hours to construct bird houses and feeding stations, several hours for observation outside during school time or to and from school, observation time of the bird feeders and feeding stations throughout the school year

LESSON DESIGN

Have students observe birds while going to and from school or arrange a field trip to observe birds. Initially, a trip out to the playground will get students interested in observing birds and show them what to look for, such as a bird's color, size, silhouette, and the way it flies. Provide a bird observation chart (see Figure 4.4) for each student so that they can write down what they observe rather than relying on their memories for later recordings.

Have the students make bird houses and suet containers to hang outside the classroom window or windows of their own homes. Suet can be bought at the grocery store. Roll it in bird seed and put it in a nylon mesh bag, or roll it into a tight ball and hang by a string, or press the suet mixture into the open cavities of pine cones to hang from tree branches. Feeders for seeds can be made out of old trash can lids set on or nailed on a post. Place a box on its side so one side acts as a roof and fill the box with birdseed. Bird feeders can be made out of almost anything. Use your imagination to attract birds to the school grounds or a home environment. Suet will attract woodpeckers, chickadees, and nuthatches, whereas seeds will attract such birds as sparrows, juncos, and finches.

Supplementary Activities

Design several different kinds of bird feeders to lure birds to students' homes or the schoolyard.

Simple feeders:

Cut a creatively designed slot out of the side of a Clorox or detergent bottle for the birds to feed from. Hang the feeder by string from the handle.

Stuff the cracks of pine cones with suet or peanut butter rolled in seeds. Hang by string from a branch in a tree.

Cut a coconut in half. Tie both halves together, cut sides facing each other. Leave a 3-inch space between the halves and hang them from a branch with a string, or, tie two wooden salad bowls together in a similar fashion and hang by string.

Milk cartons can be suspended by wire or string from a branch. Cut a small hole in the bottom of the carton, slide a dowel through from one side to the other under the hole to serve as a perch, and fill with seed.

More complex feeders:

For a ground feeder, cut a round from a downed tree any thickness and diameter. With 2-by-2s, make a frame to nail to a piece of plywood. Nail the plywood frame on top of the tree round.

String two pieces of Masonite together several inches apart and hang by wire from a tree branch.

Crimp hardware cloth into a rectangular shape. Staple to a piece of plywood. Coat the hardware cloth with suet grease before stuffing suet and seeds into the hardware cloth. The greased cloth will keep birds from sticking to the wire in the cold of winter.

BIRD OBSERVATION CHART

Name	Size	Color	Habitat	Voice	Flight Pattern	Comments

Fig. 4.4.

VOCABULARY DEFINITIONS

Abiotic—Nonliving.

Adaptation—Anything that is changed or changes to become suitable to a new situation; the ability to adjust to environmental conditions.

Asexual Reproduction—Characterizing reproduction involving a single individual.

Bacteria—Unicellular microorganisms that exist as either free-living organisms or as parasites and live in soil, water, organic matter, or bodies of plants and animals.

Biotic—Living.

Chrysalis—The third stage of development in an insects' life; enclosed in a firm case.

Cocoon—A covering spun by the larva of insects as protection for their pupal stage.

Cyst—A capsule-like membrane of certain organisms in a resting stage.

Food Chain—A series of organisms in which each organism (link) feeds on the one behind it and is eaten by the one ahead of it.

Food Web—A series of overlapping and interconnected food chains.

Habitat—The type of environment in which an organism lives.

Invertebrate—An animal without a backbone.

Limiting Factors—Too much or too little of something required for living, causing limited growth.

Metamorphosis—A change in the structure of an animal during normal growth. In insects, this includes egg, larval, pupal, and adult stages.

Nitrogen Fixation—The conversion by some soil bacteria of inorganic nitrogen compounds into organic compounds assimilable by plants.

Nodules—A small knob-like outgrowth, such as those found on the roots of most leguminous plants.

Protozoa—Single-celled microscopic organisms.

Spore—A single-celled reproductive organ characteristic of nonflowering plants, such as mosses, fungi, and ferns.

Symbiosis—The close relationship of two or more different organisms that may be, but are not necessarily, beneficial to each organism.

5

WEATHER

Weather is the state of the atmosphere at a given time and place described by such variables as temperature, precipitation, and wind. Climate is the accumulation of these conditions that characteristically prevail in a particular region and determines the kinds of plants and animals that will live in a certain place.

We should know how to record different variances in weather because it affects our daily activities. Weather is usually taken for granted, and there is nothing we can do about it. Yet there are different weather patterns of which we can learn something.

Wind, for example, is an integral part of weather. Although wind itself is not visible, the effects of wind are. Wind is air in motion and depends on several things. Air is set in motion (producing wind) where there are differences in air pressure. Without these differences, there is no wind. Wind depends upon air temperature, atmospheric pressure, and the rotation of the Earth. There are many different kinds of winds around the world. The trade winds are the steadiest winds on Earth and cover vast distances. They extend throughout the tropics and subtropics, are warm and gentle, and are accompanied by rains. Their pressure drives the sea westward in great currents north and south of the equator. The westerlies have three times the force of trade winds and extend across the land. They carry weather with them and are cyclonic. Hurricanes can move from the sea to the land, but mostly they are at sea, for their strength lies at sea. Monsoons are great masses of air that move from the sea to the land in the summer and from the land to the sea in the winter. The wind generates currents that create ocean waves and swells.

The winds of the land are different from the winds of the sea. Wind moves freely on the sea but is twisted and distorted on the land because of irregular surface features, such as mountains, plains, and valleys. Ocean winds follow long, smooth paths. The winds of the plains extend over vast distances with no change in speed or direction. The winds of the mountains and valleys are irregular. Each valley and mountain slope has its own peculiar wind pattern.

Because winds cover all surfaces of the Earth, they are constantly eroding and redistributing earth materials. Wind is unconfined; that is, winds move across the Earth in all directions and places. Water erosion, on the other hand, is confined to a specific area—a river channel, for instance. Wind-borne particles vary greatly in size from tiny dust particles to large grains of sand and rock. Not only does the wind act in an erosive manner but in a redistributive manner as well. Wind deposits materials in a variety of shapes and sizes. Several things (wind velocity, wind duration, and the size of the wind-borne particles) affect how far and how high the materials are carried.

Sand dunes are wind deposits of sand that will keep moving until the wind stops if nothing is obstructing the dune's path. Rocks or vegetation may cause a dune to stop moving and become anchored. Varied wind direction may change the shape of dunes.

Air surrounds the Earth. Air is important in many ways. It enables plants and animals to live and breathe. Clouds are part of the air. Air is invisible, but we can see things in the air, such as dust particles or smoke. Air is all around us, but it is also in the soil, oceans, rivers, lakes, ponds, and streams. Having air present in so many different places enables plants and animals to get the amount of air they need to live in a variety of places.

Air is a mixture of gases, four-fifths of which is nitrogen and one-fifth oxygen. Plants need nitrogen to grow, but it must be chemically changed before they can use it. Animals must take in oxygen in order to live. Air also contains water vapor evaporated from oceans, river, plants, and animals. Water vapor is water in the air. We cannot always see this water, but sometimes we can feel it. We can see the water when it is in the form of fog or clouds.

Air also contains invisible gases. Some, such as oxygen and carbon dioxide, are necessary for the maintenance of life. There are also gases, such as sulfur oxides, carbon monoxides, and hydrocarbons, that are harmful to life.

Air has weight and takes up space. Heavy air is close to the Earth. Light, thin air is found higher up, on tops of mountains, for instance. Warm air is light because it moves outward and takes up more space. Cold air is heavier and takes up less space. Colder air pushes warmer air upward and takes its place.

Wind is moving air. Air constantly travels and has different names, such as breezes, hurricanes, blizzards, and tornadoes. Because the sun heats different parts of the Earth with greater intensity, this heat causes air to rise. These air masses are designated as high air pressure areas. Air always moves from high air pressure areas to low air pressure areas. Air movements closer to the Earth's surface are called winds. High-level air movements are called currents.

Clouds are composed of tiny drops of water. Water goes into the air by a process called *evaporation*. That is, water in plants, the ground, rivers, and oceans is changed into water vapor with help from the sun. Warm air speeds up the process of evaporation because warm air takes up more water than cold air. As warm air cools, it is pushed into a smaller space, and these small bits of water form larger drops of mist. This mist floats in the air as clouds. Water vapor is odorless. When condensed into water droplets, clouds form and may eventually form precipitation.

There are 10 main classes of clouds, grouped according to height:

- **High**—cirrus, cirrostratus, cirrocumulus
- **Medium**—altostratus, nimbostratus, altocumulus
- **Low**—stratus, cumulus, stratocumulus, cumulonimbus

The high clouds are usually from 20,000–40,000 feet in altitude, the medium clouds from 6,000–20,000 feet, and the low clouds from 0–5,000 feet.

Stratus clouds are layered and develop when warm moist tropical air masses flow over cold polar air masses. These clouds give rainfall over a wide area. Cumulus clouds are billowing and develop in cold polar air streams. These clouds give localized showers. Cirrus clouds are so high that they are composed of ice crystals.

The billions of water drops and ice particles that are formed in a cloud must grow large and heavy before they can fall as precipitation. They can do this either by condensing, by coalescing, or by a combination of both. Condensation happens in clouds with both water drops and ice particles and can cause long periods of rain, snow, or drizzle. Some of the supercooled water drops in the cloud evaporate, and the water vapor condenses and freezes on the ice particles. These ice particles get bigger, become ice crystals, and join to make snowflakes that are large and heavy enough to fall from the cloud. If these snowflakes drop through warmer air, they melt and fall as rain. Coalescence of water drops in clouds happens because larger drops inside the cloud are blown upward by air currents. As these large water drops rise, they *coalesce*, or bump into and absorb smaller drops, and grow bigger and bigger. Upon reaching the top of the cloud, they are so large that they fall down again, absorbing more water drops and then falling as raindrops.

Hail falls from cumulonimbus clouds made of water drops and ice particles. Ice particles build into ice crystals by condensation, and the ice crystals are blown up and down inside the cloud by strong air currents, absorbing more and more water drops. These drops freeze onto the ice crystals in layers. The layers of ice in a hailstone indicate how many times it was blown up and down inside the cloud.

Dew does not fall from the sky as do other forms of precipitation. It is formed where you find it on the ground. At night the grass may cool off quickly, changing some of the water vapor in the air to drops of water on the cool grass. On dry, cold mornings in winter, frost appears because the water vapor in the air froze into ice crystals instead of remaining as water droplets.

High pressure areas, called anticyclones, are located where air sinks, and low pressure areas, called cyclones, are located where air rises. Winds blow from high pressure areas to low pressure areas and are marked on weather maps with *isobars*, or lines joining areas with the same pressure.

Huge bodies of air with the same temperature and humidity are called air masses. There are two main kinds of air masses: tropical and polar. An air mass that forms over land and comes from the poles will be cold and dry. One that forms in the tropics over the ocean will be warm and humid. Other combinations can occur.

A warm front occurs when warm tropical air rises over the cold polar air in front of it. It is characterized by a falling barometer, low stratus clouds, and rain. A cold front occurs when the cold polar air undercuts warm tropical air ahead of it. When a cold front catches up with a warm front and they merge, that phenomenon creates an occluded front.

 ### Activity 1: Measuring Snowfall

OBJECTIVE:	To determine how much water is in 1 cup of snow
MATERIALS:	Measuring cup, heat source, snow
LEVEL:	Lower to upper
SETTING:	School grounds and classroom
TIME:	30 minutes

LESSON DESIGN

Collect 1 measuring cup of snow. Measure the amount of water in the cup. Measure the depth of snow in an open area and divide that measurement by 10 to find the equivalent amount of water. Ten inches of snow is approximately equal to 1 inch of water.

Supplementary Activities

Take two sheets of copier paper. Crumple one into a ball and keep one flat. From the same height and at the same time, drop both pieces of paper and observe what happens. The flat piece of paper represents a snowflake and will fall slower than the crumpled piece of paper, which represents a raindrop. Even though both are composed of water, they are different shapes. A raindrop will drop faster than a snowflake because it takes up less space and is heavier and more dense than the snowflake.

Questions

1. Why does snow fill a greater volume than water?

2. What happens to the water when snow melts in the city in which you live?

3. What happens to the water when snow melts in the country?

 ## Activity 2: Weather Factors As Determinants of Plant and Animal Life

OBJECTIVE:	To determine if temperature, wind velocity, and relative humidity have any effect on plant and animal life found in an area
MATERIALS:	Thermometers, anemometer, hygrometer
LEVEL:	Upper
SETTING:	Classroom and outdoor settings
TIME:	2 hours to make the instruments and several hours to take and interpret measurements
PRE-ACTIVITIES:	Make a hygrometer and an anemometer as described in Activity 8 (chapter 5)

LESSON DESIGN

Record the temperature, wind velocity, and relative humidity in several different places, such as in an open field, a forest, and a lakeside. Take these measurements several times over the period of two or three weeks and compile the data in the form of a chart. While taking these measurements, observe and record the kinds and numbers of plants and animals found in the different areas and make a chart of those findings also.

Questions

1. Is there a detectable difference in plant and animal life in the different areas? If so, why? Describe the differences.

2. If there were no detectable differences between the areas, what would be the possible reasons for this?

Activity 3: Evaporation

OBJECTIVE:	To measure differences in evaporation rates
MATERIALS:	Water, several measuring cups of the same size
LEVEL:	Lower to upper
SETTING:	Classroom
TIME:	10 minutes to set up, several days to a few weeks for observation
VOCABULARY:	Evaporation

LESSON DESIGN

Measure evaporation by placing measuring cups of equal amounts of water in different places in the schoolroom. One area should be cool, one warm, one normal, and one very warm. Measure the water content in the cups after 4 days, 1 week, 1½ weeks, 2 weeks, and so forth. Record these amounts each time a measurement is taken and compare them after all of the water has evaporated in all of the cups.

Supplementary Activities

Devise a way of measuring the evaporation rate of water in different locations under different conditions and at different times of the day.

Questions

1. Which cups evaporated water the fastest? Why?

2. Which cup was the last one to have all the water evaporate? Why?

3. Which cup was the first one to have all the water evaporate? Why?

4. What does evaporation have to do with plant growth?

5. What does evaporation have to do with temperature?

Activity 4: Preservation of Snowflakes

OBJECTIVE:	To preserve snowflakes to study their structure
MATERIALS:	Small squares of glass, cardboard, lacquer spray, access to a freezer, snow, hand lenses
LEVEL:	Upper
SETTING:	School grounds and classroom
TIME:	1 hour

LESSON DESIGN

Store small squares of glass in a freezer . When it snows, rush the glass outside, holding it on the pieces of cardboard. Spray the glass with lacquer. Hold the glass out to collect snowflakes. Leave the glass outside for about an hour to dry. When the glass is dry, look at the flakes with a hand lens.

Questions

1. Do you notice any similarities between the snowflakes? If so, what are they?

2. Are each of the snowflakes completely different? How do you know?

 Activity 5: Wind Erosion

OBJECTIVE:	To demonstrate the effects of wind erosion
MATERIALS:	5 flat pans, different kinds of soil, twigs, small plants, different sizes of rocks, a hair dryer, water, heat lamp or intense light
RESOURCES:	Soil conservation service
LEVEL:	Lower to upper
SETTING:	Classroom
TIME:	1 hour
VOCABULARY:	Erosion

LESSON DESIGN

Put different kinds of soil in five different pans and label each with a number. Discuss what the materials have in common, how they are different, of what they are composed, and if their grains are large or small, coarse or smooth. Study their color and texture. Make a chart and record these observations on the chart.

Using the hair dryer, blow air on the pans, keeping the distance constant. Record your observations. Describe any differences/similarities. Spray water on each pan so that the soil is damp but not soggy, then blow air across each one. Record your observations. Place a heat lamp or other strong light above the pans. Wait until the soils are not only dry but also warmer than before, then blow air across them as before and record your observations. Now put twigs and rocks in each pan, blow air on them, and record any observable changes.

Questions

1. Does the same thing happen in each pan or do different things happen? What are these differences and similarities?

2. Which material was moved the easiest by the wind? Why?

3. How did twigs and rocks affect the winds' ability to move the soil? Which soils were affected the least and the most after twigs and rocks were added?

4. Did time have anything to do with the effect on wet soils? If so, what kind of an effect?

5. Did heat have a different effect than no heat? Explain.

6. How does a humid, arid, windy, warm, or cold climate affect the way people live?

Activity 6: Factors of Weather

OBJECTIVE:	To examine different factors of weather and develop an understanding of the role each one plays in our weather
MATERIALS:	Plastic bags, water, medicine dropper, glass, cardboard tube, paper, hair dryer, heat source, balloons, heat-resistant jar, pie pan, bicycle pump, heavy book, index card, pot, ice cubes, salt
RESOURCES:	Local weather broadcasting station or the meteorology department of a local university
LEVEL:	Lower to upper
SETTING:	Classroom and school grounds
TIME:	1–1½ hours
VOCABULARY:	Air pressure, water vapor, wind

LESSON DESIGN

The following activities are short introductions to different weather factors that need to be understood before some of the more complicated factors are discussed and dealt with.

Air occupies space: Fill a plastic bag with water. Notice the shape of the bag and the feel of its bulging sides. Empty the bag of water. Using a hair dryer, fill the bag with air and securely close it. Notice if the bag bulges as it did when filled with water. Compare the appearance of the bag with air to the appearance of the bag with water. Determine if the appearance is the same or different.

Air expands when heated: Before beginning, hold up a heat-resistant jar and discuss the fact that there is air in it. Then secure a balloon to its top. Heat some water in a pie pan on the top of a hot plate and place the jar in the pan of water. Observe what happens to the balloon. Remove the jar from the hot water and place it in a pan of very cold water and observe what happens to the balloon. Compare the two ways the balloon looked and try to decide whether warm air or cold air is heavier. (The cold air is heavier because cold air contracts.) Place the jar back in the pan of warm water and leave it there for a few minutes. Light a match to hold over the mouth of the jar as you remove the balloon. Observe what happens to the burning match and its smoke. The air from the jar is moving the smoke up and away from the jar because warm air rises, being lighter than the cooler air surrounding it.

Wind is produced because of the uneven heating of the Earth's surface: Paint a can black and another can white. Fill both with water of the same temperature. Cover the black can with a piece of black cardboard and the white can with a piece of white cardboard. Put a thermometer in each and place both in the direct sun. Record their temperatures on a chart at the beginning and every 10 minutes for approximately an hour. Discuss what color has to do with temperature. Dark areas absorb more heat than light areas, and light areas reflect more heat than dark areas. Fill a pie pan with cool water and a pie pan with sand. Record the temperatures of each and place them in a cardboard box in the direct sun. With a thermometer in each, record their temperatures on a chart every 10 minutes for approximately an hour. If the sand is the land, and the water is the ocean, the sand will absorb heat faster than the water. The air over the land is being heated and is rising. The cooler air in the cardboard box—which is coming from the water—will move toward the land to take the place of the warm air rising from the land. This air movement is wind. Next, put a piece of white paper over the pan with sand. Now the air will be warmer over the water, and the wind will blow from the opposite direction. During the day, the land heats up faster than the ocean, and air rising over the land will be replaced by cooler ocean air. Land cools faster during the night than water, and a wind will blow from the land to the ocean. To demonstrate this principle, fill a glass half full with cold colored water and very slowly and carefully pour some warm, clear water into it and observe what happens. The warmer water, which is lighter than colder water, will float on top of the colder heavier water.

Air exerts pressure: Place a heavy book on a paper bag. Pump air into the bag with a bicycle pump (or blow into it). Air pressure will cause the book to move upwards. Similarly, air pressure can be increased and decreased. Place an eyedropper in a glass of water and squeeze. Note the bubbles that make a partial vacuum inside the dropper. By releasing the bulb of the eyedropper, the water is forced up into the dropper. The greater air pressure on the surface of the water forces water into the dropper. Remove the dropper from the glass and squeeze the bulb. This squeezing compresses air inside and forces the water out. Put a crumpled piece of paper into a cardboard tube and blow really hard. The wad of paper will fly out because it was projected by compressed air.

Air contains water vapor: Heat water in a metal pot over a hot plate. Let the water boil for several minutes and observe what happens to the level of the water in the pot. When heated, the water changed to water vapor through the process of evaporation. Put several ice cubes in a pie pan and hold the pie pan over the boiling water. Observe what happens to the bottom of the pie pan. The cooler pan cools the air around it and causes the water vapor in the air to condense. This change back from a gas to a liquid is called condensation. After the pan has been held above the pan with boiling water for awhile, some of the drops will eventually fall. The drops became too heavy to remain on the pan, so they fell as precipitation. Put some more ice cubes and some salt in the pan, stir well, and again hold it above the pot with the boiling water. Observe what forms on the outside of the pie pan. The salt will lower the temperature of the ice, and frost will form on the sides of the pan.

Clouds contain water vapor: Fill a narrow-necked, heat-resistant jar one-fourth of the way full with warm water and heat it on a hot plate until it boils. Remove the jar from the heat and place an ice cube in the neck of the jar such that it stays on top and does not fall into the jar. A cloud will form in the mouth of the jar quite quickly because the warm moist air will rise and be cooled by the ice cube. This process is the way clouds are formed. The warm, moist air from the Earth rises, and as it rises it cools and forms a cloud. If the cloud gets even colder, the tiny water droplets will cling together, eventually becoming so heavy that the clouds can no longer hold them, and they fall as precipitation.

Supplementary Activities

Air occupies space: With a hair dryer, fill a plastic bag with air. Secure the end with a twist-tie. Set the bag on a table, place a book on top of the bag, and observe what is happening. What is supporting the book? Press modeling clay around the neck of a funnel, then push the funnel into the top of a soda bottle so that a seal is formed. Pour water into the funnel. What happens? Why did the water stay in the funnel and not flow into the bottle? What was in the bottle before the water was poured in?

Wind is produced because of the uneven heating of the Earth's surface: Tape a piece of black construction paper on a classroom wall. Hold a handful of flour above and in front of the black paper. Filter some through your fingers and observe what happens. Next hold a heated light bulb in front of the paper and repeat the process with the flour. What happened this time? The first time the flour fell because the air was heavier and cooler. The second time the flour rose because the air was warmer and lighter.

Air exerts pressure and pushes up as well as down: Fill a glass with a smooth rim to the brim with water. Place a piece of tag board on top of the glass and carefully turn the glass over, keeping the tag board intact. What will happen when you remove your hand from the tag board? The air pressure outside the glass is greater than the weight of the water pushing down, so it pushes up on the tag board, keeping it in place. Hold a piece of facial tissue horizontally in both hands and blow across the top of it. The outer end of the tissue will rise because the faster air moves, the less pressure it exerts. The air being blown across the top of the tissue is moving faster than the air underneath it. There is less air pressure above than below, and the greater pressure from below is push-ing the tissue up. Fill a quart jar three-fourths of the way full of colored water and place it on a stack of books on a table. Set an empty quart jar on the table next to the books so that the lip of the jar is lower than the base of the jar with the colored water. Submerge a 2-foot length of clear plastic tubing in a sink of water and fill the tube completely. Place a finger over each end of the tubing so that the water stays in and lift the tubing out of the sink. Keeping your finger over one end of the tubing, stick the other end in the quart jar of colored water on the stack of books, then put the other end in the empty jar on the table and remove your finger. Water from the top jar will move upward through the tube, then down into the lower jar because air pressure is pushing down against the water in the top jar, forcing the water through the tube.

Questions

1. Why does the balloon become inflated? From where did the air come?

2. What does the plastic bag filled with water feel like? What does the plastic bag filled with air feel like?

3. What happens to air as it is heated? Why?

4. What creates air pressure?

5. Which would absorb more heat, a snow field or a grassy field? Which would absorb more heat, water or soil?

6. Which direction does the wind blow during the day, toward the land or toward the sea? Which direction does it blow at night? Why?

7. What are evaporation, condensation, and precipitation?

8. What increases the rate at which water evaporates? What would decrease the rate at which water would evaporate?

Activity 7: Weather Forecasting

OBJECTIVE:	To study the different factors affecting weather and how they relate to weather forecasting
MATERIALS:	Maps of North America, weather maps from newspapers, water, oil, food coloring, jar with a lid
RESOURCES:	Meteorologists from local television stations or local university
LEVEL:	Lower to upper
SETTING:	Classroom
TIME:	2 hours
VOCABULARY:	Air masses, fronts

LESSON DESIGN

Weather forecasting uses information gathered about precipitation, cloud types, wind speed and direction, temperature, air pressure, humidity, air masses, and fronts. Several shorter activities follow, introducing the concepts of air masses, fronts and weather maps:

Air masses are warm, wet, dry, or cold: Discuss where each would be likely to form, and what characteristics they have in common with the area over which they form. Point out places on a map of North America where it would be possible for these different air masses to form. Continental air masses form over land and are dry. They can be warm or cold, depending on whether they were formed over the tropics or over polar areas. Maritime air masses are wet and form over the oceans. They can also be warm or cold for the same reasons. Consequently, there are four main air masses: a continental polar, which is dry and cold; a continental tropical, which is dry and warm; a maritime polar, which is moist and cold; and a maritime tropical, which is warm and moist. Discuss the kinds of weather produced by each air mass at different times of the year. Finally, discuss the fact that air masses can change as they move over different surfaces. Consequently, a warm continental air mass could become a cold wet air mass by moving over an ocean area near the poles. These movements of air masses from one area to another bring different weather patterns with them and produce changes in the weather. Cold air masses have a high barometric pressure and are therefore called *highs*. Warm air masses are called *lows* because they have a low barometric pressure.

Fronts are formed when two air masses meet: Draw cold and warm front symbols on a large piece of paper and demonstrate the development of fronts using these symbols. A warm air mass moves against a cold air mass, forming a warm front. Air masses do not mix as they meet but form a boundary layer where rapid changes in temperature and weather occur. A *front* is this boundary between two air masses. A cold air mass moving against a warm air mass forms a cold front. When a warm and cold front join, a stationary front is formed. To demonstrate what kinds of weather each front will produce, fill a jar half full with water, to which you add a few drops of food coloring. Very slowly fill the rest of the jar with cooking oil. Put a lid on the jar, tip it slightly, and observe what happens to the water and the oil. Identify which is the cold air mass and which is the warm air mass. The water is the cold air mass and the oil is the warm air mass because the oil is lighter and moves up over the water as warm air moves up and over colder air. Both fronts will produce clouds that will produce rain because the warm air will rise and cool. Take the same jar and fill it half full with cooking oil, very slowly pour some water on top of the oil, and observe what happens. Under normal conditions, the water would be under the oil—a cold air mass beneath a warm air mass. However, under different conditions, called a *temperature inversion*, the colder air holds the warmer air down and prevents it from rising.

Weather maps, called synoptic charts, are charts of the atmosphere: Using weather maps from local newspapers, discuss the various symbols on the maps, what they represent, and what they mean. Draw the various symbols on the board to discuss the different parts. Using weather maps every day for a week or two to become familiar with them, see if you can predict what the weather will be like in your area for a few days. Check a weather map and see if you are right or wrong. If possible, plot the fronts, highs and lows, temperatures, and precipitation on a map of North America. Use chalk or plastic overlay and track the weather patterns over a few weeks. In general, weather in the United States moves from west to east.

Supplementary Activities

Air masses are warm, wet, dry, or cold: Fill a condiment bottle full of hot, colored water. Fill another bottle with cold water. Place a piece of tag board on top of the hot water bottle, press firmly, and quickly turn it over and on top of the mouth of the cold water bottle. Holding the two bottles tightly together, tip them sideways, slowly remove the piece of tag board, and observe what happens. The hot water represents a warm air mass, and the cold water represents a cold air mass.

Questions

1. What is an air mass?

2. What are the four types of air masses? Why are they named as they are?

3. What are highs and lows?

4. From where does an air mass get its characteristics?

5. What is a front?

6. What are three types of fronts and how do each form?

7. What happens to the cold water? What happens to the hot water?

8. What happens when a warm and a cold air mass meet?

9. Does the same thing happen in the ocean when warm and cold water currents meet? Explain.

Activity 8: Weather Station

OBJECTIVE:	To be able to study the weather and to set up a weather station after making several weather instruments
MATERIALS:	For each group of 4 or 5 students: thermometers, drill, weather charts. One each of the following instruments: wind vane, anemometer, barometer, rain gauge, hygrometer, nephoscope, clinometer
	Anemometer: 1 5-inch square piece of paper, pin, pencil with an eraser, 2 pieces of plywood ¼-by-1½-by-24 inches, 2 small washers, 1 8-penny nail, 4 ½-pint milk cartons, glue, 1 support pole
	Wind Vane: 1 piece of plywood ½-by-3-by-5 inches, 1 small washer, 1 8-penny nail, glue, old broom handle for a support pole
	Aneroid Barometer: 1 ½-gallon milk carton, 1-pint jar, 1 balloon, scotch tape, large needle or straightened-out paper clip, thread, glue, 3-by-5 inch index card, toothpick, 2 pennies or weights
	Sling Psychrometer (hygrometer): 1 piece of plywood ¼-by-1½ inches-by-12 inches, 12-inch leather thong or heavy cord, 12-inch fine wire, 1 piece of a ½-inch dowel 6 inches in length, 2 similar thermometers, thread, relative humidity chart
	Nephoscope: 12-inch square pieces of black paper and glass, a piece of ¼-inch plywood 12 inches square
	Rain gauge: 1 #10 can, tall jar with straight sides, masking tape, ruler; OR: 1 funnel, 1 small glass jar, 1 large glass jar
LEVEL:	Lower to upper
SETTING:	Classroom and school grounds
TIME:	Several hours to construct the weather instruments and several hours for collecting and recording measurements and predicting the weather
VOCABULARY:	Anemometer, barometer, condensation, evaporation, hygrometer, nephoscope, precipitation, rain gauge, symbols from synoptic charts, thermometer, wind vane
PRE-ACTIVITIES:	Activity 6 (chapter 5) on weather factors and Activity 7 (chapter 5) on weather forecasting

LESSON DESIGN

After making the following weather instruments (see following pages), make a chart (Figure 5.1) of daily observations. From this information, predict the weather for the following day. Keep daily observations in a weather station going for several weeks during the different seasons of the year. Weather instruments include: a wind vane for measuring wind direction, an anemometer for measuring wind velocity, a barometer for measuring air pressure, a rain/snow gauge for measuring precipitation, a hygrometer for measuring humidity in the air, and a nephoscope for measuring the direction of clouds.

WEATHER INFORMATION CHART

Date: _____

Time of Day: _____

Sky Conditions: _____

Cloud Types: _____

Cloud Movement: _____

Wind Direction: _____

Wind Speed: _____

Precipitation: _____

pH of Precipitation: _____

Temperature: _____

Barometric Pressure: _____

Humidity: _____

Predictions: _____

Fig. 5.1.

Wind Vane: Cut the piece of wood to the pattern shown in Figure 5.2. Cement the washer to the top of the support pole. Slip the nail down through the hole drilled in the wind vane through the washer. Drive the nail into the support pole, only enough to hold the wind vane upright. The vane must turn freely. Because wind direction is referred to as the direction from which the wind is coming, the pointer will point to wind direction. If a north wind is blowing, the pointer will orient to the north.

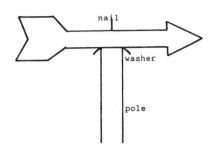

Fig. 5.2.

Anemometers: (1) To measure wind speed and direction, make a paper pinwheel. Take a 5-inch square piece of paper and make four cuts from each corner to just short of the center. Bend the four corners to the middle and fasten to the center with a pin. Push the pin through an eraser of a pencil. Color one blade of the pinwheel to use for counting revolutions. Hold the pinwheel out of a car window. Drive 5, 10, 15, and 20 miles per hour. Note the number of revolutions at each speed. From these calculations you will be able to estimate wind speed by counting the number of revolutions the pinwheel makes when set up outside. (2) Cross the wood pieces at right angles and glue them at their exact centers. Drill a hole slightly larger than the nail through both pieces of wood at their exact centers. Cut the bottom from the milk cartons and staple the tops closed. Cut a slit vertically in the gable sides of each carton and slip one on each stick end, with the open end facing in the same direction in the turning arc. Cement one washer to the top of the support pole. Assemble as shown in Figure 5.3. Leave the nail slightly loose for easy turning. Paint one carton. Wind speed is determined by counting the number of complete revolutions in 30 seconds and dividing by five. The resultant number is a good estimate of wind velocity in miles per hour.

Aneroid Barometer: Cover the top of the bottle or can tightly with the balloon. Seal the edge with rubber bands and tape. Fasten one end of the thread securely to the center of the rubber diaphragm with glue. Do not puncture the balloon. Cut the top from the milk carton. Place the jar or can upright in the milk carton. Pad paper around the jar to hold it in place, centered in the bottom of the carton. Pierce two holes in opposite sides of the upper edge of the carton walls. Pass the needle or straightened paper clip through the carton. Glue the toothpick to one end of the paper clip outside of the carton. Wrap thread one turn around the paper clip (inside

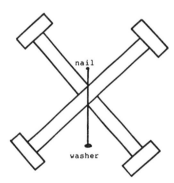

Fig. 5.3.

carton) and pass it horizontally from the pin to a third hole pierced in the carton just above and slightly forward of the paper clip or needle. Attach weights (just enough to keep the thread tight) to the thread half way down the side of the carton. Draw an arc (radius length of the toothpick) on the index card and label one end "High" and the other end "Low." Tape or glue the index card to the side of the carton under the toothpick pointer. A depressed diaphragm means high pressure. The toothpick should be centered in the arc on a relatively normal day. The instrument will now read changes in barometric pressure. High pressure usually indicates fair weather; low pressure usually indicates rainy weather. Rising pressure means clearing, and falling pressure indicates stormy weather. See Figure 5.4 for an indication of how the finished barometer should look.

Sling Psychrometer: Drill a hole large enough to accept the thong in one end of the piece of wood. Tie the thong through the hole in the wood. Fasten the other end of the thong to one end of the dowel. Fasten the thermometers to the piece of wood with one thermometer bulb projecting off the end of the stick. Use fine wire or tape to affix the thermometers, being careful not to break them. Tie gauze or wick to the thermometer bulb off the end of the wood. Calculate relative humidity as follows: immerse the wick-covered thermometer bulb in room temperature water. Swing the psy-

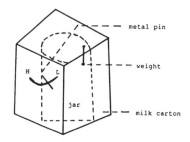

Fig. 5.4.

chrometer in a vertical, circular motion for 30 seconds. Record temperature readings from both thermometers. Subtract the wet-bulb reading from the dry-bulb reading. Using the following table and the dry-bulb and wet-bulb temperature differences, read relative humidity directly. For example, if the dry-bulb reading is 70° F and the wet-bulb reading is 56° F, the difference between the readings is 14. Read down the column under the dry-bulb temperature of 70° and read right from 14 (difference between dry- and wet-bulb readings). Where these lines intersect, read the relative humidity. This figure is 40 percent. This figure means the air has 40 percent of the water it can hold at this present temperature and barometric pressure. See Figure 5.5 for an example of a sling psychrometer and Figure 5.6 for a table on relative humidity.

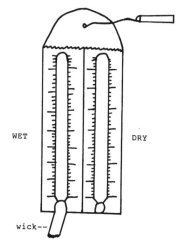

Fig. 5.5.

RELATIVE HUMIDITY (SLING PSYCHROMETER METHOD)

Diff. Between Wet & Dry Bulbs in Degrees	Dry-Bulb Air Temperature, Degrees Fahrenheit											
	-10	0	10	20	30	40	50	60	70	80	90	100
	Relative Humidity, Percent											
1	55	71	80	86	90	92	93	94	95	96	96	97
2	10	42	60	72	79	84	87	89	90	92	92	92
3		13	41	58	68	76	80	84	86	87	88	90
4			21	44	58	68	74	78	81	83	85	86
6				16	38	52	61	68	72	75	78	80
8					18	37	49	58	64	68	71	74
10						22	37	48	55	61	65	68
12							26	39	48	54	59	62
14							16	30	40	47	53	57
16							5	21	33	41	47	51
18								13	26	35	41	47
20								5	19	29	36	42
22									12	23	32	37
25									6	18	26	33

Fig. 5.6.

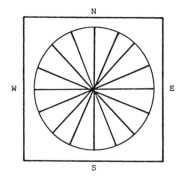

Fig. 5.7.

Nephoscope: Draw a 10-inch diameter circle on the black paper and eight straight lines crossing in the center, using the white pencil. This drawing becomes the simple compass. Label the ends of the lines "N," "NNE," "NE," "ENE," "E," and so forth. Place the paper on the plywood and cover it with the piece of glass. Bind all three together with the masking tape. Place the glass on a flat surface about waist high. Orient with a compass, reversing all directions. Turn so the N line points south. Walk around the glass, adjusting your position until a cloud is reflected in the center of the glass and seems to move along one of the compass lines. Follow the reflected cloud image until it disappears. Where the cloud disappeared out of the mirror is the direction from which it was moving (see Figure 5.7).

Rain gauge: Using Figure 5.8 as a model, collect rain and do the following calculations: Precipitation = H x d / D. H = height of rain in the glass, d = diameter of the glass, D = diameter of the funnel's top. For example, 2 x 2 / 4 = 1 inch of rain.

Supplementary Activities

Fill a glass pop bottle about three-fourths of the way full of water colored with food coloring. Insert a drinking straw about halfway into the bottle and press modeling clay around it to seal the opening of the bottle. Place the bottle in a pan of water. Put the pan on a hot plate, heat, and observe what happens.

As the liquid expands, the colored water will rise in the straw.

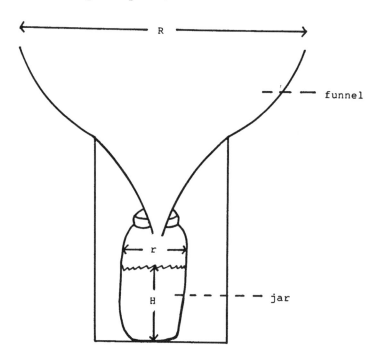

Fig. 5.8.

Activity 9: Tornadoes and Hurricanes

OBJECTIVE:	To demonstrate how tornadoes and hurricanes form
MATERIALS:	2 2-quart soft-drink bottles, duct tape, paper towels, 1 ruler, 1 8-ounce jar, water, vinegar, liquid dish soap, glitter, salt, soda water, lazy Susan, eye dropper, food coloring or cold milk, bowl
LEVEL:	Lower to upper
SETTING:	Classroom
TIME:	30 minutes

LESSON DESIGN

A tornado is a funnel cloud that touches the ground. Most tornadoes are formed from super cell thunderstorms—cool, dry air aloft and warm, humid air on the surface.

Hurricanes form over warm, tropical oceans, have wind speeds that can be 125 miles per hour or more, and dissipate over cool water or land. Storms of this magnitude are called *typhoons* if they form in the western Pacific.

Fill one plastic soft-drink bottle half full of water, then cover the mouth of the bottle with tape. Punch a hole in the middle of the tape approximately ¼ inch in diameter. Tape the second bottle on top of the first so that they are neck to neck. Turn the bottles over so that the bottle with water is on top of the empty bottle. Holding the bottles by their necks, quickly rotate them in circles, then set them on a table (keeping the empty one on the bottom). The water will fall from the top bottle into the bottom bottle and resemble a tornado.

Fill the 8-ounce jar three-fourths of the way full of water. Put in a teaspoon of vinegar and a teaspoon of dish soap. Add a small amount of glitter. Put a lid on the jar and swirl it around and around to make a tornado.

Fill a glass almost to the top with water. Place the glass in the center of a lazy Susan and spin it. As it spins, add a couple drops of food coloring to the water and watch the tornado move.

Fill a glass almost to the top with soda water. Place the glass in the center of a lazy Susan and spin it. As it spins, add a teaspoon of salt to the water and watch the movement of the tornado.

To simulate a hurricane, fill a large bowl three-fourths of the way full with warm water. Carefully stir the water to set up a circular motion. Add a few drops of food coloring or a teaspoon of cold milk in the center of the swirling water and observe how the movement resembles a hurricane.

Activity 10: Dew Formation

OBJECTIVE:	To study the causes of dew formation
MATERIALS:	Drinking glass, thermometer, water, ice, 2 sheets each of black and white construction paper, bottle, jar, paper towels
LEVEL:	Lower
SETTING:	Classroom and home
TIME:	1 hour and overnight
VOCABULARY:	Condensation, dew, dew point

LESSON DESIGN

Place a glass jar in a pan of ice water for 5 minutes. Remove the jar from the water and dry it off. Quickly breathe on the jar and observe what happens. Water vapor from your warm breath condenses on the cool jar. Because cool air holds less water vapor than warm air, the water vapor in the air forms into water droplets. This process is called *condensation*.

Heat some water in an aluminum pie pan on a hot plate. When heated, pour a small amount of hot water in a plastic cup. Place an identical cup on top of the first one so that the lips match. Tape the two cups together where they meet and observe them. Water vapor will rise from the cup of hot water and form a small cloud in the top of the second cup.

Fill a drinking glass with ice, then pour in enough water to just cover the ice. Place a thermometer in the glass. Observe the outside of the glass and record the temperature when water drops begin to collect on the glass. Depending on humidity levels, water will condense on the glass at different temperatures—higher humidity requires a higher air temperature to form dew.

Place a piece of white construction paper and a piece of black construction paper on the grass in your yard. Let them sit for several hours, examining the grass underneath every couple of hours. Dew forms when an object cools enough to condense water vapor. Because dark materials lose energy faster than light colors, the dew point is reached sooner by the black paper than by the white paper. The white paper may not have any dew on it at all.

Perform a similar experiment using two pieces of black paper. Loosely cover one piece of paper with a piece of cloth and leave the other piece of paper out in the open. After a couple of hours, check each piece of paper to see if and where dew formed. Heat radiates away from both pieces of paper but only collects on the unprotected piece because it loses enough energy to cool to the dew point. The covered paper also radiates heat outward, but its covering radiates some heat back down to the paper, thus keeping it warmer and less likely to reach the dew point. For this reason, cloudy nights are warmer than clear nights.

Supplementary Activities

Make a hygrometer to measure humidity with the following materials: two thermometers, a piece of cardboard, one glass, a piece of muslin. Tape two thermometers to a piece of cardboard so that they hang approximately 4 inches from its bottom edge. Stand the cardboard up on a table and lean it against a wall so that it is stable. Wet a piece of muslin and wrap it around the bulb of one of the thermometers. Fill a small glass three-fourths of the way full of water and place the muslin-wrapped thermometer in it. Let the thermometers sit for approximately 30 minutes, then record their temperatures. Compare the two temperatures on a relative humidity chart such as the one in Activity 8 in chapter 5 to determine the percentage.

To predict the dew point, the temperature at which air becomes saturated, use the wet- and dry-bulb hygrometer to take the temperature of the air and to determine the relative humidity. Then use the dew point table to locate the dew point temperature.

Questions

1. How does a hygrometer compare with a sling psychrometer, such as the one used in Activity 8?

2. Where would a hygrometer work best? Under what conditions would a sling psychrometer work better?

Activity 10 continues on page 134.

Table 5.1.
Dew Point Table

To find the dew-point temperature, use the hygrometer to find the wet-bulb temperature and also find the current temperature. The difference between the two temperatures is the wet-bulb depression. Find the numbers in the current temperature row and the column under the wet-bulb depression.

DEW-POINT TEMPERATURE

Wet-Bulb Depression

Current Temperature °F	1.8° F	3.6° F	5.4° F	7.2° F	9.0° F
14.0°	5.9°	-6.3°	-33.3°		
18.5°	11.5°	1.9°	-13.9°		
23.0°	16.9°	9.0°	-2.2°	-24.3°	
27.5°	22.1°	15.4°	6.6°	-6.7°	-42.3°
32.0°	27.1°	21.4°	14.4°	4.6°	-11.0°
36.5°	32.2°	27.1°	21.0°	13.5°	3.0°
41.0°	37.0°	32.5°	27.3°	21.0°	13.3°
45.5°	41.9°	37.8°	33.3°	27.9°	21.6°
50.0°	46.6°	42.8°	38.8°	34.2°	28.8°
54.5°	51.3°	47.8°	44.1°	40.1°	35.4°
59.0°	55.9°	52.9°	49.2°	45.7°	41.5°
63.5°	60.6°	57.7°	54.5°	51.1°	47.3°
68.0°	65.3°	62.4°	59.5°	56.3°	52.9°
72.5°	70.0°	67.3°	64.4°	61.3°	58.3°
77.0°	75.7°	72.0°	69.3°	66.3°	63.5°
81.5°	79.2°	76.6°	73.9°	71.4°	68.5°
86.0°	83.7°	81.3°	78.8°	76.3°	73.6°
90.5°	88.2°	85.8°	83.5°	81.0°	78.4°
95.0°	92.8°	90.5°	88.2°	85.8°	83.3°
99.5°	97.3°	95.2°	92.8°	90.5°	88.2°
104.0°	101.8°	99.7°	97.5°	95.2°	93.0°

Activity 11: Cloud Formation

OBJECTIVE:	To understand how clouds form
MATERIALS:	Glass jar, ice, metal pan, hot water, matches, plastic soft-drink bottle with cap
LEVEL:	Lower to upper
SETTING:	Classroom
TIME:	30 minutes to 1 hour
VOCABULARY:	Cloud condensation nuclei

LESSON DESIGN

Heap ice cubes in the metal pan and set it aside for about a half hour or until the pan is well chilled. Pour about 2 inches of hot water into the jar. Set the pan of ice on top of the jar of hot water and observe what happens.

Pour about 2 inches of warm water into the soft-drink bottle and screw on the lid. Immediately squeeze the bottle several times to make the air inside contract and expand. Observe any changes. Now light a match, blow it out, drop it in the bottle, and recap it. Squeeze the bottle once and release it. Observe any new changes.

At 100 percent relative humidity, water vapor condenses into clouds. Water vapor condenses onto small particles of soot or dust called *cloud condensation nuclei*. The air is cooled below its dew point temperature, and cloud condensation nuclei are present. Rising air cools, and water vapor begins to condense.

Questions

1. What happened when the bottle was squeezed the first time?

2. What did you see when the match was added to the bottle? Why?

VOCABULARY DEFINITIONS

Air Masses—Huge masses of air with the same temperature and humidity.

Air Pressure—The weight of air on an area that exerts a force and is measured with a barometer.

Anemometer—An instrument for measuring wind speed.

Barometer—An instrument for measuring atmospheric humidity.

Cloud Condensation Nuclei—Tiny particles that water vapor condenses on to form cloud droplets.

Condensation—The process by which water vapor changes into liquid vapor because saturated air cooled to the point where it could no longer hold as much water vapor.

Dew—Moisture condensed on cool surfaces, especially at night.

Dew Point—Temperature at which water vapor will condense.

Erosion—The process of wearing away the land by weathering, abrasion, and corrosion.

Evaporation—The process of giving off water vapor from bodies of water.

Fronts—The boundary between two air masses.

Hurricane—A severe tropical storm with wind speeds of more than 75 miles per hour, blowing around an area of low pressure and usually including heavy rain.

Hygrometer—An instrument that measures atmospheric humidity.

Nephoscope—An instrument that measures cloud direction.

Precipitation—Any form of rain, sleet, hail, or snow that has condensed from atmospheric water vapor and that gets sufficiently heavy to fall to the Earth's surface.

Rain Gauge—An instrument that measures rainfall.

Synoptic Charts—Weather maps with symbols representing cloud cover, wind direction and speed, temperature, air pressure, and precipitation.

Thermometer—An instrument for measuring temperature.

Tornado—A forceful rotating column of air extending from the base of a cumulonimbus cloud to the ground and whirling at speeds of up to 300 miles per hour.

Water Vapor—Water in its gaseous state in the atmosphere.

Wind—The movement of air blowing from one of the four cardinal directions: north, south, east, or west.

Wind Vane—An instrument for measuring wind direction.

6

ENVIRONMENTAL PROBLEMS

Sixty-five percent of the people in the United States live in cities. Neighborhoods are communities within the larger community of a city. They are important for the growth of the people living in those communities. Neighborhoods provide most of the things people need, such as food; shelter; other people; and sometimes fire and police protection, recreation facilities, and hospitals. Different people perform different functions and share their skills and resources. Because an *environment* is everything surrounding a person (people, buildings, natural resources, air, sun, and climate), an urban environment should provide people with all of their needs—material needs as well as emotional needs—supplied by nature. If wildlife areas are not near enough to be used, parks should be evenly dispersed throughout the city. Materials used to build cities all come from the earth and are used either in their natural state or refashioned by people.

Human and natural communities are analogous in certain ways. Both have living and nonliving components all coexisting. Both communities are also constantly changing, some naturally and others adversely because of the effects of people. Living things in a community interact with each other and with their environment. After examining an urban community sociologically and ecologically, one can better understand these interactions. An urban environment contains more than just buildings, people, and simple, natural things. Many plants and animals share cities with people. These living things have their needs, their interdependencies, their adaptations, their life-supporting cycles, and their reactions to crowding. All of these things can be studied in the city as well as in the country.

Plants and animals must either adapt, die, or relocate if their environment does not supply them with their needs. Some plants and animals can adapt to city life; others cannot. Living things need food, air, water, sunlight, and space to grow. The quantity and quality of these things determine the plant and animal life found in a particular area.

Population growth is becoming a more serious problem, especially in the underdeveloped countries of the world. People cannot reproduce indefinitely and expect a decent standard of living. Our finite food supply, our increasingly poisoned earth, or the exhaustion of our finite fuels may ultimately limit growth. Overpopulation will become a more severe problem in the future because of the depletion of our natural resources, such as reduction of cultivable land for food production, pollution of our waters and air, and overusage of our fuels. Overpopulation decreases standards of living and creates sanitation, education, and housing problems. Animals, including people, need a reasonable amount of space in which to live in order to be mentally and physically healthy. Therefore, if space is decreased for every person, increased anxiety and stress will result, creating such changes as reduced individualism and diminished aesthetic resources (wilderness and wildlife).

Directly related to overpopulation is food production. Each new baby consumes resources, but as the number of babies increases, the supply of resources decreases. It is important for children to understand that land areas vary in their suitability for cultivation; that often fertile agricultural lands are withdrawn from cultivation for other uses, such as housing and industrial parks; and that undernourishment, low food production rate, and a high population growth rate are interrelated. The use of natural resources has increased to serve larger numbers of people. All of these problems are interrelated and are a direct corollary of population growth.

The study of population leads naturally to discussion and exploration of pollution and people-made problems, such as waste disposal and fuel shortages, as well as good accommodations for the existing people on Earth. Since people first discovered how to use fire, we have polluted the air. Burning provides us with power, but the process pours wastes into the air. Not until recently has air pollution been considered a threat to our biophysical environment. This change has occurred for two main reasons: rapid population growth and increased technological activities. Our technology has created massive waste problems, producing products detrimental to the growth of living things, aesthetically unpleasing, and economically expensive.

Pollution means the addition of foreign matter to the natural environment to such a degree that the cleansing actions of winds, precipitation, and mixing cannot keep the biosphere balanced. The major source of pollution is combustion, mainly from car exhaust, factories, power plants, and incinerators. These pollutants are in the form of carbon monoxides, nitrogen oxides, sulfur oxides, hydrocarbons, and particulate matter. Pollutants are of three basic types: gases (sulfides and carbons); liquids (aerosols and fumes); and solids (dust, ashes, and particulate matter).

Air pollution has been around longer than people but in a different form than generated by people. Natural air pollution has always existed in the form of contamination by sand and dust storms, fires and volcanic action, and gases given off by decaying materials. Yet manufacturing technology has increased air pollution, surpassing nature's output. Consequently, people are becoming more aware that something must be done. Individuals as well as organizations are concerned and putting forth an effort to help solve our environmental problem of air pollution.

Air pollution not only threatens human health but the health of every living thing as well. Millions of people are subjected to polluted urban air every day. Pollution has a cumulative effect, working slowly and insidiously, eventually leading to sicknesses or death. The most adverse effects of air pollution on health occur in urban communities having the highest concentrations of people and industry.

Air pollution not only affects living organisms internally but externally as well, such as their vision. Reduced vision of motorists and aircraft pilots has been attributed to air pollution. Sulfuric oxides lower visibility by defusing light. Nitrogen dioxides absorb sunlight in the blue region of the light spectrum, which results in a brown haze that fills the air over cities. Economic losses are a result of this reduction of visibility. If sunlight is reduced, lighting bills increase, transportation hazards increase, and an unattractive gloominess pervades a city.

Air pollution also severely damages material objects. Pollutants can corrode, tarnish, soil, crack, erode, weaken, and discolor such materials as silver, rubber, fabrics, car finishes, house facings, and a host of other goods. Particulate matter in the air speeds up the destructive qualities of oxidants.

Air is a thin layer of mixed, odorless, colorless, and tasteless gases that surround the Earth. These gases are mostly nitrogen and oxygen. Air is indispensable because life could not exist without it. Pure air is essential to life, but in the United States we charge our air with a tremendous amount of pollution each year. This pollution comes from the following sources and produces the following pollutants:

1. Automobiles—carbon monoxide. This poisonous gas drives the oxygen out of our bloodstreams. Large amounts, of course, can kill; small amounts can cause adverse effects, such as dizziness, fainting, or impairing a person's driving abilities.

2. Factories—sulfur oxides and nitrogen oxides. Sulfur oxides come from oil- or coal-burning factories. They irritate eyes, noses, and throats; damage the lungs, kill plants; and affect visibility. Nitrogen oxides occur when nitrogen and oxygen are converted to nitrogen dioxide as a result of fuel burning. This poisonous gas can result in a brown haze that irritates the eyes, reduces visibility, and diminishes sunlight.

3. Other sources—particulates, smoke, fly ash, dust, and fumes from both liquids and solids. Some may settle to the ground; others remain suspended in the air. Particulates soil clothes, dirty houses and cars, scatter light, and carry poisonous gases. They come from cars, incinerators, building materials, and fertilizers.

4. Photochemical smog—A mixture of gases and particulates (derived from burning fuels, such as gasoline) oxidized by the sun. They irritate the eyes, nose, and throat, making breathing difficult. They corrode materials and damage crops.

Air pollution will only get worse because more people are coming into our world every day and fewer are dying. These new people will drive more cars, use more fuel and power, and consequently produce more waste material.

Air pollution control is being worked on. Government standards are imposed upon factories to limit emissions. Control techniques are implemented, such as precipitators and centrifuges, to help eliminate particulates and poisonous gases. More national standards are being enforced regarding exhaust emissions of cars and trucks. Inefficient methods of burning trash and open burning can be replaced with efficient incineration or sanitary landfills. Helping to control and alleviate air pollution is everybody's duty, but it starts with the federal government, which provides research on the effects of air pollution and the development of improved methods of air pollution control. The federal government sets standards to protect the people, and it assists counties and municipalities in setting up and maintaining air pollution control systems.

Acid precipitation is one of our major environmental problems and a major contributor to air pollution, water pollution, and land pollution. It is a great challenge to scientists from such diverse disciplines as meteorology, bacteriology, botany, agriculture, and engineering because acid precipitation affects many aspects of the environment. Acid precipitation can damage flora, fauna, buildings, statues, and people. Because its effects are so widespread, we need to find and implement suitable controls.

The term *acid deposition* is a more correct term than *acid rain* or *acid precipitation* because it includes all forms of precipitation (rain, sleet, snow, and hail) as well as dry particulate matter, such as fly ash and dust. Acid rain is the more common name by which we refer to acids falling to the Earth.

Acid rain is a direct result of energy production and motorized transportation, which are two of the most vital activities of an industrialized nation. Acid rain occurs when acid molecules fall from the atmosphere onto land, water, and physical objects. Acid rain forms when sulfur oxides (SO_x) and nitrogen oxides (NO_x) in the atmosphere combine with water to make sulfuric acid (H_2SO_4) and nitric acid (HNO_3). Sulfur oxides and nitrogen oxides can originate from natural sources, such as volcanoes, forest fires, and geothermal activity, and from human-made sources, primarily from the burning of fossil fuels. Sulfur oxides and nitrogen oxides are produced when coal and oil are burned by electrical power generating plants, paper mills and other industries, and ordinary people heating their homes; as well as from exhaust emissions from cars, trucks, airplanes, and other vehicles. Consequently, combustion is the greatest source of air pollution contributing to acid rain. A drop of acid rain can be formed when a sulfate particle acts as a nucleus around which a raindrop forms, or when the particle is simply absorbed by a falling drop of rain, subsequently referred to as "washout" and "rainout." Sulfur dioxide emitted from smokestacks eventually returns to Earth, sometimes caught and "washed out" of clouds by rain falling from above, or carried downward as the clouds condense into rain. The "washout" of sulfur dioxide by rain falling through a concentration of sulfur dioxide is influenced by the size of rain droplets, the pH of rain, and the extent of sulfur dioxide concentrations. Small raindrops are more effective than large raindrops in capturing and dissolving atmospheric sulfur dioxide. Because heavy rain is characterized by large raindrops, it will tend to have lower sulfur dioxide concentrations than a light rain, falling through the same atmosphere. "Rainout" probably accounts for most of the sulfate in precipitation in remote areas because "washout" has been found to be dominant close to the source of pollution.

Normal precipitation is slightly acidic because atmospheric carbon dioxide reacts with rain to produce carbonic acid. On the pH scale (0.0–14.0), 7.0 is neutral, and normal precipitation is about 5.6. Acid rain has a pH of 5.0 or less. The pH of substances is found by dipping a piece of litmus paper into the substance, observing the color, and comparing it with the pH color chart to determine if it is acid or base.

The effects of acid rain are as pervasive as the rain; many are detrimental and irreversible. The most dramatic and concentrated effects of acid rain are to our lakes and rivers. Acidic pollutants may enter an aquatic ecosystem in different forms, either as dry deposition, or gases, but mostly as acid rain. The result of this influx of acidic pollutants is a change in the equilibrium of the aquatic ecosystem, mostly through an alteration in its pH. Acid rain produces chemical changes in the blood of fish. Their basic body metabolism is altered, which results in a failure to breed or deformity. In many cases, fish can not reach maturity. They cannot grow at a normal rate because their respiratory systems are unable to process oxygen in the water passing over their gills, and their blood is unable to transfer proteins to the flesh and bones. Acid is selective in its decimation. Not all organisms are equally vulnerable. Organisms decline in a particular order as acid intensity increases. For instance,

- at pH 5.8, shrimp and minnows vanish;
- at pH 5.5, leeches disappear;
- at pH 5.0, all snails and most clams are extinct, and insects that breathe air increase;
- at pH 4.2, the common toad is extinct;
- at pH 4.0, little is left but chub, rock bass, and lake herring;
- at pH 3.5, almost all frogs, fish, and crayfish are extinct;
- at pH 2.5, only a few species of acid-tolerant midges and some bacteria and fungi are alive; and
- at pH 2.0, the water is, practically speaking, sterile.

As fish, insects, and amphibians disappear, so, too, must the predators that depend on them for food. When the food is gone, wildlife populations must also decline. In this way, acid from acid rain goes through the whole food chain.

Forest ecosystems change more slowly than aquatic ecosystems in response to acid precipitation. The neutralization process strips away such invaluable nutrients as calcium, magnesium, sodium, and potassium. As the buffering minerals are stripped away from the soil, acid begins to mobilize aluminum to invade the root hairs of trees, through which the plants normally extract water from soils. The aluminum ravages the cells of the roots' endodermis, the inner cellular passageway through which water moves, and the trees begin dying of thirst from the crown down. With the root system weakened, fungi and bacteria invade, and the trees have little hope for survival. Other problems include visible leaf damage, or *necrosis*, and *chlorosis*, or the absence of chlorophyll, and reduction of species per unit area.

Acid can interfere with fertilization, stunt or kill the growth of seeds, or render them sterile. The length of time an acid raindrop clings to a leaf, the number of times it happens in a rainstorm, the number of rainstorms, the time of day, and the time of year—all influence how soon stunted needles, wilted leaves, and thwarted fertilization and germination will result. Trees also become weakened and have less resistance to insects and disease. Increased stress from acid rain has weakened trees so that they have difficulty recovering from natural stresses, such as harsh winters, insects, plant and tree diseases, and shifts in rainfall and temperature.

Acid rain can probably not be stopped. Therefore, the only logical approach to acid rain lies in its control and reduction. There are several options available:

1. Coal Switching—Factories could switch to lower-sulfur coal, which would require little modification to their plants. However, there is not as much lower-sulfur coal, which mainly comes from mines in the eastern United States, available. The use of Western coal, which is lower in sulfur, takes money away from the East, and Western coal doesn't burn as hot.

2. Coal Cleaning—This method relies on crushing and washing of coal to reduce transportation and waste-disposal costs. It reduces operating and maintenance costs in the boiler and coal-handling equipment caused by incombustible impurities and reduces emissions.

3. Smokestack Scrubber—Air polluted with sulfur dioxide from coal fire is sent to the scrubber, where it is sprayed with water containing limestone dust that converts sulfur dioxide gas to sludge. Clean air goes up the stack, and often the sludge is recycled.

4. Liming—This process entails the addition of lime to acidified lakes to neutralize them and increase their pH to improve fish survival. This method treats the symptoms and not the problem.

5. Energy Conservation—People would use less energy and use it more efficiently, which would result in reduced fuel consumption. This method includes lifestyle changes, such as carpooling, and using less electrical energy for heating, air conditioning, and electricity. It also includes tapping energy from solar, tidal, nuclear, biomass, and geothermal sources.

If these measures are not employed, our world will surely be devoid of aquatic organisms, viable lakes, and unproductive croplands and forests. This result means we can look forward to even more polluted skies and aquatic and terrestrial ecosystems.

A natural result of population is sewage, its treatment, and its disposal. Chemicals in water come from two sources: naturally, from rocks and soils over which the water travels, and sulfates, phosphates, nitrates, and chlorine, which come from the effluent discharged from sewage treatment plants. Detergents, chlorine, phosphates, and surface water runoff (containing garden fertilizers and pesticides) flow back into the streams to become a part of domestic water supplies again.

There are three kinds of sewage treatment plants. Primary treatment plants compose approximately one-third of sewage treatment plants in the United States. They remove sticks, paper, sludge, and debris that can be trapped by screens. Secondary treatment plants use screens and a process of chlorination that removes approximately 90 percent of degradable organic waste and 99 percent of the germs in water. Tertiary treatment plants use filtration, flocculation, and other mechanical and chemical processes to remove almost all contaminants from water. This treatment is a very expensive process.

Sewage treatment plants remove suspended solids and oxidize organic wastes in the water to form carbon dioxide, nitrogen oxides, sulfur oxides, and water. Sewage treatment speeds up natural bacterial oxidation processes by adding vast amounts of oxygen. A typical sewage treatment plant works like this. First, water flows into large settling tanks and is given a suitable amount of time for solids to settle out. The solids are removed by a machine, and the water is sent to an aeration tank where it is mixed with active bacterial sludge, aerated, and agitated. This mixture goes to another settling tank, and more sludge is removed. The water is filtered and goes into a river, lake, or ocean. Another method sprays the water over a bed of stones covered with microorganisms. Left in the open air, the organisms oxidize the organic matter. Sludge and sediment from settling tanks often is put into a tank with anaerobic bacteria that will change it into methane gas, which can be used to generate electricity. Leftover sediment can be dried and used as fertilizer.

Discussions on air pollution, population, and sewage disposal ultimately lead to discussions on conservation, or how to protect the totality of our natural resources: our air, water, land, plants, and wildlife. Conservation means self-preservation for us all. It means preserving Earth's many life forms and the balances of nature. The balances of nature are disrupted by people more quickly than the changes brought about by nature. When these balances are upset, everything on Earth is endangered, including people. With our advanced technology, we have assumed the right to destroy, but we also have the responsibility to preserve and keep Earth livable. Our intelligence must supercede our greed.

Because of humankind's avarice and unconcern, many species are extinct or are now endangered. An endangered species is one that is in jeopardy of becoming extinct, either because of a reduction in number or because of a change in habitat.

Increasing atmospheric greenhouse gases could cause global warming, a gradual rise in the Earth's temperature. The atmosphere absorbs about 20 percent and reflects about 30 percent of the solar energy that passes through it. The Earth reflects about 10 percent and absorbs 40 percent of the solar energy that hits the Earth's surface.

To keep the temperature of the Earth's surface stable, an equal amount of heat energy must be reradiated back into space from the Earth's surface. Greenhouse gases, water vapor, carbon dioxide, methane, and ozone naturally trap heat near the Earth's surface. However, as fossil fuel consumption, burning of tropical forests, and urban development increase, so do the greenhouse gases, most especially CO_2. If, indeed, global warming does occur, the consequences will include partial melting of polar ice caps, expansion of deserts, and a rising sea level.

During the past hundred years, global temperatures have risen approximately 1.2° F (0.7° C). That doesn't sound like much, but significant warming could have disastrous results. Because of increased evaporation, lower water levels in fresh-water lakes could concentrate pollutants. If the level of the oceans were raised, polar ice caps could melt, coastal cities could flood, and barrier islands and reefs could disappear. Scientists project that the average global temperature will rise 2–6° F by the year 2100, more than temperatures have risen in 10,000 years. Carbon dioxide is responsible for about 55–60 percent of global warming, chlorofluorocarbons (CFCs) 25 percent, methane (CH_4) about 12 percent, and nitrous oxides (N_2O) about 6 percent. Carbon Dioxide (CO_2), methane (CH_4), and chlorofluorocarbons (CFCs) are by-products of burning fossil fuels. They absorb and reflect heat to the Earth and prevent heat from escaping into the atmosphere. Eventually they will raise the Earth's temperature in a greenhouse effect.

Some recommendations to help reduce these pollutants include reducing the production of CFCs, reducing the use of fossil fuels by increasing the use of alternative sources of energy, stopping the burning rain forests, planting more trees and other vegetation, using more air-pollution devices, and slowing population growth.

As we have gained more and more people in the world, we've also gained more and more garbage. Solid waste, household garbage, yard wastes, construction wastes, and ashes end up in landfills that are becoming increasingly fuller. Then what do we do? Forty-five billion bottles and jars are disposed of each year. Three and three-fourths billion tons of paper are discarded each year. More than 800 billion steel and aluminum cans are put into landfills each year. More than 20 billion plastic containers are tossed out each year, any of which are biodegradable but still are not able to be broken down because there is no sunlight and air to help decompose them. Approximately 200 million tires are thrown away each year. Also, approximately 50 billion pounds of yard and food wastes are discarded annually. Where does all this trash go? Into our landfills, which is land that could be used in a more productive way—for agriculture or wildlife, for instance.

A renewable resource is one that, if managed properly, can be reused or replaced naturally. For instance, after trees have been cut down, they can be replanted. A nonrenewable resource is one that is available in limited quantities and is nonreplaceable. Fossil fuels—coal, oil, and natural gas—are nonrenewable resources. Because trash can be both renewable and nonrenewable, our goals should be conservation of natural resources and reduction of trash to keep our landfills from getting overfull and to preserve some of our needed resources.

A sanitary landfill is not just a dump. It is a dump where trash is crushed and pushed together, ground into layers, and covered with soil. Then bacteria, moisture, and protozoans decompose the trash. Unfortunately, not everything decomposes because not enough air circulates through the different layers to allow the bacteria to work properly. If an item decomposes in a landfill, it is biodegradable. Aside from the fact that not everything decomposes, there are other problems associated with landfills. Toxic water from a landfill, called *leachate*, can seep into the ground water and spread to other water sources, such as rivers and lakes, and harm humans, other animals, and fish.

Recycling is the process of recovering materials from a used object and using that material over again to make new objects. By recycling aluminum, we use 90–95 percent less energy than making it from raw materials. Recycling one aluminum can can save the energy equal to 6 ounces of gasoline, a nonrenewable resource. Recycling can save energy, money, and natural resources and can reduce waste. We must practice the three Rs—reduce, reuse, and recycle.

Landfills work on the principle of decomposers, such as bacteria, protozoa, and molds. These microbes digest and oxidize, or burn, garbage, which results in good, rich humus that enriches the soil and provides a more fertile medium for plants to grown in. A compost heap is a way of recycling household waste. Almost 20 percent of our household garbage could be recycled through a compost pile. By mixing composted materials with soil, a great amount of organic matter is being returned to the soil. This rich humus loosens and aerates the soil, enables the soil to hold water better, and adds necessary nutrients to the soil. By composting, we reduce the amount of garbage put in landfills and lessen the amount of methane gas produced by organic matter, a strong leachate that could contaminate ground water.

Each person in the United States uses approximately 600 pounds of paper a year. Overall, that is about 60 million tons of paper. Seventeen trees are needed to make one ton of paper. Paper production also requires a great deal of energy—one ton of paper needs 16,320 kilowatt hours (KWH) of electricity, whereas recycled paper requires 5,919 KWH, a savings of 64 percent. Recycling also reduces air and water pollution associated with paper production from virgin wood; recycled paper creates 35 percent less air pollution than paper made from virgin wood.

In one day in the United States, we dispose of the following: 90 million bottles and jars, 46 million cans, and 26 million television sets. Aluminum is the most abundant metal on Earth. The largest use of aluminum is for cans. If 250 people saved one can a day, that would equal 3,000 gallons of gas each year. Fifty percent less energy is required to make paper with recycled paper, and it reduces air pollution by about 95 percent. 850 billion trees each year go into making newspapers. Two hundred fifty million trees could be saved if each person recycled each paper every day. One hundred forty-four million pounds of plastic would be eliminated from our landfills if 10 percent of us would purchase products with less plastic 10 percent of the time.

Activity 1: Population

OBJECTIVE:	To define population and determine the effects of overcrowding
MATERIALS:	Stopwatch, a lot of children
LEVEL:	Lower to upper
SETTING:	Classroom
TIME:	30–45 minutes
PRE-ACTIVITIES:	Discuss the term *population*. Draw two ovals of different sizes on the blackboard and draw or list the names different types of organisms inside the ovals (people, cows, fish, and so forth). Discuss the fact that when the word *population* is used alone, it usually refers to people, and that it is possible to have many different populations in one area. Show that there are two different populations because there are two different boundaries. Draw a bridge between the two ovals, uniting the areas. Illustrate how changing the determining boundary changes the population.

LESSON DESIGN

Have half the students in the class crowd into a small area. Using a stopwatch or a second hand, add one child every eight seconds until the other half of the class is also in the crowded area. This rate is proportional to the growth rate in the United States for the next 70 to 100 years. Discuss with the students how they felt about being crowded physically and emotionally, and how they felt toward the other students in the crowded area.

Divide the classroom in half for the day. Put all the students in half the space to illustrate the effects of overcrowding (more humans on less land space). Take 10 students and have them represent 10 different countries, one of which is the United States. Use something like cookies or jellybeans to represent natural resources and divide them up according to how much of the world's resources are used by the different countries. Use an encyclopedia to obtain current facts and information. Remember that the United States uses about 50 percent of the world's resources with only about 7 percent of the world's population.

Go out to the playground at various times of the day and have the students take note of the number of children who are on the playground at that particular time. Have them imagine what it would be like if each child brought another child. Discuss their reactions to these crowded situations. Have the students apply the idea to a swimming pool area, a vacant lot, a riverbank, and a favorite place.

Questions

1. How can we improve crowded situations and make them more enjoyable and not feel so crowded?

2. How would the environment change if space was expanded for additional play areas, rivers, and the like?

3. How would the environment change if more space was expanded for parking lots, buildings, and roads?

4. How can our country and other countries conserve on natural resources?

 ## Activity 2: Overcrowding

OBJECTIVE:	To determine the effects of overcrowding
MATERIALS:	1 cup and 1 bowl for each student, 1 quart container and 1 gallon container, water. *Sambal recipe*: onions, chilies, garlic clove, anchovies, rice, oil, water
	Optional: drawing paper, papier-mâché, clay
RESOURCES:	Information specialists on nutrition and malnutrition to discuss the world's food problems and nutrition in general.
	UNESCO—write for pamphlets on world hunger and malnutrition.
	UNICEF—write for information on their Halloween programs as well as general information on world hunger and children specifically.
LEVEL:	Upper
SETTING:	Classroom
TIME:	1 hour for the first activity and several days for the models
VOCABULARY:	Famine, malnutrition
PRE-ACTIVITIES:	Activity 1 (chapter 6) on population

LESSON DESIGN

Have the students split up into groups of varying sizes. Give each child a glass and give each group the same amount of water (1 quart to 1 gallon). Then have the groups divide the water equally among the group members. Compare the amounts of water each child received. Discuss how the students feel about receiving the different amounts of water. Do the same thing with a bowl of rice.

Plan the following simple meal of Sambal (serves approximately four persons): two chopped onions, one crushed garlic clove, three chopped chilies, one cup dried anchovies, rice, oil, and water. (Adjust the recipe to suit the number of students you have.)

Fry the onions, garlic, and chilies together in 2 tablespoons of oil, add the anchovies, and fry until hot. Eat the mixture on top of rice. This recipe should be thought of as a flavoring for rice, which is the main ingredient of the meal. This meal is a staple for many Southeast Asian countries. After eating the meal, discuss with the students how they would like to eat this same meal every day. How would they like eating only this every day, sometimes as many as three times as day?

Supplementary Activities

Make a model city out of papier-mâché, clay, or paper. Then increase the number of buildings, shopping areas, parking lots, and so forth without increasing the size of the city. Discuss the effects both physically and aesthetically.

Have the students make posters or collages illustrating the effects of overcrowding.

Have the students write stories about crowded conditions. For example: "My Crowded School," "Crowds in the Street," or "The Day the Earth Became Too Crowded."

Have a school-wide Halloween campaign for UNICEF. UNICEF will send a lot of wonderful information to schools concerning hunger and children and how to implement a Halloween collecting program in your school. Included is a film on UNICEF and its concerns.

Questions

1. Does the amount of space people have affect their health and happiness?

2. What kind of a situation is created when there are too many people in one place?

3. How is your life different than a child who lives in Southeast Asia, Africa, Europe, a major metropolitan city, or a rural town?

Activity 3: Litter

OBJECTIVE:	To be able to distinguish between biodegradable and nonbiodegradable materials
MATERIALS:	Large boxes (liquor or fruit), soil, spade, plastic wrap, newspaper, trash bags, items to bury—aluminum foil, orange peel, a piece of plastic, a piece of newspaper, toothpick, can, cloth, and so on— clear container, aluminum foil, organic (potato peels, coffee grounds) and inorganic garbage (plastic milk jug, pop can)
LEVEL:	Lower to upper
SETTING:	Classroom and outdoors
TIME:	45 minutes
VOCABULARY:	Biodegradable, decomposition, inorganic, organic, recycle

LESSON DESIGN

Take a short walk around the playground or into the community with trash bags, collecting litter. Take the litter back to the classroom and spread it out on newspapers. Hypothesize about which items might disintegrate over time if buried and which items would not disintegrate. Write hypotheses in a science notebook. Line four large boxes with plastic wrap and fill it three-fourths of the way full with soil. Bury three rows of identical items of litter in each box, making sure that each box contains different items. For example, Box 1 could contain three rows of apple cores, toothpicks, a plastic lid, and a pop can. Box 2 could contain a piece of aluminum foil, a cookie, a piece of newspaper, and a hairpin. All three rows in each box are identical, but the different items will decompose at different rates. Keep the soil damp at all times. After one week, carefully dig up one row in each box, laying the contents on pieces of newspaper. Analyze each item and record observations in a science notebook. After two weeks, carefully dig up the second row in each box, analyze the items as in the first week, and record any observations. After the third week, dig up the third row of items and analyze them. Record all observations in a science notebook and discuss conclusions based on original hypotheses.

Visit the city dump, sanitary landfill, or waste disposal area to see how garbage is handled in your community. Discuss different ways garbage can be disposed, such as sanitary landfill, open burning, incineration, and so forth. Discuss their pros and cons and any effects they may have on the environment, such as air pollution, water pollution, or land pollution.

Supplementary Activities

Fill a clear plastic or glass container with garbage alternately layered with soil. Keep the soil moist at all times. Cover the container with aluminum foil or a lid. Once a week write about the following observations in a science notebook:

- Sketch and describe any molds present.

- Identify any empty spaces. Are there any? Are they really empty?

- For what could this landfill be used?

- What helps materials decay?

- Is there any difference between organic and inorganic decomposition? If so, what?

- Make some generalizations about decomposition.

Questions

1. Did any of the items show any signs of breaking down? If so, which items?

2. Did any of the items remain the same? If so, which ones?

3. Which materials were organic, and which ones were inorganic?

4. Which materials were biodegradable, and which ones were not?

5. Which materials could eventually pollute our environment?

6. Could any of the materials be worn down in any other way, by burning, for instance? If so, are there any environmental repercussions because of that method?

7. Could any of these materials be reused or recycled instead of put into dumps or burned? If so, how?

8. What are cities going to do with all the garbage they collect in future years? How will it be possible to get rid of all this waste without infringing on other countries for possible dump sites, polluting the ocean by dumping our wastes there, or polluting our air by burning our wastes?

Activity 4: Waste Production and Reduction

OBJECTIVE:	To demonstrate the effects of waste on the environment and some ways of reducing it.
MATERIALS:	Chart paper, pencils, paper
RESOURCES:	Water and sewage sanitation personnel of your municipality, state legislature, or literature
LEVEL:	Upper
SETTING:	Classroom and field trip areas
TIME:	1 hour of classroom time, several hours for the field trips
VOCABULARY:	Renewable resource, waste

LESSON DESIGN

Visit a supermarket and make a list of examples of excess packaging. Discuss ways in which packaging could be controlled and used more wisely.

As a class activity, chart each student's waste, including paper, aluminum, water, electricity, and so forth (see Figure 6.1). Show the students how to reduce their and their family's waste production with a few of the following suggestions: don't let the water run while brushing your teeth; don't leave appliances (television, lights) on when not in use; write on both sides of a piece of paper; and recycle paper, cans, and bottles. Have a weekly follow-up or one of several months on students' waste and their progress, if any, on conserving.

Write to the state legislature and national organizations, such as the National Wildlife Federation, the Acid Rain Foundation, and the Environmental Protection Agency, for information on waste and pollution. From the file of resources collected, make a bulletin board depicting the perils of overpackaging, pollution, and overconsumption of resources.

Visit a water processing plant and a sewage disposal plant and get qualified personnel to give you a guided tour with a lot of explanation. Discuss water treatment and the possibility of recycling sewage water for drinking. Discuss the present water treatment conditions in terms of a doubled population. Visit the river above and below the treatment plants. Discuss the impact the treatment has had on the environment and the possible reasons.

Supplementary Activities

Visit a major factory (papermaking, automobile, cannery, and so forth) located on a river. Observe the visible impact of that factory on the immediate environment and hypothesize the long-term impact on the same environment as well as the down-river environments that are out of sight from the factory.

Collect aluminum cans as a recycling project for your classroom. As a classroom, choose to what the money from the cans will go: a new game for the classroom, UNICEF, a classroom wastebasket (for recycling cans or bottles), a charity, or some other worthy cause.

Questions

1. In what ways can we reduce the amount of waste we create?

2. In what ways can we reduce the amount of packaging that is seen in grocery stores (e.g., Styrofoam for tomatoes, boxes for toothpaste, and plastic wrap for apples)?

3. What will your municipality's water/sewage treatment facility be like in 15 or 20 years? Will it be able to withstand the demands of more and more people, or will it be working under capacity? What would be the effects of a sewage/water treatment plant working under capacity?

4. How can a papermaking plant or an automobile plant add waste to a river? What is that waste doing to the environment around it—now and in the future?

SOLID WASTE CHECKLIST

Name:			Number in Family:					
Kind of Waste	Mon	Tue	Wed	Thu	Fri	Sat	Sun	Total
aluminum								
plastic								
glass								
paper								
wood								
Styrofoam								
metals								
other??								

Fig. 6.1.

Activity 5: Community Land Use

OBJECTIVE:	To become aware of the land usage in and around your community
MATERIALS:	Community land use map
RESOURCES:	Town manager or town planner
LEVEL:	Upper
SETTING:	Classroom
TIME:	1½–2 hours
PRE-ACTIVITIES:	Ask the town manager or town planner to give a talk to the class on present and future needs of the community.

LESSON DESIGN

From the land use map, evaluate the following:

1. Where do most people live?

2. Where are the shopping areas located?

3. Where are the industrial areas located?

4. Where are the recreational areas located?

5. What other types of buildings are available?

Choose an area of your community around which to walk and take note of the following:

1. What is the most common land use?

2. What houses or buildings look out of place?

3. What is the percentage of residential areas?

4. What is the percentage of industrial areas?

5. Are there signs of change? What kinds?

6. Count the number of buildings per block for:

    Commercial use

    Residential use

    Industrial use (list the types)

    Public use (list the types)

What other features are visible? List them:

Open space (playgrounds, lots, parking spaces, other)

Natural features (trees, gardens, parks, other)

Environmental health (trash collection, litter, dead animals, pests, other)

7. How would you rate the area? (Check the appropriate line.)

As a place to live?	_____Good	_____Fair	_____Bad
As a place to go to school?	_____Good	_____Fair	_____Bad
As a place to play?	_____Good	_____Fair	_____Bad
As a place to work?	_____Good	_____Fair	_____Bad

Investigate the streets in your community. What damages streets? (Examples might be salt, extremes of heat and cold, heavy traffic, extremes of precipitation). Are streets level from one side to the other? Place a string across the street. Are they level at the curbs? Pull the string taut. Measure with a tape measure the distance from the string to the ground in several places to determine if the street is on a single plane or not. Would shape assist runoff? When it precipitates in your city, where does the excess water go? Into what body of water do your city's sewers flow?

Make a study of your school building as a mini-watershed. Visually examine the roof to determine how many surfaces it has for water runoff and locate the rain gutters and downspouts. Trace the route water would take from the roof's surface to the gutters to the downspouts to the ground to the sewers. After a fairly heavy rain, walk around the school grounds and locate areas of low spots where water could collect. Repeat this activity for several main buildings in your town or neighborhood. See if you can determine how the construction of streets affects the drainage of water from them and the pattern established for the creation of the city's watershed.

Supplementary Activities

Take a walking video tour of your surrounding community. With the video camera mounted on a tripod on wheels, or just carrying it, the class can visually record their impressions, comments, and questions. A still camera can be used instead and a slide presentation set up later. Either method can be used later to present your findings to other classes.

Questions

1. In walking around your community, did you find it to be well planned? In what ways?

2. What would you do to improve that particular area of your community?

3. What would you remove to improve the area? What would you add to improve the area?

4. Are streets a waste of water resources? If so, how can this waste be reduced?

5. Does gutter water affect litter and soil in the gutter? How?

6. What are the environmental problems of your community?

7. What kinds of information on soil and water would city planners need to plan well-developed housing projects, recreation areas, shopping centers, and industrial areas?

 ## Activity 6: Land Usage and Community Planning

OBJECTIVE:	To design and build a model city using land use and community planning concepts
MATERIALS:	Paper, pencils, paints, scraps of cloth, Styrofoam, wood, plastic, anything reusable rather than new
LEVEL:	Upper
SETTING:	Classroom
TIME:	1 hour of initial planning and several days for construction
PRE-ACTIVITIES:	Activity 5 (chapter 6) on community land use and the information gained from the talk by the town manager or city planners

LESSON DESIGN

Divide into groups from two to six and design a model city of the future based on the information you have gained from some of the activities on land usage, population, and soil. Assume that you have a limited amount of space because of the increase in population. Dwellings should probably be multifamily; vegetation is not only nice but necessary; some sort of power is needed to run machines, vehicles, industry, subways, and recreational vehicles but that pollutes very little; and aesthetics are just as important as function. Groups should work together to design and implement their plans, seeing which group can come up with the best overall plan according to the criteria described.

The following specifications should be considered: size and kind of housing, major industry/minor industries, transportation, shopping areas, government buildings, parking areas, green spaces, such as parks and gardens, cultural and recreational areas, streets and highways, bicycle paths and walking paths, schools, libraries, fire and police departments, and water and sewage treatment plants. There are many more considerations, but these are the basics that need to be incorporated in each plan. Not only must these items be included in the plans, but the plans must designate where some of these things will be located. For instance, a retirement home does not need to be next door to a singles bar or a car manufacturing plant.

Latitude and longitude, climate, soil types, and water availability need to be considered. Major industry is not as feasible in an area without a river, for instance, and soil type might dictate the kinds of building materials or architectural styles used.

When the models are finished, have each group review the other groups' models to see that they adhered to certain guidelines for soil, water treatment, and land usage specifications. The models can then be displayed for other classes or schools to enjoy, and the students can explain their models to interested classes to let them know what they have been studying.

 ## Activity 7: Overpopulation of Plants

OBJECTIVE:	To show the effects of overpopulation of plants
MATERIALS:	Birdseed, pint milk cartons, water, potting soil, rulers, graph paper
LEVEL:	Lower to upper
SETTING:	Classroom
TIME:	30 minutes to plant the seed, several weeks of observation

LESSON DESIGN

Growing plants in crowded and uncrowded situations will show the effects of overpopulation. Fill the milk cartons about three-fourths of the way full of soil. Plant several cartons with seeds—some with two or three seeds, several with a small handful, and several cartons with a large handful. Varying the amounts of seed in the different cartons creates different conditions under which the plants will grow. After the seeds have become seedlings, measure and record their heights on a piece of paper and draw a line graph on graph paper to represent each group of seedlings. Evaluate the plants' growth periods in terms of the number of plants under the different conditions.

Supplementary Activities

Repeat the same process as above. When the seedlings are fairly well established and the overcrowded groups seem to be failing, thin some of the plants in those groups. Document any changes in the plants left in the cartons. What does it have to say about space requirements for plants?

Questions

1. Did all of the seeds sprout equally well? Explain.

2. After the seeds became seedlings, which group or groups seemed to be growing the best? Why?

3. Did any group die? For what reason?

4. How are plants similar and dissimilar to people in their needs for space and suitable conditions under which to grow?

Activity 8: Oxygen in the Air

OBJECTIVE:	To determine the amount of oxygen in the air
MATERIALS:	Large round cork, birthday candle, glass to fit over the candle, magic marker, pan, water
LEVEL:	Lower to upper
SETTING:	Classroom
TIME:	30 minutes

LESSON DESIGN

Measure to find the center of the cork and secure the candle to the cork with some hot wax. Put some water in the pan and see if the candle on the cork will float on the water. If it doesn't float, redo it until the exact center is found and the cork and candle float. Light the candle and place the glass over the candle and cork, being careful not to push the glass to the bottom of the pan. After a minute or two, mark the glass to indicate water level on the inside of the glass. As it uses up the oxygen in the glass, the candle will eventually go out. Because of the absence of oxygen in the glass, the air becomes lighter inside than outside the glass and presses down on the water in the pan with more strength than the air in the glass. Consequently, this force pushes the water up into the glass in proportion to the difference in pressure. To determine the amount of oxygen originally in the glass, measure from the rim of the glass to the line drawn on the glass. A 2-inch mark in a 10-inch glass means oxygen took up $\frac{2}{10}$ (or $\frac{1}{5}$) of the original air. Approximately 20 percent of the air was oxygen because $\frac{1}{5}$ equals 20 percent. The water in the glass will rise as the candle burns and will cease to rise when the candle goes out.

Questions

1. Why does the candle eventually go out after the jar is placed over it?

2. Why does the water level rise in the jar as the candle is burning?

3. Why does the water level stop rising after the candle goes out?

4. Approximately what percentage of air is oxygen?

 Activity 9: Smoke in the Air

OBJECTIVE:	To determine amounts and kinds of smoke in the air
MATERIALS:	3-by-5 inch index cards, pencils or crayons, paper
RESOURCES:	Air pollution experts
LEVEL:	Upper
SETTING:	Classroom and observation sites
TIME:	1 hour
VOCABULARY:	Air pollution, density
PRE-ACTIVITIES:	Talk by an air pollution expert, from the EPA or some other organization, on air pollution, its effects, and probable solutions

LESSON DESIGN

To estimate smoke density, make a Ringelmann Smoke Density Chart. On an index card, draw four squares of equal size across the top. Draw the same number and size of squares on the bottom of the card. In the middle of the card, draw a rectangle, 4 inches long and ½ inch wide. Starting with the first square, shade it light gray with a pencil or crayon. Shade the second square a little darker, the third square even darker, and so on, through all eight squares. Number the squares by order of gradation, 1–8. Cut out the center rectangle. Now you have a Ringelmann Smoke Density Chart with which to observe smoke from smokestacks. The gradations of density will approximate that of professional charts. On a piece of paper, record the date, time, location, and number from the smoke density chart that is closest to the color of the smoke coming from the smokestack. Hold the chart up and sight through the slit to determine the best number. Record the same data every day for a week or two and average the numbers. Find out if this number meets air pollution standards for your area.

Supplementary Activities

Discuss colors associated with air pollution. Make an air pollution color chart—black, gray, red, yellow, orange. Place pictures with representative colors on a chart as examples. Collect magazine pictures and so forth, showing smog, smokestacks, temperature inversions, and car exhaust. Post them on a bulletin board next to the color chart. Discuss the pictures and colors, their causes, effects, and possible solutions.

Interview people on the street about their opinions on air pollution, causes, effects, and solutions. Ask them if pollution affects them physically or mentally or both.

To observe particulate matter in the air, put several glass slides coated with Vaseline outside in several different locations. Make a data sheet to record the information. After one day, bring in one slide. After two days, bring in another and so forth, until all slides are inside. Record the differences and the differences in locations. Two or three slides for each area will be needed to make the experiment more reliable.

Cut a hole in the middle of several large index cards. Cover the hole with transparent tape so that one side remains sticky. Write on the cards the following: date, time, and location. Thumbtack or hang three different cards in several locations around town. After a specified amount of time, collect the cards—maybe one card after one day, the second card after four days, the third card after one week. Each time you collect the cards, examine them under a microscope or with a hand lens. Make a chart to display the differences in particulate matter found in the various locations. The chart could include data as well as the index card with the particulate matter.

Have the students repeat the procedure in their own homes. Are different rooms susceptible to different amounts of particulate matter? Would a wood-burning stove have any effect on particulate matter as opposed to electric heat? What about kitchen fumes? Discuss some of these possibilities.

Questions

1. Which index cards collected the most particulate matter? Did location affect the amount of particulate matter collected? Why?

2. What would be the sources of particulate matter in the different locations?

3. Would there be any way to reduce particulate matter in any of these locations? Explain.

Activity 10: Smog

OBJECTIVE:	To demonstrate how smog is formed
MATERIALS:	Large jar, ice, aluminum foil, paper, matches
LEVEL:	Upper
SETTING:	Classroom
TIME:	45 minutes
VOCABULARY:	Smog, temperature inversion

LESSON DESIGN

Smog is a combination of smoke and fog (or moisture). Often it is trapped near the ground by a temperature inversion: cold air trapping warm air (and pollution) near the ground. Set up the following, as in Figure 6.2. Wash the jar, leaving moisture on the sides of the jar. Tear pieces of paper into strips and light them on fire. Place them in the bottom of the jar and seal the top with aluminum foil. Place ice cubes on top of the aluminum foil and watch the air in the jar. As the air cools, the smog should thicken.

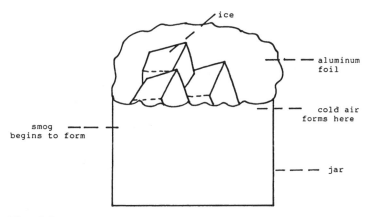

Fig. 6.2.

From *Consider the Earth*. © 1999 Gates. Teacher Ideas Press. (800) 237-6124.

Supplementary Activities

Smog can contain many combinations of chemicals. To observe one of these chemicals, place two dishes side by side. Place a few drops of concentrated hydrochloric acid into one dish and place a few drops of ammonia in the other. Put both dishes in a large glass jar. Light some pieces of paper and place these in the jar with the dishes. Seal the top with aluminum foil and watch what happens. A cloud of white particles, ammonium chloride, will form in the air where the two evaporating chemicals meet.

Questions

1. What would it be like to breathe all the different chemicals that form in the air?

2. Is it possible not to be bothered by the chemicals we breathe in the air?

3. If we can't see air pollution, is it still dangerous to our health?

4. If we can't smell pollutants in the air, are they dangerous to our health?

 ### *Activity 11: Temperature Inversion*

OBJECTIVE:	To demonstrate a temperature inversion and to observe what happens to pollutants in this situation
MATERIALS:	2 aquariums or 2 large glass jars, plastic bags, food coloring, hot plate, pin, water, ice
LEVEL:	Upper
SETTING:	Classroom
TIME:	1 hour
VOCABULARY:	Pollution, temperature inversion
PRE-ACTIVITIES:	Activity 10 (chapter 6) on smog

LESSON DESIGN

This activity is divided into two sections, one that stresses atmospheric conditions under normal conditions and one that demonstrates a temperature inversion.

To create a normal atmospheric condition, heat a pan of water on a hot plate and add a few drops of food coloring to the water. Fill the aquarium about three-fourths of the way full of cold water. Make the water even colder by adding several ice cubes. Half fill a plastic bag with the warm water that was heated on the hot plate and remove the ice cubes from the aquarium. Seal the plastic bag as carefully as possible so that no air remains in the bag. Lower the bag with the warm, colored water into the cold, colorless water of the aquarium. When the water is calm, poke a hole in the bag with the pin and observe the interaction of the warm water with the cold water.

To simulate a temperature inversion, add several ice cubes and several drops of food coloring to a pot of water. Heat several quarts of water with which to fill the aquarium about three-fourths full. Half fill the plastic bag with the cold, colored water and close it so that no air remains inside. Lower the bag with the cold, colored water into the aquarium with colorless, warm water. When the water is calm, poke a hole in the bag with the pin and observe the interaction of the warm and cold water.

Questions

1. Why would a temperature inversion make air pollution problems worse?

2. Under normal atmospheric conditions, where does a cool air mass lie—above or below a warm air mass?

3. In a temperature inversion, where is a warm air mass located? Why does this create a problem?

Activity 12: Acid Rain

OBJECTIVE:	To understand acids and bases by testing different solutions
MATERIALS:	pH paper (or red and blue litmus paper), jars, common substances (soap, ammonia, coffee, soda, aspirin, distilled water, vinegar, lemon juice, and baking soda, for example)
LEVEL:	Upper
SETTING:	Classroom
TIME:	1 hour
VOCABULARY:	Acid, alkaline, litmus paper, pH

LESSON DESIGN

Fill small jars with common substances, such as lemon juice, vinegar, baking soda with water, soda pop, distilled water, and so forth and measure their pH by dipping a piece of pH paper (or litmus paper) into each solution. Record the color on a piece of paper. When all of the solutions have been tested, make a chart from 0.0 to 14.0 to show the relative positions and pH levels of each substance. Acids are substances that turn blue litmus paper red. Bases are substances that turn red litmus paper blue, and neutral substances have no effect on either color of litmus paper. pH paper turns different colors, from dark blue to green to yellow-orange (alkaline to acidic on a scale from 14.0 to 0.0). Write your observations in an acid rain notebook and include your hypothesis and inferences.

Questions

1. What does pH mean, and what does it measure?

2. On a pH scale of 0.0 to 14.0, what is neutral, what is acidic, and what is alkaline?

Activity 13: Acid Rain 2

OBJECTIVE:	To determine the buffering capacity of soil in your area
MATERIALS:	3 or 4 soil samples from different areas, water, vinegar, coffee filters, jars, funnels or plastic jugs cut to make funnels
RESOURCES:	Soil conservation service
LEVEL:	Lower to upper
SETTING:	Classroom
TIME:	30 minutes
VOCABULARY:	Buffering capacity
PRE-ACTIVITIES:	Talk to the soil conservation service to make sure that the soil samples you want to collect are all different and help you identify the kinds of soils; Activity 10 (chapter 6) on smog.

LESSON DESIGN

To a certain degree, the amount of damage acid rain does to an area depends upon its soil. Alkaline soils can buffer or partially neutralize acid rain. More acidic soils do not have this buffering capacity. Partially fill the coffee filters with the different soil samples. Place the coffee filters in the funnels and place each in a separate jar. Pour a small amount of distilled water over the soil samples and measure the pH of the water that has dripped into each jar. When all of the water has dripped through, remove the muddy water. Make an acidic water solution by mixing 50 milliliters of vinegar with 150 milliliters of water (approximately pH 4.0). Pour this acidic water over the soil samples and again take the pH of the dripped water in the jars. Compare the "before" and "after" pH measurements to decide which soil samples have the best buffering capacity.

Questions

1. What does buffer mean?

2. Why does one kind of soil buffer acid rain better than another kind of soil?

3. How can a lake buffer itself from acid precipitation?

Activity 14: Acid Rain 3

OBJECTIVE:	To determine the pH of acid precipitation by collecting samples of rain or snow
MATERIALS:	Clean glass jars, pH paper with color charts, tape, pens, one data sheet per group, plastic wrap or plastic bags
RESOURCES:	Department of Wildlife personnel or Environmental Protection Agency (EPA) personnel, written information from the Acid Rain Foundation or Acid Precipitation Awareness Group
LEVEL:	Upper
SETTING:	Classroom, playground, and other outdoor areas
TIME:	30 minutes to compile data, indefinite amount of time to collect samples of precipitation
PRE-ACTIVITIES:	Talk by someone from either the wildlife department or the EPA on acid precipitation; Activity 10 (chapter 6) on smog.

LESSON DESIGN

Divide the class into groups of four or five students. In distilled water, wash equal numbers of jars as there are students. Wrap jars in plastic wrap or put in plastic bags so that they don't get contaminated. During a rainstorm, set the jars on the playground or at various sites around the community. Label and tape the group's number and location of collection on the jar. Measure the pH of the collected samples by dipping a piece of pH paper in the sample and comparing the color with the color chart to determine the pH. Record this information on the data collection form (see Figure 6.3).

Immediately following a snow storm, have each student take a jar home and collect samples of snow from their neighborhoods. Measure the pH of the samples the following day and record this information on their chart. Several samples should be collected periodically throughout the year in order to make comparisons.

Supplementary Activities

Collect samples of rainwater at the beginning of a storm and at the end of a storm. Measure the pH of each sample to determine if the rain at the beginning of the storm was any more or less acidic than at the end of the storm.

Questions

1. What is the pH of normal rain? Is it acid or alkaline?

2. Acid rain can come in many forms. What are they?

3. Acid rain starts at approximately what pH level?

4. How and why do we measure acid precipitation?

5. Is it possible for the same rain or snowfall to have different pH values?

RAIN (pH) DATA SHEET AND WEATHER INFORMATION

Sample Location: _____

Time and Date: _____

Wind Direction: _____

Sample Accumulation: _____

Kind of Precipitation: _____

pH of Sample: _____

Cloud/Sky Description: _____

Comments: _____

Name: _____

Group Number: _____

Group Members: _____

_____

_____

_____

_____

Fig. 6.3.

Activity 15: Acid Rain 4

OBJECTIVE:	To demonstrate the effects of acid rain on seeds and plants
MATERIALS:	Radish and bean seeds, small pots or paper cups, pH paper and color chart, water mixtures that vary in pH from 2.0 to 6.0, vinegar, potting soil
LEVEL:	Lower to upper
SETTING:	Classroom
TIME:	45 minutes to set up, several days for germination, and several weeks for observation
PRE-ACTIVITIES:	Activity 10 (chapter 6) on smog

LESSON DESIGN

Fill paper cups three-fourths of the way full of potting soil and plant equal numbers of seeds in each cup. Plant both radish seeds and bean seeds but in separate cups. Each group should plant two cups of each kind, one for the seed experiment and one for the plant experiment. One cup will get watered with normal water, and the other cup will get watered with a pH mixture. Label each cup with the group number, date, and pH of water being used to water the seeds. Wet the soil, but do not saturate it. Make daily observations and records of seed growth, which cups germinate, which ones do not, and any differences between those that do germinate. When the cups that have been watered with normal water have germinated, place them in a well-lighted area so that they can grow well. After the plants are fairly well established, water them with the mixed pH solutions. Make careful observations and records of the plants' growth patterns, heights, and number of leaves.

Supplementary Activities

Collect several different kinds of deciduous leaves, either from outside or from house plants. Make a water solution of pH 4.0 (acid rain). Place a few drops of normal water on a leaf's surface and a few drops of pH 4.0 water on a second leaf's surface. Let the leaves stand for awhile and record any observations or changes occurring in the leaves.

Questions

1. What effect do different pH mixtures have on a seed's ability to germinate?

2. What effect do different pH mixtures have on plant growth?

3. How would plant growth be affected if the soil used was alkaline instead of sterilized potting soil?

4. Do you think acid rain would have the same affect on aquatic plants as terrestrial plants? Why or why not?

 ## Activity 16: Acid Rain 5

OBJECTIVE:	To demonstrate the effects of acid rain on aquatic and terrestrial ecosystems
MATERIALS:	20-gallon aquarium, glass or plastic to cover the aquarium, gravel, soil, grass seed, water, sulfuric acid, goldfish, atomizer
LEVEL:	Upper
SETTING:	Classroom
TIME:	1 hour to set up the simulation, several weeks of observation

LESSON DESIGN

In one end of the aquarium, make a pond with a plastic or glass bowl lined with and surrounded by gravel. Contour the gravel up to the other side in a gentle slope. Place soil on top of the gravel and contour more severely so that a hill is created, sloping down toward the pond. Plant grass seed in the soil and put two goldfish in the pond. When the grass is well established, start sprinkling it with a water/sulfuric acid mixture (pH of 4.0) every couple of days. Keep the aquarium covered after this to create a simulated hydrological cycle containing acid rain. Make daily observations and record any changes in the aquatic or terrestrial part of the system.

Questions

1. What effects does acid rain have on an aquatic ecosystem and a terrestrial ecosystem? Are there any differences or similarities?

2. Is it possible for ecosystems to adapt to differing amounts of acid rain over time? If so, how?

 ## *Activity 17: Recycling*

OBJECTIVE:	To learn the process of making recycled paper
MATERIALS:	Scraps of construction paper, newspaper or whatever is handy, blender, cornstarch, tempera paint, premade plaster mold or screening
RESOURCES:	Paper or pulp factory
LEVEL:	Lower to upper
SETTING:	Classroom
TIME:	45 minutes to make, 2 to 3 days to dry
VOCABULARY:	Landfill, precycle, recycle, reuse
PRE-ACTIVITIES:	Activity 4 (chapter 6) on waste production and reduction; if possible, visit a paper factory so that the students can see first-hand how paper is made

LESSON DESIGN

Tear the scraps of paper into 1-inch pieces. Fill the blender three-fourths of the way full of water. Add 1 teaspoon of cornstarch to the water. If you want the finished product to be colored, also add a squirt or two of tempera paint. Add scraps of paper, secure the lid on the blender, and blend for approximately 4 or 5 minutes until you have a thick slurry. Either pour the liquid paper pulp into a plaster mold and sponge off the excess water or spread it on top of a piece of screening and press out the excess water. Flip the paper out of the mold or off the screening and onto a piece of newspaper to dry. After a day, flip the paper over onto another piece of newspaper to dry the other side. Total drying time is about two days.

Activity 18: Garbage and Landfills

OBJECTIVE:	To understand how much solid waste we produce
MATERIALS:	Large plastic garbage bag, 4.5 pounds of household waste, scale, newspapers, calculators, classroom waste
RESOURCES:	Town manager, water and sewage sanitation personnel of your municipality
LEVEL:	Lower to upper
SETTING:	Classroom and field trip sites
TIME:	1 hour initially, varied time for class visitations and field trips
VOCABULARY:	Biodegradable, decomposition, hazardous waste, landfill, nonbiodegradable, nonrenewable resource, recycle, renewable resource, solid waste
PRE-ACTIVITIES:	Activity 4 (chapter 6) on waste production and reduction; have a person from the local water and sewage sanitation department or town management visit your classroom to speak about solid waste management, waste water treatment, and recycling; visit the local landfill and talk with the person in charge.

LESSON DESIGN

Fill a large trash bag with household trash. Weigh the bag to make sure it contains 4.5 pounds—the average amount of trash a person produces each day. Create a table to represent the amount of trash generated by each family of each child in the class. Then calculate the average amount of trash generated by the town and state in which you live, based on rounded census figures.

Supplementary Activities

Keep a chart to calculate the type and amount of trash that is thrown away in your classroom each day. Before school's end each day, weigh the trash in your trash cans. Dump the trash on a newspaper and sort it by type. Record your results on your chart. Record and calculate on your chart how much trash is thrown away in your entire school each day, then how much is thrown away by your class and school in a week, a month, and a year.

Have each child keep every scrap and morsel of trash he or she throws away for a day. Everything from food scraps to pieces of paper and pencil shavings should be placed in a paper bag, saved until the next day, and weighed. Record the results on a chart. Stash, save, and weigh trash every day for a week so that averages can be calculated and recorded on the chart. Calculate the percentages of trash that can be recycled, reused, or composted as opposed to what has to be thrown away. Sometimes we automatically throw things away without thinking about recycling, reusing, or composting. Look into starting a recycling program at your school.

At Christmas time, calculate the amount of space, volume, a Christmas tree would take up in a landfill. Multiply that by the number of households in your community, school, neighborhood, and so on to determine the massive amount of space that would be occupied by dead Christmas trees.

Questions

1. Where does all the trash go?

2. What is a sanitary landfill?

3. Aside from taking up space that could be used for other purposes (parks, golf courses, open space), what adverse effects could landfills have on the environment?

4. What can be done with a landfill once it is full?

5. What could be done with some of the waste aside from throwing it away? Can it be composted, recycled, or reused? Brainstorm. What can be done to reduce the amount of trash thrown away each day at school and in the home?

6. What kinds of things can be recycled? Find out from your local sanitation department/recycling center what things they will take.

7. What can be done with Christmas trees aside from dumping them in a landfill? Research the possibilities that are feasible for your area (chippers or shredders for mulch, wave break on the beach to prevent erosion, and the like).

Activity 19: Sanitary Landfills

OBJECTIVE:	To construct a model of a sanitary landfill to understand how one works
MATERIALS:	Deep pan or large box, gravel, soil, garbage (Styrofoam, plastic, newspaper, food, leaves, grass, wood, and so on), spoon
LEVEL:	Upper
SETTING:	Classroom and actual landfill
TIME:	20 minutes
VOCABULARY:	Aerobic, anaerobic, biodegradable, decomposition, landfill, nonbiodegradable
PRE-ACTIVITIES:	A visit to a local sanitary landfill

LESSON DESIGN

Place a shallow layer of gravel in the bottom of a large box or deep baking pan: about 3 inches of soil; a layer of small, chopped-up garbage (a combination of foods, paper, Styrofoam, plastic, and so on); and more soil to cover. Sprinkle with a little bit of water and set in a warm, dark place. Once a week add water, if necessary, to keep it moist but not wet. After six to eight weeks, dump the contents of the box or pan onto sheets of newspaper, examine the results, and compare the rate of decomposition.

Supplementary Activities

Divide the bread slice into four equal pieces. Place one-quarter slice in each plastic baggie. Sprinkle the bread square with water to make it wet but not soggy. Squeeze the air out of one baggie and zip it closed. Do not zip the other baggie closed but place it inside the jar, fold the top of the baggie over the lip of the jar, and cover with the nylon stocking. Secure with the rubber band. Place both baggies in a dark place and make daily observations and records.

Do the same experiment using nonbiodegradable objects and compare your results with the original experiment.

Do the same experiment but vary the temperature. Place the baggies in a really hot place and also in a really cold place. Are there any differences? Why?

Questions

1. How are the mini-landfills similar or different from real landfills?

2. In the mini-landfills, why did some of the garbage look untouched but other pieces of garbage seemed to be disintegrating? Which things are better for our environment? Why?

3. How can landfills be hazardous to the environment?

4. How can landfills reduce the risk of pollution?

5. Most landfills can be used for approximately 15–20 years. What can the land be used for after the landfill has served its purpose?

 ## *Activity 20: Hazardous Wastes*

OBJECTIVE:	To determine how harmful hazardous wastes are
MATERIALS:	4 paper cups, water, lemon juice, ammonia, salt, bean seeds
LEVEL:	Upper
SETTING:	Classroom
TIME:	30 minutes initially, several days of follow-up
VOCABULARY:	Hazardous waste, landfill
PRE-ACTIVITIES:	Activity 18 (chapter 6) on garbage and landfills; Activity 19 (chapter 6) on sanitary landfills

LESSON DESIGN

Fill four paper cups about three-fourths of the way full of potting soil. Label one Cup A, one Cup B, one Cup C, and one Cup D. Plant a couple of bean seeds in each cup. Place all cups in a sunny location and water regularly until the bean seeds sprout. When the cups have small plants growing in them, start watering Cup A with plain water, Cup B with salt water, Cup C with ammonia water, and Cup D with lemon water. Record your observations. Even though salt and lemon juice can be ingested by animals, and ammonia is poisonous to animals, all are harmful to plants. Substances that are harmful to plants, such as salt and ammonia, can leach into the soil from decomposing trash in landfills and poison the soil as well as living things in and around the soil.

Supplementary Activities

Do a comparison test with some of the following alternative cleaning methods, then discuss their feasibility.

Alternatives to Household Hazardous Wastes

INSTEAD OF THIS:	DO THIS:
Drain cleaner	1/4 c. baking soda + 1/2 c. vinegar
Ammonia-based cleaner	1 gal. hot water + 1/4 c. vinegar
Toilet cleaner	Baking soda + a toilet brush
Disinfectants	1/2 c. Borax + 1 gal. water
House plant insecticide	Liquid soap + water to spray on plants' leaves

Questions

1. What do such things as paint thinner, vinegar, oven cleaner, and fertilizers have in common?

2. Why should we be concerned about throwing away these kinds of products?

3. Why is it important to reduce household hazardous wastes?

4. Did the alternative household cleaners work just as well as the standard cleaners? Why or why not?

 ## Activity 21: Composting

OBJECTIVE:	To learn about the importance of composting by making a compost pile
MATERIALS:	Large, bottomless wooden box; dry plant matter (hay, straw, dry leaves, sawdust, wood chips, or dry weeds = 50 percent); moist organic matter (manure, green weeds, grass clippings, kitchen wastes = 35 percent); (soil, humus, or old compost = 15 percent); wood ashes, crushed shells, or limestone sprinkled on top to help neutralize acidity; pitchfork; water; thermometer
LEVEL:	Upper
SETTING:	Outdoors
TIME:	1–2 hours to set up, many months to "ripen"
VOCABULARY:	Compost

LESSON DESIGN

Directly on top of the soil (not on sod or grass) lay 3–4 inches of your chosen dry plant matter. The next layer will consist of 6–8 inches of moist organic stuff—mixed kitchen scraps and manure. In layer three, spread garden soil, humus, or old compost. Finally, add a fine layer of damp wood ashes, crushed limestone, or crushed shells. Repeat the layers in the same order until the box is full. Cover with a layer of dry straw or plastic. Keep the compost moist but not soggy. Let the compost sit for about a week, then turn it. Using a pitchfork, turn the heap over so that the outside of the old pile is now the center of a new heap. Once again sprinkle the new heap with water to moisten it but not make it soggy. Cover the turned heap and wait another few days before turning it again.

Questions

1. What benefits are derived from composting?

2. Are there any negative aspects to composting? If so, what are they?

3. What is the purpose of each layer? Could composting be a complete cycle without one of the layers? Why or why not?

Activity 22: Greenhouse Effect

OBJECTIVE:	To understand the basic concept of the Greenhouse Effect
MATERIALS:	2 glass thermometers, test tube with a 1-hole rubber stopper
LEVEL:	Lower to upper
SETTING:	Classroom
TIME:	5 minutes to set up, at least 1 hour to record temperatures
VOCABULARY:	Chlorofluorocarbons (CFCs), global warming, Greenhouse Effect

LESSON DESIGN

Slide one thermometer in the one-hole rubber stopper, then insert it into one of the test tubes. Record the temperature of each thermometer, then put both the test tube and the second thermometer in the sunshine. Every 10 minutes, record the temperature of each thermometer for approximately an hour or until the temperatures remain constant.

Supplementary Activities

Place 2–3 cups of soil in a 1-gallon glass jar. Put a thermometer inside the jar and put a lid on it. Place the jar and a second thermometer in a sunny place. Record the temperatures of both thermometers before placing them in the sunshine, then again every 10 minutes for approximately an hour.

Tape thermometers to the insides of two glass jars. Record the temperatures of each thermometer. Cover one jar with plastic wrap or a clear lid. Place both jars in the sunlight and record their temperatures every 10 minutes for approximately an hour.

Vary any of the above experiments by adding plants, different types of soil, water, and so forth, to see if and why the results can be altered.

Questions

1. Which thermometers had the highest readings? Why?

2. How is heat trapped by glass similar to heat trapped by the Earth's atmosphere?

3. Does the soil have any effect on the temperature? Why or why not?

Activity 23: Global Warming

OBJECTIVE:	To study the effects of carbon dioxide on the environment
MATERIALS:	2 fish aquariums, heavy-duty plastic wrap, soda-lime crystals, heat source, 2 thermometers, soil, water, bowl
LEVEL:	Upper
SETTING:	Classroom
TIME:	15 minutes to set up, several hours to observe
VOCABULARY:	Carbon dioxide (CO_2), chlorofluorocarbons (CFCs), global warming, greenhouse gases
PRE-ACTIVITIES:	Activity 9 (chapter 8) on solar energy; Activity 22: (chapter 6) on the Greenhouse Effect; visit a greenhouse and take temperature readings during several hours, from early morning to late day. Record temperatures outside the greenhouse for the same hours. Make a chart of readings for the two environments.

LESSON DESIGN

Cover the bottom of both aquariums with a couple inches of soil. Label one Aquarium A and one Aquarium B. Set a thermometer in both aquariums and a bowl of soda-lime crystals in Aquarium A. On a chart, record the temperature of each aquarium. Cover both aquariums with heavy-duty plastic wrap so that they are sealed tightly. Either set both aquariums in bright, direct sunlight or place a lamp above each one. On your chart record the temperatures of each aquarium every half hour for several hours.

Supplementary Activities

To demonstrate the effects of carbon dioxide from a forest fire on the atmosphere, line one of the aquariums from the original experiment with soil. Place a thermometer in one corner of the tank and one outside the tank. Then place one jar of lime water in a different corner of the tank and a second jar of lime water outside the tank. Stick a tight clump of birthday candles in the soil in the aquarium. All at one time, light the birthday candles and as quickly as possible cover the aquarium with a piece of Plexiglas or glass so that the aquarium is sealed tightly. Leave the cover on the tank, let it sit for at least a week, and record your results.

To demonstrate the effect global warming could have on the polar ice caps, use both of the aquariums from the original experiment with soil in the bottom. Place a large bowl of water in one end of both aquariums. Cover one aquarium with heavy-duty plastic wrap or a piece of Plexiglas. Keep the other aquarium uncovered. Observe the tanks over a week's period and record any differences or changes between the two. Tank A with the cover should mimic the greenhouse gases, trapping heat and preventing it from radiating back into the atmosphere. To represent the Earth's icecap, place a large, whole chunk of ice in each aquarium at the opposite end from the bowls of water. Replace the cover on Tank A, but leave Tank B open. Place the aquariums in a sunny location or position a lamp to shine above each in an indirect manner. Observe the tanks over a period of several hours and record your results.

Questions

1. What effect did the soda-lime crystals have on Aquarium A?

2. Compare the simulation with the effects of carbon dioxide in the atmosphere.

3. Were the temperature differences great or small?

4. What eventually happened to the birthday candles in the aquarium?

5. Forest fires put out tremendous amounts of carbon dioxide. What does this do to the atmosphere? How would many forest fires add to the Greenhouse Effect?

6. Which tank trapped more water vapor? What effect would the trapped water vapor have on the Earth?

7. Which ice melted more quickly, those in Tank A or Tank B? Why?

8. If the bowl were an ocean, what would happen to the level of the ocean as the polar ice cap melted? What effect would it have on the ocean shoreline?

 ## Activity 24: Global Warming 2

OBJECTIVE:	To explore the principle of global warming
MATERIALS:	Vinegar, baking soda, bottles, balloons, drinking straw, bromthymol blue
LEVEL:	Upper
SETTING:	Classroom
TIME:	1 hour
VOCABULARY:	Carbon dioxide (CO_2), chlorofluorocarbons (CFCs), global warming, greenhouse effect, ozone
PRE-ACTIVITIES:	Activity 23 (chapter 6) on global warming; Activity 4 (chapter 2) on absorption of CO_2.

LESSON DESIGN

Pour ½ cup of vinegar into a soda pop bottle. Spoon ⅓ cup of baking soda into a balloon. Secure the balloon on top of the bottle containing the vinegar. Tilt the balloon so that the baking soda slips into the vinegar. As an alternative, put baking soda in the vinegar and put the balloon on top of the bottle.

Pour 1 tablespoon of bromthymol blue solution into a jar of water. Place a straw in the glass and blow into the bromthymol blue-water solution.

Pinch the balloon shut with your fingers, then twist a straw into its end. Place the open end of the straw into the bromthymol blue-water solution and slowly let the gas from the balloon leak into it.

Supplementary Activities

Discuss ways you can reduce the amount of carbon dioxide you put into the atmosphere. Some examples: (1) car pool or combine errands into one trip instead of three or four separate trips; (2) recycle; (3) plant trees; (4) keep thermostat turned down low; and (5) have family car tuned-up and tires properly inflated.

Questions

1. What happened to the balloon? Why?

2. What happened to the bromthymol blue-water solution? Why?

3. Which had the most effect on the bromthymol blue-water solution: your breath or the vinegar-baking soda solution? Why? What does this have to say about the CO_2 in the atmosphere?

VOCABULARY DEFINITIONS

Acid—An aqueous substance with a pH less than 5.0.

Acid Deposition—Pollutants mixed with any form of precipitation, rain, snow, sleet, or hail and dry particulate matter, such as dust or soot.

Aerobic—Processes that use air.

Air Pollution—The contamination of the atmosphere with noxious substances

Alkaline—An aqueous substance with a pH greater than 7.0.

Anaerobic—Processes that do not use air.

Aquatic—Living or growing in or on the water.

Biodegradable—Capable of being decomposed by a natural biological process.

Biosphere—The totality of regions of the earth that support self-sustaining and self-regulating ecological systems.

Biotype—A group of organisms having identical genetic but varying physical characteristics.

Buffering Capacity—The ability of soils and bodies of water to neutralize acidification.

Carbon Dioxide (CO_2)—Carbon dioxide is a colorless, odorless gas formed during respiration, combustion of fossil fuels, and organic decomposition.

Chlorofluorocarbons (CFCs)—Chlorofluorocarbons are human-made substances used in coolants, are one of the greenhouse gases, and can destroy ozone.

Compost—A controlled decaying process in which billions of organisms break the organic wastes down into forms usable by plants.

Conductor—A substance that transmits heat, light, or electricity.

Conservation—Preservation of natural resources, such as topsoil, water and wildlife, from loss, waste, or harm.

Decomposition—To cause to rot, decay, or putrefy.

Density—Thinkness of consistency or impenetrability.

Ecosystem—An ecological community with interacting biotic, or living, factors and abiotic, or nonliving, factors.

Endangered Species—A species in danger of extinction.

Famine—A drastic and wide-reaching shortage of food. Severe hunger and starvation.

Global Warming—The heating of the lower atmosphere due to the buildup of greenhouse gases that comes from the combustion of fossil fuels.

Greenhouse Effect—The buildup of heat in the lower atmosphere because of the absorption of radiation from the Earth's surface by molecules from such gases as water vapor, carbon dioxide, ozone, chlorofluorocarbons, and nitrous oxides.

Greenhouse Gases—Carbon dioxide, chlorofluorocarbons, ozone, water vapor, nitrous oxides.

Hazardous Waste—Waste material that is poisonous or dangerous to living things.

Insulator—A material that prevents the passage of heat, sound, or electricity.

Landfill—A garbage dump with a layer of soil on top.

Litmus Paper—A paper treated with litmus (a blue, amorphous powder derived from lichens) and used as an acid-base indicator.

Malnutrition—Poor nutrition because of an insufficient or poorly balanced diet.

Nonrenewable Resource—A resource that cannot be used again, such as oil.

Organic—Pertaining to or derived from living sources.

Ozone—Ozone in the upper atmosphere results from the bombardment of upper atmospheric oxygen with ultraviolet radiation and screens us from this harmful radiation.

Ozone Gas—Ozone gas (O_2), a bluish gas with a pungent odor, is a form of naturally occurring oxygen in the upper atmosphere and is poisonous.

pH—Potential of hydrogen. A measure of the acidity or alkalinity of a solution.

Pollution—The contamination of soil, water, or the atmosphere with noxious substances.

Population—Total number of organisms in a specified habitat.

Population Density—Number of inhabitants per unit of geographic region.

Precycle—Refusing to buy products packaged in wasteful ways, such as fibrous egg cartons and plastic and Styrofoam containers for vegetables and fruits.

Recycle—To extract useful materials from something and reuse them.

Renewable Resource—A resource that can be used or made new again, such as trees.

Reuse—To use something again instead of throwing it away.

Sewage—Liquid and solid waste carried off with ground water in sewers or drains.

Smog—Fog that has become mixed and polluted with smoke. Blend of smoke + fog.

Solid Waste—Waste that is solid such as household wastes (glass, plastics, metals, etc.).

Temperature Inversion—A layer of warm air that lies above a layer of cooler air that keeps polluted air from rising higher and dispersing with the winds. Upper air is usually colder, thus the term temperature inversion.

Terrestrial—Of or pertaining to the Earth or composed of land.

Waste—Worthless by-product of a process. Refuse or excess material. Garbage or trash.

Watershed—A regional drainage pattern. The region draining into a river or other body of water.

7  OCEANS

Oceans cover approximately 70.8 percent of the Earth, 140 million square miles (361 square kilometers), in an unevenly distributed pattern. Even though ocean bottom features are similar to those on land, with hills, valleys, plains, and mountains, they have some distinctive physical features too.

The continental shelf is a shallow platform that borders continents and extends outward from the shore to a depth of approximately 500 feet. It accounts for 8 percent of the ocean's surface, or about one-sixth of the Earth's total land area. The continental slope extends from the edge of the continental shelf to a depth of approximately 6,000 feet. The slope is steep—three to four degrees on mountains and two degrees on the coasts. It may be smooth, hilly, or terraced. The basin floor extends from the continental rise to the other side of the ocean. Much of the ocean basin consists of flat plains with slight irregularities called *abyssal plains*. They lie at depths of between 9,000 and 16,000 feet. More than 30 percent of the ocean basin is occupied by ridge and rise systems. The mid-oceanic ridge is the largest mountain system, extends 40,000 miles, can be one and half to two miles high, and is approximately 620 miles wide. Trenches, or deeps, account for less than 2 percent of the ocean bottom. They are found near coasts or submarine ridges, are flat bottomed, usually narrow, and V-shaped. Some isolated peaks of the ridge and rise system extend above sea level, forming islands. Other islands are formed by volcanic action. *Seamounts* are volcanic mountains whose tops have not reached the surface.

Marine sediment can be deposited in shallow water, on the continental shelf, or in the deep sea. It is inorganic and usually comes from the land, carried to sea by runoff and erosion. It is found on open coast lines, transported by waves and currents. It consists of the calcareous remains of organisms, salt, glauconite (an iron-potassium silicate), and material eroded from rocks and older sediment from wave action. Most are *pelagic*, from the upper layers of the open ocean, formed from skeletons of planktonic plants and animals, of wind-blown dust, and of clay.

Light from the sun heats the oceans. Ocean water, however, is a barrier to light, preventing light from penetrating more than 2,000–2,500 feet, depending on if the water is clear or turbid. Approximately 65 percent of the sun's rays reach the Earth's surface on a normal day.

Water has a high heat capacity that limits ocean temperatures to a narrower range than land temperatures. Temperatures vary with depth and location: approximately 28° F near the ice caps and 86° F in tropical oceans. The oceans are the Earth's greatest heat reservoirs because of their high specific heat, the capability to absorb and retain heat. Therefore oceans are a thermostatic control of climate. The Earth receives approximately the same amount of heat from the sun that it loses by radiation and reflection. Tropical areas absorb more solar heat than they radiate or reflect. The opposite is true for high latitudes. Ocean and air currents move heat from low latitudes to high latitudes. Oceans also control the moisture content of the atmosphere through evaporation.

Density of ocean water is dependent on both temperature and salinity. Density increases as temperature decreases or as salinity increases. The densest water is found on the ocean bottom, created by evaporation, freezing, or cooling, then sunk from the surface. This sinking process helps circulate water in the deeper areas of the ocean.

Pressure increases with depth because of density. At sea level, air pressure equals approximately 14.5 pounds per square inch (one atmosphere). Pressure increases one atmosphere for every 33 feet of depth.

Pure distilled water at 4° C at atmospheric pressure is the base for determining the density of sea water. Temperature, salinity, and pressure determine density. Surface sea water density is determined by measuring temperature and salinity. Below the surface, density is determined by measuring temperature, salinity, and pressure. The density of sea water measured against the density of distilled water at 39.2° F (4° C) is its specific gravity. Approximately 3.5 percent of seawater is composed of dissolved compounds from the breakdown of dead organisms, eroded rock and soil, and the condensation of rain from the atmosphere. Salts account for the majority of these dissolved compounds. This total amount of dissolved salts is called *salinity* and is measured in parts per thousand. The salinity of average seawater is about 35 parts per thousand. Temperature and salinity in water masses vary from the surface downward and are altered by processes that can add or delete salts or water from the ocean. These processes include evaporation, precipitation, river runoff, and freezing or thawing of ice. If evaporation exceeds precipitation, salinity is increased because the remaining salts are concentrated. If precipitation increases, then salinity decreases because the remaining salts are diluted.

There are different types of ocean currents. Some currents cover small areas and last a short amount of time; others cover great distances and are permanent. Currents are produced by variations in density and temperature and by the drag of the wind on surface layers. As water begins to move, it is deflected due to the Coriolis effect, and a surface current circulation pattern is established. Surface water circulates in opposite directions on both sides of the equator.

Because of the Earth's rotation, objects on the Earth's surface are deflected to the right in the Northern Hemisphere and to the left in the Southern Hemisphere. Water is moved on shore by winds coming in at an angle. In the Northern Hemisphere, surface currents can be deflected as much as 45° to the right of wind direction. Conversely, in the Southern Hemisphere, currents are deflected 45° to the left.

El Niño, Spanish for the Christ Child, is a term originally used by South American fishers to refer to a warm ocean current that usually appears around Christmas time. In 1904, Sir Gilbert Walker, a British scientist, was in India trying to predict Asian monsoons. He discovered that when barometric pressure rises in the east, it falls in the west, an event he called the Southern Oscillation.

Under normal conditions, trade winds, which are strongest in winter, push the equatorial current westward in the South Pacific, off the coast of South America. High pressure in the central Pacific Ocean makes the water warmest as well as creates the strongest storms in the western Pacific Ocean as the trade winds push the warm water westward. During a typical El Niño year, approximately every two to seven years, the trade winds weaken, causing warm water to flow eastward rather than westward. Instead of cold water flowing along the coast of South America, warm water does, reversing the whole process. What we get is an area of high pressure over the western Pacific Ocean and strong thunderstorms over the central Pacific Ocean.

Accompanying El Niño is a change in atmospheric circulation called a Southern Oscillation. When a Southern Oscillation occurs, the equatorial current in the Pacific Ocean reverses. An El Niño and a Southern Oscillation together are called *ENSO*. The temperature of the ocean off South America can rise as much as 18° F, which prevents the cold, nutrient-rich waters from penetrating the deeper layer of warmer water. This effect in turn reduces the amount of phytoplankton, fish, and animals in the surface waters.

In a normal year, the warmest water is in the western Pacific Ocean, with the strongest thunderstorms forming above this warm water. The coldest water is along the South American coast. High atmospheric pressure is in the central Pacific Ocean, causing strong trade winds to push the warm water westward.

During a normal year, the storm tracks follow a normal west to east pattern, but during an El Niño year, the storm tracks are shifted because the high and low pressure areas have changed. This effect creates a warmer than average winter in the western United States and a wetter than average winter in the southeastern United States.

Land near the coast of Peru is a desert, but the ocean nearby is a highly productive fishing grounds. Sea life is abundant because of upwelling, cold, nutrient-rich water that comes up from below to replace the warmer surface water.

Winds determine sea surface temperatures, differences in sea levels, and heat content of the upper oceans. Winds mix the nutrient-rich water with the surface water, thus increasing production of phytoplankton and affecting the growth of zooplankton.

Consequences and effects of El Niño are flooding (in U.S. Gulf states and western South America), hurricanes (in the western Pacific Ocean), and droughts and fires (in southern Africa, Asia, and western South America). Changes in oceanic conditions can bring about an increase in hantavirus in drought-ridden areas because of an overpopulation of rodents, an increase in meningitis because of airborne bacteria related to dryness and heat in the desert, an increase in schistosomiasis and such diseases as yellow fever and cholera due to abundant rainfall in some areas of the world.

Tides are the rise and fall of ocean water. At the same time that the moon's gravity pulls the water closest to the moon away from the Earth, the moon also pulls the Earth away from the water on the opposite side. As the Earth rotates, there is always a tidal bulge on the side facing the moon and one on the opposite side. Therefore, two high and two low tides occur each day in most places on the ocean. The maximum elevation of the tide is high tide; the minimum elevation is low tide. Exceptionally high and low tides are known as spring tides; moderate tides are known as neap tides.

Uneven heating of the Earth's atmosphere produces winds. Winds that blow across the ocean's surface produce waves. Wind exerts two forces—a direct force on the backside of a wave and an eddy, or suction, on the front side of the wave. A wave's height and length are determined by the speed and duration of the wind and by the distance the wave travels. As a wave moves forward, the surface water remains stationary but the water within the wave travels in a circular motion. As a wave nears a beach, the lower part of the wave drags along the bottom, which makes the wave rise more steeply because the top moves faster than the bottom, then falls as a breaker.

Life in the oceans is very diverse. The most abundant form of life is the tiny planktonic plants and animals that are carried by the currents. *Nektonic* animals include porpoises, whales, sharks, squid, and fish. They swim on their own power. Plants and animals that live along the shore and bottom comprise the *benthos*. They cannot swim well or not at all and include crabs, lobster, snails, seaweed, and algae. As on land, plants are the basis of life in the ocean. They use nutrients dissolved in seawater and live anywhere there is enough sunlight to carry on photosynthesis. Food chains in the ocean can be simple or complex. The transfer of energy is a three-way process between producers, consumers, and decomposers. *Autotrophs*, self-nourishing organisms, are the primary producers. The second tropic level is the *heterotrophs*, or herbivores, that feed on the autotrophs. The third level is occupied by the animals that prey on other animals, or carnivores. The final link in the food chain is occupied by the decomposers that exist on detritus: waste products of all organisms and dead organisms.

Marine organisms are classified according to where they live. The *epifauna*, bottom-dwelling organisms, and the *infauna*, sediment-dwelling organisms, occupy the benthos. The *nekton* includes the actively swimming animals, such as fish, mammals, and some crustaceans. Phytoplankton, autotrophic organisms, and zooplankton, heterotrophic organisms, are small and microscopic and are carried by the currents.

Unlike once thought, foods from the seas are not inexhaustible. We must practice conservation and management and avoid pollution. Regulations are needed to determine the amounts of fishing that should be allowed in order to learn the level of exploitation that will produce a maximum yield. Because international waters can be fished by all nations, management regulations are difficult to impose. Fishery yields can be increased if new resources are discovered and utilized, productivity is increased, the present catch is more completely used, and farming of the seas is intensified. More complete use of fishery resources could result in fewer fish being wasted. For example, fish caught with shrimp that are thrown away could be ground up into fish flour—a high-protein flour for both livestock and humans.

The area that lies below the photic zone is hardly touched. Deep-sea squid, bottom-dwelling crabs, and other crustaceans are as yet unexploited. Productivity of the sea is determined by sunlight and nutrients. By increasing phosphates, nitrates, and other elements in a fishing area, the fish yield may also increase. Another way to increase productivity is to use a thermal pump to circulate the water from down deep to lift nutrient-rich waters to the sunlight or to divert the course of some currents toward more favorable areas. The oceans could be more fully used by farming the seas.

Plants and animals are not the only resources in the sea. One major resource is the 140 million square miles of water contained in the oceans. Yet because sea water contains salt and other chemicals, it must be purified before it can be used for irrigation, drinking water, and other household uses. Desalination plants supply fresh water to many cities in the world. Many minerals can be found in sea water that could help supplement the dwindling supplies on land—minerals such as magnetite, tin, thorium, cobalt, and silica.

Sources of ocean pollutants include waste water and sewage discharge, oil, hot water, and agricultural runoff, to name just a few. Polluted waters can not only destroy the pristine environment of our oceans but create health risks for people by contaminating our food sources. Through the years, we have used the oceans as a dumping ground for waste that we didn't want or were not able to dump on land.

Human sewage sludge, the end product of municipal wastewater treatment plants, pollutes beaches, bays, and inlets through pipelines or barges. Under ideal conditions, there is nutritional value in sewage sludge for zooplankton and benthic detritus feeders, but so much sludge is being dumped in the water that it is becoming diluted. Some cities even barge sludge to offshore sites for dumping.

Toxic pollutants enter the ocean because of industrial discharge and sewer systems. These include such substances as mercury, copper, lead, and chlorinated hydrocarbons.

DDT is almost insoluble in water and is rapidly absorbed by suspended particles in seawater. It blocks normal nerve functions in vertebrates and interferes with calcium deposition in the eggshells of birds.

Another chlorinated compound is dioxin. Dioxins can cause cancer and malformations in animals. They enter the oceans through the effluent from pulp and paper factories. These toxic pollutants enter the food chain at the lowest trophic level and as they spread through each successive level become more concentrated and toxic.

Great reserves of oil lie buried deep beneath the ocean floor. Many offshore oil rigs are spread throughout the world, providing us with a lot of much-needed oil. Yet they also pose problems with oil leaks and spills.

Petroleum is a fossil fuel formed millions of years ago when organisms died, were buried in mud and soil and rock, and were compressed until they formed petroleum, or oil. Petroleum is very useful. It is used to make gasoline, jet fuel, heating oil, and diesel fuel. Most oil is transported by ocean tanker or pipeline. If a tanker spills oil, the spilled oil floats on the surface of the water because it is less dense than water. These oil spills create serious problems. They block sunlight from penetrating the surface, which keeps plants from making their food. They suffocate animals, prevent birds from flying, and poison animals that eat oil-covered objects.

Oil spills cause massive problems. Benthic organisms are suffocated because their gills get clogged. Birds' feathers and mammals' fur become so soaked with oil that they lose insulation and buoyancy. Not only is the toll on wildlife in the area of an oil spill devastating, but the oil spreads with the currents and waves. Oil also enters the oceans through parking lot runoff, underground storage tanks, and illegally dumped oil, as well as from fishing, military, and cruise ships.

Marine debris includes any discarded object that is manufactured and comes from dumping garbage at sea by merchant, fishing, military, hospital, and recreation ships. Many of these items dumped at sea are plastics, which not only decompose very slowly but float on the surface of the ocean and therefore are carried by currents and waves and continue to litter beaches and harm animal life. Common plastic products include jugs, bags, life preservers, buoys, six-pack yokes, fishing gear, nets, traps, and setlines. Many animals get entangled in the floating debris and can be seriously injured or even die.

The following is a partial list of debris discarded each day in the ocean and how long it takes those items to decompose:

paper towel	2–4 weeks
newspaper	6 weeks
apple core	2 months
cardboard box	2 months
waxed milk carton	3 months
cotton gloves	1–5 months
cotton rope	3–14 months

plywood	1,1963 years
biodegradable diaper	1 year
wool gloves	1 year
tin can	50 years
Styrofoam	50 years
Styrofoam buoy	80 years
aluminum can	200 years
six-pack holder	400 years
disposable diaper	450 years
plastic bottle	450 years
monofilament fishing line	600 years
glass bottles	undetermined

 ## Activity 1: Physical Features

OBJECTIVE:	To construct a 3-dimensional model of the ocean floor
MATERIALS:	Large box, plastic wrap, plaster of Paris, papier-mâché or modeling clay, tempera paint
RESOURCES:	Encyclopedias and books on the ocean
LEVEL:	Lower to upper
SETTING:	Classroom
TIME:	1 hour to several days
VOCABULARY:	Abyss, abyssal plain, continental rise, continental shelf, continental slope, guyot, oceanic ridge, rift valley, sea mount

LESSON DESIGN

Get as many books on the ocean as possible that contain diagrams of the ocean floor. Study the diagrams carefully. Discuss the vocabulary associated with the various features. To create a model of the ocean floor, line a box with plastic wrap so it won't get soggy. With the clay, papier-mâché, or plaster of Paris, make the ocean features and press them into the box. When dry, paint them with tempera paints.

Draw and label the main ocean features on a piece of poster board. Hang the poster board maps on the wall in front of where you display the three-dimensional models so that you can compare the two displays.

Supplementary Activities

To make a profile of the ocean floor, fill an aquarium three-fourths of the way full with water, then cover the bottom with sand and rocks of various sizes and heights. Tape a ruler to the top of the aquarium. Cut a piece of string 1 foot long. With permanent marker, mark the string at half-inch intervals. Tie a weight to one end of the string. On graph paper, draw a horizontal axis to represent distance across the aquarium (one square = ½ inch) and the vertical axis to represent the depth (one square = ½ inch). Measure the depth of the water on the outside of the aquarium. Mark zero on the graph for the water line. Mark and number a vertical axis below the water level.

Drop the weighted string into the aquarium so that the weight rests on the sand and rocks. Starting at one edge of the aquarium, count the number of lines on the string that are underwater. Put a dot on the coordinates on the graph to represent each depth as you make your way across the aquarium at half-inch intervals. When finished, connect the dots, and you will have a profile of the ocean bottom.

Questions

1. Which display shows the ocean floor in a more accurate way? Why?
2. Which display creates a more visual picture? Why?

Activity 2: Salinity

OBJECTIVE:	To observe different factors related to the salinity of sea water
MATERIALS:	Salt, 2 heat-resistant flat dishes, water, Bunsen burner
LEVEL:	Lower to upper
SETTING:	Classroom
TIME:	1 hour to set up, 1–2 days for observation
VOCABULARY:	Buoyancy, condensation, density, evaporation, precipitation
PRE-ACTIVITIES:	Activity 10 (chapter 8) on solar energy

LESSON DESIGN

To see what materials are dissolved in sea water, add 2 tablespoons of salt to an 8-ounce glass of water. Stir to dissolve. Pour 4 ounces of salt water into one dish and 4 ounces of fresh water into the other dish. Heat both dishes until all the water evaporates. Examine this material under a microscope or with a hand lens. If possible, classify the materials.

To see how the ocean gets its salt, mix equal parts of salt and soil (about 2 tablespoons of each). Put a coffee filter inside a glass beaker. Secure it by wrapping a rubber band around the rim of the beaker. Put a tablespoon of the salt-soil mixture in the coffee filter. Slowly sprinkle 1 to 2 tablespoons of water over the salt-soil mixture. A small amount of the water will seep through the mixture and drip into the beaker. Remove the filter from the beaker. After the water has evaporated, examine the residue on the bottom of the beaker. Water dissolves salt from the soil and takes it to the ocean, thus making the ocean salty.

Supplementary Activities

Try the first experiment using the sun as the evaporating power. Pour a very thin layer of fresh water on a pie pan and the same amount of salt water on another pie pan. Place both pie pans in the sun for several days. Observe daily to see what changes are taking place. Some countries in the world get their salt this way rather than mining it.

Questions

1. Which sample had the most material left over after evaporation? Why?

2. Why don't we see these particles in the liquid sea water?

3. If both experiments were performed, one with the Bunsen burner and one with the sun, were the results the same? Why or why not?

Activity 3: Density

OBJECTIVE:	To demonstrate that ocean water is denser than fresh water
MATERIALS:	Salt, measuring cups and spoons, plastic egg, modeling clay
RESOURCES:	If possible, have an oceanographer demonstrate the use of a hydrometer, an instrument used to measure specific gravity
LEVEL:	Lower to upper
SETTING:	Classroom
TIME:	20 minutes
VOCABULARY:	Buoyancy, density

LESSON DESIGN

Pack clay into both sides of a plastic egg and stick the pieces together to make a whole egg. Fill a glass three-fourths of the way full with water. Place the clay-filled egg in the glass of water and observe its position. Bit by bit, add a tablespoon of salt to the same water and observe what happens. Because salt water is denser than fresh water and therefore has greater buoyancy, the egg will rise higher in the water as more salt is added.

Make a simple hydrometer. Fill a graduated cylinder to the 100 mm line with fresh water. Put an eye dropper, upside down, in the water. Record where the top of the inverted eye dropper comes to rest in the cylinder. Replace the fresh water with exactly 100 mm of salt water and record its reading. Repeat the process with liquid soap, cooking oil, rubbing alcohol, and any other liquids you want to test. Finally, repeat the process with very hot and very cold water.

Cut clear plastic drinking straws in two. Either cut raw potatoes into 1-inch thick slices or mold plasticine clay into 1-inch thick slices. Mix the following solutions: salt water (1 cup of water, 4 tablespoons of salt, food coloring); water (1 cup of plain tap water and food coloring); and alcohol (1 cup of alcohol and food coloring); glycerin (1 cup of glycerin and food coloring). Fill 4 cups half full with one of each of the solutions. Each solution will have a different color. Remember which color represents which liquid and make the liquids dark enough for the layers to stand out. Insert a straw into each potato or clay slice and begin experimenting with the different colored liquids. With an eyedropper, squeeze a small amount of liquid into the straw. Add approximately equal amounts of liquid from each cup to see which liquids are more or less dense than the others. If done carefully, some of the liquids will layer themselves from most to least dense; otherwise, some will mix with others. Some experimenting is necessary.

Make three different colored salt water solutions of varying intensities and one colored plain water solution: $\frac{1}{8}$ cup of salt, $\frac{1}{4}$ cup of salt, $\frac{3}{8}$ cup of salt each in 2 cups of water. Repeat the same procedure with straws and clay or potato slices to see how the colored salt solutions layer themselves.

Supplementary Activities

Add soil to fresh water and find its specific gravity with the simple hydrometer.

To see which is denser, salt water or fresh water, do the following. Fill a bowl with cold water. Slowly lower an egg into the bowl. Does it sink or float? Take the egg out of the bowl and add a large amount of salt to the water (½–¾ cup). Once again slowly lower the egg into the water.

Questions

1. Which liquid was the most dense? The least dense? Why?

2. What effect did adding soil have on the density of the water? Why? What does that tell you about the density of the ocean? Would it be possible to have differences in density in different parts of the ocean?

3. What happened to the egg once salt was added to the bowl of water? Why? What does that tell you about the density of ocean water compared to fresh water?

Activity 4: Density, Turbidity, and Convection Currents

OBJECTIVE:	To see how density, turbidity, and convection currents form
MATERIALS:	Soil, water, salt, food coloring, plastic tub, jar
LEVEL:	Lower to upper
SETTING:	Classroom
TIME:	45 minutes
VOCABULARY:	Convection, current, density, turbidity
PRE-ACTIVITIES:	Activity 3 (chapter 7) on density

LESSON DESIGN

Fill the plastic tub about three-fourths of the way full of fresh water, then set it on a table so that one end is higher than the other by about an inch. In a jar of water, mix 3 tablespoons of salt and a few drops of food coloring. Starting at the elevated end of the tub, slowly pour the colored salt water into the fresh water as close to the side of the tub as possible. Observe how the heavier salt water moves below the lighter fresh water, creating a density current.

Pour the water out of the tub. Now fill it three-fourths of the way full with salt water and elevate it like before. Mix several tablespoons of soil in a jar of fresh water and mix well. Starting at the elevated end, slowly pour the muddy water into the salt water as close to the side of the tub as possible. Once again, observe how the heavier muddy water moves below the lighter salt water, creating a turbidity current.

Supplementary Activities

To demonstrate a temperature density current, such as the cold water that travels from the polar regions to the warm waters of the tropics, pour cold, colored salt water into a plastic tub of warm salt water. Observe the cold water as it flows under the warm water.

Chill a plastic cup of water with ice cubes, then add several drops of food coloring. Fill another plastic cup with hot water. Fill an eyedropper with water from the ice water cup. Slowly add a few drops to the warm water and observe what happens. Reverse the process but follow the same steps—add warm water from the eyedropper to cold water in the cup and observe what happens. Once again, the cold, denser water will sink, and the warm, less dense water will rise, causing a convection current.

To observe what happens when a current of salt water meets a current of fresh water: Place salt water in one bottle, fresh water in another bottle, and food coloring in either one. Repeat the same process of fitting the jars together and sliding the card away from them so that the water from the top jar slips into the bottom jar. Observe what happens.

To observe a temperature inversion: Fill one bottle with warm water, the other with cold water. Place the one with cold water on top of the one with warm water and repeat the process of fitting the jars together and sliding the card away from them so that the water from the top jar slips into the bottom jar. Repeat with the process reversed—place the warm bottle on top and the cold bottle on the bottom. What happens? Why?

 Activity 5: Pressure

OBJECTIVE:	To compare water pressure at different depths
MATERIALS:	2- or 3-pound coffee can, nail, water, masking tape
LEVEL:	Upper
SETTING:	Classroom
TIME:	30 minutes
VOCABULARY:	Density, mass, pressure

LESSON DESIGN

With the nail, drill three holes in the top, middle, and bottom of the coffee can. Place a piece of tape over the holes. Pour water into the coffee can. Remove the masking tape and observe the distance the water spurts from each hole. The bottom hole, which has the greatest pressure, will spurt the farthest.

Activity 6: Coriolis Effect

OBJECTIVE:	To understand the Coriolis effect
MATERIALS:	Lazy Susan, glass pie pan, water, two colors of food coloring
LEVEL:	Lower to upper
SETTING:	Classroom
TIME:	15 minutes
VOCABULARY:	Coriolis effect

LESSON DESIGN

Fill the glass pie pan about half full of water. Center the pan on the lazy Susan and slowly spin it clockwise. After a few seconds, stop the turntable and add one drop of food coloring to the very center of the pan of water. Then add a drop of a different color to the outside edge of the water. Observe what happens. Repeat the process with clean water, but spin the turntable counterclockwise. Observe what happens.

If the Earth didn't spin, the winds would blow in a straight line. Because the Earth does spin, winds blow along a curved path. The water on the edge of the pan travels faster than the water in the center because it has farther to go for each rotation. Winds in the Northern Hemisphere act as if they're being pushed to the right. Therefore, the food coloring spreading from the outer edge toward the center of the pan deflects to the right when the turntable is spun counterclockwise, and to the left if spun clockwise. Looking at the Earth's rotation from above the North Pole, the Earth spins counterclockwise. Looking at it from above the South Pole, the Earth spins clockwise. Winds in the Southern Hemisphere act as if they're being pushed to the left, whereas winds in the Northern Hemisphere act as if they're being pushed to the right.

Supplementary Activities

Cut a strip 1 inch wide from the long end of a piece of 12-by-18 inch tag board. From the rest of the tag board, cut out the largest circle possible. Place a thumbtack through the strip and into the center of the circle as well as a thumbtack through the outside end that overreaches the circle. Be sure the circle will turn freely. While one person slowly turns the circle, another person should draw a straight line down one edge of the strip all the way across the circle. Observe the effect.

If you can find a merry-go-round, have two students sit on opposite sides of it. To begin, have the students toss a ball back and forth not only to see how easy it is but to see the straight path the ball takes. Slowly start to spin the merry-go-round and have the students continue to toss the ball back and forth. Now observe the path the ball takes. Finally, have one student stay on the merry-go-round and one stand on the ground and toss the ball back and forth.

Activity 7: Land and Sea Breezes

OBJECTIVE:	To demonstrate the difference between land and sea breezes
MATERIALS:	2 shallow pans, ice, sand, water, long matches, heat source, 2 thermometers, 2 glasses, lamp
LEVEL:	Upper
SETTING:	Classroom
TIME:	30 minutes to set up, 2–3 hours to observe

LESSON DESIGN

Fill one glass half full of water. Fill the other glass half full of soil. Put a thermometer in each glass and let both glasses sit for about a half hour before reading each thermometer. Place both glasses directly under a heat source so that they receive equal amounts of heat. Now record the temperature on each thermometer and do so every half hour for the next two hours. Turn off the light and once again let the glasses sit for about a half hour, then record the temperature in each glass every half hour for approximately one more hour. The glass of soil should cool faster than the glass of water because water has a higher heat capacity than soil. On a warm day, these differences will produce a land breeze at night and a sea breeze during the day. Land cools faster than water during the night. Cool air sinks over the land and flows toward the ocean. Warmer air rises over the ocean and moves toward the land as a replacement. This phenomenon is a land breeze. A sea breeze is the opposite. During the day, air that was cooled by the ocean sinks and flows toward the land to replace the low pressure area that was created by the warm land.

Supplementary Activities

Fill a pan with soil. Heat this pan of soil in the oven or with a heat lamp. Fill another pan with ice cubes. Place both pans on a table, side by side, and erect a cardboard barrier around them on three sides. Light a long fireplace match and hold it between the two pans. Observe what happens. A sea breeze has been created because the warm soil warms the air above it, making it rise. It is replaced by the cool air from above the ice. To simulate a land breeze, replace the ice with warm water and the warm soil with soil that's been in the freezer overnight.

Activity 8: ENSO— El Niño and the Southern Oscillation

OBJECTIVE:	To demonstrate the effects of ENSO—El Niño/Southern Oscillation
MATERIALS:	2 deep plastic tubs, thermometers, water, pitcher, food coloring, aquarium, tiny blow dryer or hand-held fan, ruler
LEVEL:	Upper
SETTING:	Classroom
TIME:	30 minutes
VOCABULARY:	Current, El Niño, Southern Oscillation, trade winds
PRE-ACTIVITIES:	Activity 4 (chapter 7) on currents; Activity 6 (chapter 7) on Coriolis effect.

LESSON DESIGN

To demonstrate the effects of trade winds during an El Niño, fill an aquarium three-fourths of the way full with cold water. Add several drops of food coloring to a pitcher of hot water. Slowly pour some of the hot, colored water into the aquarium to form a thin layer on the surface of the cold water. Measure the depth of the colored surface layer at both ends of the aquarium. It should be the same. Now, from one end of the aquarium only, direct the fan on the colored water so that it moves toward the other end. Turn off the fan and watch what happens to the warm water. When the fan is shut off, the effect of the pile-up of warm water at the opposite side can be observed. Once again measure the depth of the warm surface layer at both ends of the aquarium and record your observations.

Supplementary Activities

Compare the temperatures before and after an ENSO event by putting equal amounts of the same temperature of cool water into two plastic tubs. Feel the water in each tub. Hold a thermometer in one tub and pour hot water into it until the thermometer rises 18° F (10° C). Again feel the water in each tub.

Questions

1. What did the difference in water temperature feel like? What effects could this warm water have on the coastal areas of South America?

2. After the onset of the trade winds, where was the warm surface layer the deepest?

3. How would the difference in water temperature affect sea life? Why? Could the reverse also be true? If warm water suddenly turned colder, what effect could that have on marine life?

VOCABULARY DEFINITIONS

Abyss—The deep ocean basin.

Abyssal Plain—A large, open, sediment-covered area of the abyss.

Buoyancy—The ability to stay afloat in a liquid or to rise in air.

Condensation—The process by which vapor changes into liquid because saturated air cools to a point where it can no longer hold the water vapor.

Continental Rise—An underwater mountain chain.

Continental Shelf—Extends seaward from the shoreline and is part of the landmass.

Continental Slope—The steep slope that is the boundary between the continental landmass and the abyss.

Convection—The transfer of heat by movement of molecules between materials or regions of unequal density.

Coriolis Effect—The apparent deflection of air masses and ocean currents toward or away from the equator due to the Earth's rotation.

Current—A steady onward movement of water.

Density—The amount of something per unit measure.

El Niño—A warm current that flows eastward across the Pacific in the Southern Hemisphere and is associated with a weakening of the trade winds.

ENSO—Name used for a combination of El Niño and the Southern Oscillation.

Evaporation—The process of water vapor being given off from bodies of water.

Guyot—A sea mount with a flat top.

Oceanic Ridge—A continuous underwater mountain chain.

Precipitation—Any form of rain, sleet, hail, or snow that has condensed from atmospheric water vapor and becomes sufficiently heavy to fall to the Earth's surface.

Rift Valley—A central valley running the length of a ridge.

Salinity—The total amount of dissolved salts in something.

Sea Mount—Underwater mountains.

Southern Oscillation—As trade winds weaken and the temperature changes, the equatorial current in the Pacific Ocean reverses itself.

Trade Winds—Prevailing easterly winds found on both sides of the equator. They blow north-easterly in the Northern Hemisphere and southeasterly in the Southern Hemisphere.

Turbidity—Sediment or particles suspended in a body of water so that it looks cloudy.

8

ECOSYSTEMS

Ecology is the interaction of living things with their respective environments and the physical factors that affect their distribution and success. Certain basic factors, such as sunlight, water, air, temperature, atmospheric gases, and substratum, affect this quality and distribution. These are not only success factors but limiting factors as well. These factors do not operate independently on or with the biological existence of organisms. Each of these things is dependent upon one another and is important in the life process of an organism.

The sun is the basic source of all energy and is imperative for green plants to carry on photosynthesis. Because plants depend upon the sun for their energy, animals are directly or indirectly dependent upon them for their energy. Many aspects of sunlight—intensity, duration, and wavelength—are important in the regulation of life processes.

Each organism has a different capacity or tolerance for heat, which enables it to live in only a certain environment. Daily and seasonal temperature changes limit and determine the quantity and quality of organisms inhabiting a certain area. Moisture is as necessary to growth as sunlight. Without water, plants could not grow, and without plants, animals could not survive. The substratum is the material in which organisms grow. The type of soil in an area determines the kinds of organisms that will be supported.

Ecosystems are an integral part of our natural environment. An ecosystem is a self-sustaining natural system. It has two parts: a *biotic*, or living, part and an *abiotic*, or nonliving, part. The abiotic part is divided into three parts: the *lithosphere*, or solid earth; the *hydrosphere*, or liquid earth; and the *atmosphere*, or the gaseous earth. The solid biosphere is made up of rocks, sediment, and soil. Flora and fauna, plants and animals, constitute the biotic part. The components of an ecosystem are completely interrelated. No part is independent. Therefore, each plant and animal performs a specific function in that particular community and fills a particular niche. If one organism were destroyed, the whole ecosystem could eventually fall apart. In other words, nothing can be changed without eventually affecting the whole system. Almost everything in nature works in cycles. The same is true of ecosystems. Plants and animals live and die and decompose, only to be recycled into a new form of life again.

Ecosystems have three main components. Producers are green plants that produce their own food. Consumers are organisms that get their food energy from other living things, either plants or other animals. Decomposers are plants and animals that live off once-living materials and cause them to rot or decay.

Ecosystems are more than food cycles. They contain a carbon cycle, a nitrogen cycle, and a water cycle as well. Decay bacteria break down the remains of dead plants and animals. By doing so, those decay bacteria are returning carbon to the atmosphere. Carbon is in every living thing, obtained from carbon dioxide in the atmosphere, manufactured during photosynthesis by green plants. This substance is passed along to other organisms as chemical energy through the food chains. The carbon is returned to the air by animals and by plants. Plants give off oxygen during the day, but at night they release carbon dioxide. If there were no decomposers, all carbon would remain in organic material and never decay. Consequently, oxygen would not be returned to the atmosphere. Without carbon dioxide, vegetation would disappear. Animals need oxygen and plants need carbon dioxide to live. As plants get older, they consume as much oxygen as they give off. When they die and decay, they give off no oxygen at all, but they do contribute to the carbon dioxide level.

Nitrogen is just as essential to living organisms as carbon. The nitrogen-fixing bacteria and algae in the soil use nitrogen and convert it to nitrogen salts or *nitrates*. These nitrates are released into the soil when the bacteria die. Plants' roots can absorb these nitrates once they are dissolved in the soil. The nitrates are then passed on to animals as they eat the plants. The nitrogen cycle continues to move from living organisms to the soil and back to living things again.

When precipitation occurs in the form of rain, sleet, hail, or snow, the water either sinks into the soil or runs off, eventually ending up in a river, lake, or ocean. The water that sinks into the soil is taken up by plants. The water moves up plant stems to their leaves and is then transpired into the air. A great deal of water is also evaporated from the soil and bodies of water. Evapotranspiration is water transpiring from trees and water evaporating from the soil and bodies of water. A forest with a river or a lake is a good example of evapotranspiration.

Three important elements of all ecosystems are niche, habitat, and ecological succession. A *niche* is the total role of a species within a community. It is a particular place of an animal within its community; its relation to its habitat, its food, its partners, and its enemies. Every population has an ecological niche. This niche determines the structural, physical, and behavioral adaptations of the population. A niche is the place in the community the population inhabits. Ecological equivalence is the occurrence of similar but unrelated species in almost identical niches in different geographic areas resulting from evolutionary adaptation. Because of competition, no two species can occupy the same niche in the same community. One species will always be superior to the other. For different species to survive in one community, their niches must be different.

A population is also affected by location, whether this be geographic location or range, or environmental location or habitat. A habitat is the specific location within a range. Habitats can be highly specialized or generalized; one part of a leaf or the forest floor, for instance. A microhabitat is a highly specialized habitat, such as the upper photosynthetic cell layer of a leaf of a certain species of plant. The environmental variables of a microhabitat are referred to as a *microenvironment* or a *microclimate*.

Many ecosystems have populations highly specialized to their habitats because of a constancy of abiotic environmental factors, such as climate. This specialization increases the efficiency of a population in meeting its requirements. High diversity in an ecosystem implies smaller populations.

Communities constantly change. They are not static. These changes occur on several levels. The simplest level consists of the growth, interaction, and death of organisms passing through their life cycles. Change may occur quickly or slowly and may be minute or large scale. Larger scale changes include ecological succession, community evolution, and community reaction to alterations in regional abiotic factors.

Every organism occupying the same habitat affects the plant and animal life of that region. The number, variety, and interrelationships between the plants and animals sharing the same habitat are infinite. Each living organism exerts visible as well as invisible influences upon some or all of the other organisms.

Ecological succession is a process of continuous community change. Ecological succession is a characteristic of all ecosystems. Change is continuous until a final state of equilibrium is reached. It is brought about when one or several conditions of an area changes. Changes may be due to the enrichment of the soil or the addition or loss of moisture. Finally, the area will be populated by a new group of organisms that dominate and stabilize in an area. This stage is the climax stage. A climax is characterized by the plant life best capable of prospering under existing climatic conditions; soil content, water supply, and the organic environment. Succession may also reverse itself because of floods, fire, human intervention, or any other cataclysmic event. Certain conditions necessary for the success of the climax stage may then take over. The regular succession will again follow once the essential conditions are reestablished. The environment will then be restored to its stable state.

Pioneers are the first plant species or organisms to become established in an ecosystem experiencing succession. Climax is reached when the equilibrium community ends the succession. Succession is a dynamic interaction among the community participants inhabiting the ecosystem, the existing state of the whole ecosystem, and time. Ecological succession occurs because the array of niches changes with the maturation of the system.

There are six types of interrelationships of organism within an ecosystem. Two are favorable or *symbiotic*, one is neutral, and three are unfavorable or *antagonistic*. The favorable ones include mutualism and commensalism. *Mutualism* is when two organisms depend upon each other and cannot survive without their partner. It may exist between two animals, such as a termite and a protozoa, or between plants and animals, such as a honeybee and flowers. Inside a termite's digestive tract lives tiny protozoan that eat the woody part of the cellulose and release a sugar that the termite is able to digest. Without the aid of the protozoan, the termite would be unable to digest the wood it eats. Pollen is carried by bees for fertilization of flowers, nectar for honey, and nourishment for the inhabitants in the hive. Another example of mutualism involves a certain species of ant that deposits leaves in a damp spot. The leaves decay, and fungi sprout and flourish. Then the ants eat the fungus as their main diet. Mutualism between two plants is also common. Lichens are a combination of an alga and a fungus. The alga is capable of manufacturing food. The fungus is unable to manufacture food but is capable of support and protection against desiccation. Each supplies the other with an important necessity the other lacks.

Commensalism is another type of symbiotic relationship. For one partner the relationship is essential, for the other it is neutral. Examples are a turkey vulture and the carrion it eats, vines growing on trees for support, birds' nests on tree branches, or an animal taking shelter in a thicket.

Antagonistic interrelationships include amensalism or antibiosis, predation or parasitism, and competition. *Amensalism* is when one partner is harmful to the other but is not affected itself, such as a reaction of an antibiotic on a disease-producing bacterium, for example. *Predation* or *parasitism* can be exemplified by mistletoe deriving water from a tree and eventually killing the tree. *Competition* is when one organism vies with another for habitat, food, or growing space. One is at the expense of the other. *Neutralism* is when two plants or animals living in the same habitat tolerate the other's presence but do not affect each other directly.

The following describes two different ecosystems, an aquatic ecosystem and a terrestrial ecosystem.

Water covers three-fourths of the Earth's surface, either as salt water or as fresh water. Aquatic ecosystems are historically the source of life on Earth. Water is the basis for all aquatic life, it is the medium within which all aspects of the ecosystem coexist, and it is the nutrient source for aquatic life. It is also the medium by which organic and inorganic wastes and sediments are distributed throughout the system. Ninety-nine percent of the surface water of the Earth is in the oceans. Water has the same general relationship to all other factors in the environment in an ocean, lake, or river. Consequently, aquatic ecosystems are simpler than terrestrial ecosystems.

An estuary is the traditional zone between a river and the sea and is intermediate in dissolved content between fresh and marine waters. Estuarine waters are variable dynamic environments and are impoverished in comparison to either a river or a sea community. They are semi-enclosed coastal bodies of water where seawater is diluted with fresh water from the rivers. Not all rivers open out into estuaries. Some discharge directly into the ocean. Estuarine environments are subject to tides because their openings are relatively free. The tidal action flushes out the estuary and mixes the fresh water with the salt water. Because of the tidal effects, the salinity of the water varies greatly. At low tide, most of the water passing through is fresh water from the river, thereby creating a low level of salinity. However, at high tide, most of the water is of marine origin, and the salinity level is correspondingly high. Salinity may also vary from one location to another. Consequently, an estuary is a variable environment. In an estuary, the amount of dissolved oxygen tends to be high because of the shallowness and turbulence. The tidal action concentrates nutrient energy materials that wash in from upriver. In this way, the estuary acts as a nutrient trap, with a nutrient level higher than either a river or the sea. An estuarine community is a combination of three parts: the marine water, the fresh water, and the brackish water. Because estuaries have served as conduits for shipping and as sites for cities, they are particularly vulnerable environments.

Lakes have a thermal stratification. The *epilimnion* is the warm top layer, heated by the sun and affected by wind and currents. The *hypolimnion* is the lowest layer, is not heated by the sun, and is too deep to be circulated directly by wind. A *thermocline* is the transition zone or *metalimnion*. An *overturn* is the period of circulation of a lake. Lakes with only one overturn per year are *monomictic*.

Oceans—The largest and most stable ecosystems on earth are oceans, suitable habitat for autotrophs and heterotrophs, or green plants and animals. The volume of water in which photosynthesis can occur is small compared to the total area. Photosynthesis can occur only in the uppermost layers where sunlight is available.

Stream Communities—Streams support many varieties of communities as they flow from their various sources to their outlets. Some communities occupy surface waters, some only bottom habitats, and others both land and aquatic habitats. Because of the moving current, plankton are not as abundant in streams as in lakes or oceans. Plant and animal life of streams have adapted themselves to the flowing water. They have developed suckers, claws, or threads to attach themselves to stationary objects. Because a stream flows through different biomes, the water carries with it plant and animal organisms different from those of the surrounding biome.

Lakes—Lakes are affected by the biome within which they are situated. There are three types of lakes: oligotrophic, eutrophic, and dystrophic. Dystrophic lakes support a limited variety of species, all slow growing, because of the presence of great amounts of decayed humic matter. This activity results in a high consumption of oxygen. During decomposition, after the oxygen has been exhausted, great amounts of unrotted material remain with the decomposed matter at the bottom of the lake. This decayed matter colors the water brown, preventing the penetration of sunlight into the depths, thereby forcing most of the plants to grow in the surface waters. Dystrophic lakes eventually become bogs because they are invaded by shore plants. Bogs are able to support only plants tolerant of these conditions. The depth and surface area of a lake influences the life it supports. A large, shallow lake will support more life than a large, deep one. Depth prevents lakes from harboring a lot of organisms. These lakes are *oligotrophic*, or little-producing, because they are lacking in nutrients. A *thermocline* is a stratified layer separating surface waters from bottom waters. Shallower lakes are richer in organic life and have a higher volume of warm surface waters. These are *eutrophic*, or well-nourished lakes, rich in dissolved nutrients.

Some ponds are temporary bodies of water. Others may be in a successional stage from aquatic to dry land. Ponds contain less open water than lakes and are usually invaded to their center by shore plants. Without an inflow of oxygenated stream water, a pond must depend upon surface water for oxygen renewal. Without an outlet, a pond soon fills with silt. There is no stratification in ponds because only during the spring is the pond's center relatively free of plant life.

Terrestrial ecosystems are much more variegated than aquatic ecosystems, even though they comprise only one-fourth of the Earth's surface. Terrestrial ecosystems are diverse and not uniform at all. Water is the main determinant of aquatic ecosystems, whereas in terrestrial ecosystems there are three main determinants of life: atmospheric and climate, soil, and the biotic community itself.

Regional climate, of which there are various aspects, such as temperature, water, rainfall, and evapotranspiration, is the chief determinant of terrestrial ecosystems. Twelve climatic regions are present in the world: polar, tundra, mountain, marine, savanna, desert, semi-arid, Mediterranean, humid subtropical, humid continental, tropical wet, and tropical wet and dry.

Conditions of habitat are dependent upon climate, which is determined by latitude. Habitats are dependent upon the quantity and quality of air they receive. Air moves in air masses characterized by uniform conditions of temperature and humidity. There are five types of air masses: polar continental, polar maritime (polar Pacific and polar Atlantic), tropical continental, tropical maritime (tropical Pacific and tropical Atlantic), and equatorial.

Continental air masses originate over the continent and are dry. Polar continentals come from polar regions, and tropical continentals originate in areas bordering the tropics. Maritime air masses originate above the ocean, drawing up great amounts of moisture by evaporation. Therefore, they possess a higher amount of humidity in contrast to the continental air masses. Warm air holds more moisture than cold air and, therefore, the tropical air masses are more humid than the cold polar air masses. Equatorial air masses are the highest in humidity and temperature. However, there are nonclimatic factors that are important as well. One of these is the landform of the region. Landforms range from mountains to hills, from plateaus to flatlands.

Soils are the most characteristic feature of any terrestrial environment. Soil is a mixture of weathered rock materials and organic detritus. *Detritus* is organic wastes and dead matter. Soil is also the means of support for all terrestrial organisms. A soil profile is a cross section of the layers of which soil is composed. These layers are called *horizons*. The upper horizon is the litter zone. It consists of decomposed plant and animal matter in varying degrees of decomposition. Underneath the litter zone is the topsoil, or the *zone of eluviation* (the zone in which materials are brought into aqueous suspension). Below the topsoil is the *zone of illuviation*. Much of the material leached out of the eluviation zone, such as the minerals removed by percolating gravitational water, is precipitated and enriched in this zone. Below this horizon is the weathered rock or sediment. This zone is usually lacking in organic matter. All soils do not contain all of these horizons, and some soils may have more complex horizons.

A biome is a specific geographic area with a somewhat uniform climate throughout. Conditions are such that certain plants have adapted themselves to living there. Consequently, a biome usually derives its name from the dominant plant life. The plant environment creates an environment in which certain animals can live. A biome is an independent area of interdependent plant and animal life. The major biomes of the world are the tundra, the coniferous forest, the temperate deciduous forest, the great plains or temperate grasslands, the desert, the tropical forest biomes, rain forests and deciduous-tropical forests, the grasslands or savanna, the chaparral, and the equatorial.

Arctic Tundra Biome—Bogs or muskegs are a result of the melting and thawing of snow and ice and from the underlying permafrost, which is a layer of permanently frozen soil. In the summer a shallow top layer, exposed to sunlight, thaws but extends only a few into the ground.

Coniferous Forest Biome—This is the biome in which the cone-bearing, needle-leafed trees grow. It is also called the *taiga* (a Siberian word, equivalent to "boreal forest").

Prairies or Grasslands Biome—Grasses are more tolerant than trees and are able to survive where precipitation is neither regular nor dependable. Various grasses grow in specific areas on the prairies. Near the edges of the deciduous forest, where large amounts of water are found, the tall grasses grow. The mid-length grasses grow farther west. Nearer the mountains are the shorter grasses.

Deciduous Forest Biome—Deciduous trees require a lot of rain. Precipitation is high and evaporation low, creating a rather damp forest. These are the trees with leaves that fall off in the autumn.

Desert Biome—High temperatures, low rainfall, and extremes of temperatures day and night describe this biome. The climatic conditions are a result of high air pressure, high latitudes, and mountains that cut off the water supply and winds from the sea. Desert plants had to adapt to survive such extreme conditions. These adaptations are effected in three ways: plants may *aestivate*, or cease growing, during periods when moisture is lacking; they may lose their leaves, the surface of which is covered with a material that retards evaporation; or they may store water in their succulent stems and leaves. Desert animals are well camouflaged, blending with the color of the substratum upon which they are found, somewhat protected when unable to hide among the widely spaced desert plants.

Tropical rain forests are very diverse. Warm temperatures exist, and photosynthesis occurs throughout the year. Rain is abundant and well-distributed, creating copious plant and animal life.

An ecological pyramid is a basic function of any ecosystem. A habitat can support only so many of one species. Plant life is the main food factor of any environment. In aquatic environments, the basic plant growth is called *phytoplankton*, or microscopic plant life.

Microscopic animal life, or *zooplankton*, feeds off the phytoplankton. All animal life, whether large or small, depends upon this phytoplankton. The same sort of food chain exists on land. A far greater quantity of plant life exists on land. Biomass is living weight, including stored food and rate of reproduction. A biomass pyramid is the living weight of each group of organisms in the food chain. The pyramid explains the tapering proportion of each successive group of feeders to their food supply.

An energy or production pyramid deals with available energy for use by life processes. To produce a certain amount of plant food, a large amount of solar energy is needed. Some of this energy is wasted, and a lot is used up by life processes, such as keeping the body warm and supplying energy to move. Therefore, less energy is available to the animal that feeds upon the primary consumer of plant material. There is less available energy the higher one goes up the pyramid.

Activity 1: Sand Dunes

OBJECTIVE:	To study the effects of wind on sand dunes
MATERIALS:	2 large boxes, sand, hair dryer or fan, stones, plants (artificial or real)
LEVEL:	Upper
SETTING:	Classroom
TIME:	30 minutes

LESSON DESIGN

Open one end of one box and place enough sand in it to form hills and valleys. Put several stones and plants (artificial or real) in various places on the hills and in the valleys. Place the other box at the open end of the first box to catch blowing sand. Set up the fan or hairdryer at the closed end of the box containing sand. Set the fan on low to create wind and observe how this wind affects the hills, valleys, and areas around the stones and trees. Vegetation helps keep the sand from eroding and blowing away quickly and in large volume. Sand dunes located along lake shores and ocean shores help reduce the damage done by hurricanes or other strong winds because they lessen the severity of the winds and act as barriers against them. Once the vegetation is stripped away because of drought, careless management, or misuse, the sand dunes will erode and blow away.

Supplementary Activities

Design two coastlines along a seashore or a lakeshore with sand dunes on one side. The models can be drawings or paper. Design the coastlines such that one is a good example of an ecologically sound coastline with sand dunes that are well managed not only to protect themselves from erosion but to protect the shoreline and houses along the shoreline. The other example should be designed such that it is a poor example of sand dunes and coastlines. The dunes have been used by pleasure-seekers with all-terrain vehicles who have torn up the dunes, ripped up vegetation, and laid them bare to the ravages of erosion. As the dunes erode, they are virtually useless; they blow away, and the area is destroyed.

Questions

1. What are sand dunes, and how are they formed?

2. In the sand box, what happened to the sand in front of the dune?

3. In the sand box, what happened to the sand on the far side of the dune?

4. In the sand box, what happened to the sand on the top of the dune?

5. What happened to the sand around the stones?

6. What happened to the sand around the plants?

7. If you visited a sand dune today and took a picture of it, would it look exactly the same a year from now? Why or why not?

8. What does question number 7 have to say about the fragile nature of sand dunes?

 Activity 2: Food Webs

OBJECTIVE:	To develop an understanding of a food web by constructing one
MATERIALS:	Aquatic food web: Aquarium, sand, algae, aquatic plants, daphnia, snails, guppies, freshwater crustaceans
	Terrestrial food web: aquarium, lid or porous material to fit the aquarium, soil, seeds (radish, bean, grass), small lizard or salamander, ant lions, crickets, spider, ladybugs, flies, water
LEVEL:	Lower to upper
SETTING:	Classroom
TIME:	1 hour to set up, several weeks for observation
VOCABULARY:	Carnivore, consumer, decomposer, food chain, food pyramid, food web, herbivore, producer, terrarium, vivarium
PRE-ACTIVITIES:	Discuss food chains, food webs, and food pyramids; construct several on the chalkboard as a class. Each group of four or five students should construct a food web of a different ecosystem on a piece of construction paper (see Figure 8.1). Mount these food webs on a bulletin board for everybody to share. Make a food web with students as the component parts. Make signs to represent each part of the food web and use string to connect the various parts. Eliminate one student (organism) from the food web, then another, and observe the effect on the total system. Discuss the different interrelationships and the effect of eliminating various organisms from the system.

FOOD CHAIN

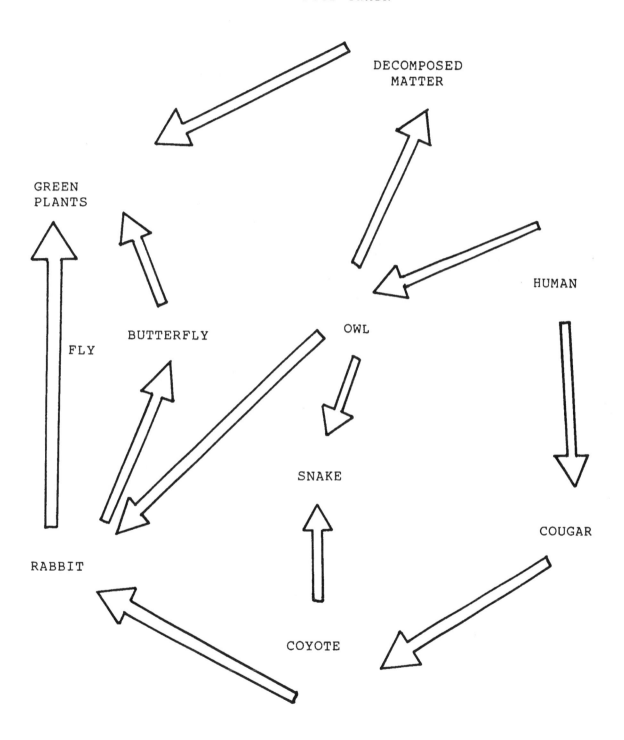

Fig. 8.1.

LESSON DESIGN

Wash the sand well before putting a 2- to 3-inch layer of it on the bottom of the aquarium. Fill the aquarium with water and let it stand for a couple of days to dechlorinate. Plant the aquatic plants in the sand, add some algae, and add some snails.

Let the system sit for a couple of days, then add equal numbers of daphnia and ostracods and half as many amphipods, and observe them for one week. Do not feed any of these organisms. Instead, the ecosystem will balance itself naturally. At the end of one week, count the numbers of each species of organisms left. Record all of this information in a science log. Now add a couple hydras and observe the system for one more week. Record any predator-prey relationships that you observe. After the second week, add two pairs of guppies and observe any new effects on the ecosystem. After the third week, count the numbers of each species of organisms left, make any other observations that seem pertinent, and draw diagrams of the food web in this ecosystem.

Put 3 inches of soil on the bottom of the aquarium and plant the grass, bean, and radish seeds. Water them well and place the aquarium in a well-lit place to enhance germination. When the plants are well established and about 4 inches tall, add some aphids and ants and cover the vivarium. After a week, add some crickets, ant lions, and ladybugs and observe how each organism behaves in response to the other organisms and any discernible feeding relationships. At the end of week two, add a spider. Finally, after another week, add the lizard or salamander and diagram the food web that was observed in the ecosystem. Don't forget that abiotic factors, such as sunshine, soil, and water, are extremely important aspects of food webs also and need to be included in the diagrams.

Supplementary Activities

Locate a natural area somewhere in your community to study. It may be an aquatic ecosystem or a terrestrial ecosystem. Have the students spend as much time as possible in this area to observe interrelationships. From the students' observations, have them construct food webs of the area in groups of two to four. Compare food webs and discuss any similarities and differences among them. If possible, do the same thing with three or four different ecosystems, once early in the year and once later in the year, and compare the observations. Note any variations from one time period to the other.

Questions

1. Is any one part of a food web not connected to any other part? Why or why not?

2. What effect did removing an organism have on the food web? What would the effect be if two or more organisms were removed?

3. What roles do producers, consumers, and decomposers play in an aquatic ecosystem? What role does each play in terrestrial ecosystems, such as forests or grasslands?

4. How might people's use of natural resources affect the soil, water, and air in relation to the equilibrium of an ecosystem?

5. In the aquatic and terrestrial ecosystems you set up, which organisms are the producers, and which organisms are the consumers, the predators, and the prey?

6. If the terrestrial and aquatic ecosystems you set up were left alone for a long time, say several months, would they stay in balance, or would they get out of balance and everything die?

7. In these same ecosystems, when and how would decomposers be introduced into them? Would they eventually take over the whole system? Why or why not?

 ## *Activity 3: Ecological Succession*

OBJECTIVE:	To study the effects of succession on an aquatic ecosystem
MATERIALS:	Quart jar with lid, pond vegetation, sterile pond water, microscope, slides and covers, eyedroppers; all of this for each group of 4–5 students.
LEVEL:	Upper
SETTING:	Pond for collecting water and plant materials, classroom for the main experiment
TIME:	Time varies for collecting water and plant materials. Approximately 2–3 weeks for the organisms to get established and succeed each other, and 1 hour of classroom time for microscope work.
VOCABULARY:	Climax community, dominant species, pioneer stage, primary succession, secondary succession
PRE-ACTIVITIES:	Discussion of the vocabulary and if possible a field trip to an area of ecological succession. If the field trip is not possible, several photographs or pictures from books on ecological succession or a talk by a forester about succession with photographs of representative examples of succession.

LESSON DESIGN

Into a clean glass quart jar, place some dried vegetative material from a pond. Fill the jar with boiled pond water and put a lid on it. Place each group's jars in areas of the room that vary in temperature and light and observe them from time to time. When the water turns cloudy, remove portions of it from different parts of the jar to examine under the microscope. Record your observations in a science log every day for several days.

Questions

1. Where did the organisms that were observed under the microscope come from?

2. How long did it take for the water to get cloudy? Why did it get cloudy?

3. Was there any evidence of succession in the jar? If so, what kind?

4. After several days of observation, were there any changes in community populations?

5. What kind of a food web existed in the jar? Explain the different organisms associated with the food web.

6. Were all of the jars from the different areas of the room the same, or did they each have different characteristics?

7. Did the community in the jar reach a climax stage?

8. Did the community in the jar start a new successional community once the climax stage was reached?

 ## Activity 4: Limiting Factors

OBJECTIVE:	To observe tree growth to determine if there are factors present that are limiting their growth
MATERIALS:	Paper, pencils, cloth tape measure, materials from previous activities (see pre-activities that follow)
RESOURCES:	A forester
LEVEL:	Upper
SETTING:	Two forested areas
TIME:	2 hours of observation time once a month for the whole year
VOCABULARY:	Circumference, diameter, limiting factors
PRE-ACTIVITIES:	Environmental problem Activity 1 (chapter 6) on population; Activity 2 (chapter 6) on overcrowding; Activity 7 (chapter 6) on overpopulation of plants; and plants Activity 12 (chapter 2) on tree measurements. Ask a forester to point out two areas with similar tree species growing under two different conditions.

LESSON DESIGN

Locate two areas with the same species of trees growing under two different conditions or ask a forester to locate them for you. Select 10 trees in each area to study and make the following calculations about each tree in each area every month:

1. Approximate height of the trees, using the method described in Activity 12 (chapter 2) on tree measurements.

2. Circumference of the trees, using the method described in Activity 12 (chapter 2) on tree measurements (diameter = circumference divided by pi [3.14]).

3. Approximate age of the trees—a forester can take a core with a tree borer and you can count the rings, or you can skip this part because age is difficult to determine unless the tree is dead and rings can be counted from a tree cross section.

4. Species of tree, either described by a forester or identified in a tree book.

5. General health of the trees—healthy-looking with no visible signs of decay and fungus, or yellowing needles and leaves, sparse leaves and needles, or spotted leaves.

6. Soil moisture—if it is wet or dry (take into account any recent storms).

7. Light—if it is severely restricted or if the area is open with a lot of light.

Compare the monthly calculations and notations and see if you can pinpoint why one area is healthier than another.

Supplementary Activities

Plant two miniature gardens with plants well spaced. When the plants are well established, limit a factor, such as sunlight, water, or space, for one garden only. Record any observable changes as well as reasons for the changes. Then, return what was limited and see if the plants reestablish their original healthy state.

Questions

1. What things can limit how well a species grows?

2. What can be done to improve an area that is suffering because certain factors (sunlight, water, or space) have been limited?

3. Is it possible for a species to dwindle in health, then have its health restored because certain factors were no longer limited? How, in what way, and to what extent?

Activity 5: Interdependence of a Balanced Ecosystem

OBJECTIVE:	To learn how plants and animals depend upon each other and to observe the interdependent aspects of a balanced ecosystem
MATERIALS:	Aquarium or other large container; sand, gravel, or soil; water; plants and animals suited to a particular environment; container for water; water
RESOURCES:	Encyclopedias, plant and animal identification books
LEVEL:	Upper
SETTING:	Classroom
TIME:	1 hour to set up and several weeks or months of observation
VOCABULARY:	Ecosystem, interdependent, vivarium
PRE-ACTIVITIES:	Activity 2 (chapter 8) on food webs

LESSON DESIGN

Set up a vivarium with plants and animals to show the interdependent aspects of a balanced ecosystem. Choose a particular environment to represent in your vivarium, such as the desert, a grasslands, or a woods. Research the kinds of plants and animals that would live there.

This vivarium will focus on a desert environment. Cover the aquarium bottom with gravel and 2 to 3 inches of a sand/soil mixture. Add a few rocks and build up the soil to form hills and level areas. Make a pond out of a small dish surrounded by soil and gravel and fill it with water. Plants and animals should be hardy, warmth loving, and small. These could include lizards, horned toads, cacti, sedum, aloe vera, crassula, ants, flies, and spiders. Loosely cover the container so that air can circulate and the animals cannot escape, then observe what interactions take place. Experiment with the numbers of different organisms needed in the vivarium to achieve the right balance so that the animals don't have to be fed.

An environment halfway between wet and dry, such as a woods, would include tree frogs, crickets, salamanders, ladybugs, aphids, turtles, grasses, philo-dendrons, fittonia, pepperomia, and wandering jews. A bog environment, which is very damp, would include mosses, ferns, carnivorous plants, ants, tree frogs, salamanders, newts, mealworms, and mud turtles.

Supplementary Activities

After the vivarium is well established, change one element to observe the effect on the other organisms and the whole system. For instance, remove one of the producers, all of the producers, or one particular consumer. Record your observations as well as how long it takes for certain changes to occur.

Questions

1. Is the vivarium a balanced ecosystem? If so, how? If not, why and what could make it balanced?

2. If the ecosystem was balanced, how could it be upset?

3. Which cycles are occurring in the vivarium, and what evidence do you have to support your hypothesis?

4. Are there producers, consumers, and decomposers in the vivarium? What are they, and how are they important to the existence of the vivarium?

5. Would a succulent desert plant be able to live in a boggy vivarium with a salamander? Why or why not?

6. Are the same plants and animals able to live in different environments with different climatic factors, or are they restricted to living in a particular area? Explain.

7. Do all organisms (plants, animals, and people) depend on their respective environments as well as on each other to live? Explain.

Activity 6: Abiotic Factors

OBJECTIVE:	To observe the effect of light on an aquatic ecosystem
MATERIALS:	Pond water, 4 jars, plastic wrap, thermometers
LEVEL:	Upper
SETTING:	Pond to collect water and the classroom for observation
TIME:	Water collecting time will vary, 1–2 weeks for observation

LESSON DESIGN

Collect pond water in the four jars, or have students bring pond water to school from a pond near their homes. Record the water temperatures in each jar. Cover the jars with plastic wrap and place two of them in direct sunlight and two in an area with very little light, but not in total darkness, such as in a closet. Make daily observations of the jars as well as temperature readings and record your findings. After a week or two, there should be some noticeable differences.

Questions

1. What differences were observed in the various jars during a period of several days to several weeks?

2. What were the differences in temperature between the four jars? Why were there differences?

3. What effect does light have on the growth of organisms?

4. What effect does temperature have on the growth of organisms?

 Activity 7: Oxygen and Fire

OBJECTIVE:	To discover why oxygen is necessary to keep fire burning
MATERIALS:	Large jar, smaller jar, candle, matches, small plant cutting
LEVEL:	Lower to upper
SETTING:	Classroom
TIME:	10 minutes to set up and several days for observation

LESSON DESIGN

Light a candle and place a jar over it. Observe carefully and time how long it stays lit. The candle will burn for a short while, then go out because the fire used up all the oxygen. Place a small plant cutting in a smaller jar of water and put this under the larger jar with the candle. Let the jars sit for a few minutes, then relight the candle. The candle should stay lit for a much longer time because the plant has restored the oxygen that the candle took away.

Questions

1. Why did the candle go out fairly soon after placing the jar on top of it?

2. Why did the candle burn longer after the plant was placed with it in the jar?

3. Why would a forest fire burn more quickly with a strong wind than at a time with no wind?

4. What are the sources of oxygen on Earth?

5. In how many ways do people use oxygen?

6. How does the amount of oxygen determine the quantity and quality of life on Earth?

 Activity 8: Adaptation

OBJECTIVE:	To determine what plants and animals need and what characteristics they posses to live in, and adapt to, a certain environment
MATERIALS:	Pencils and paper
LEVEL:	Lower to upper
SETTING:	Classroom, school grounds, natural settings (woods, pond, grassland), and a vacant lot
TIME:	Several hours of observation and several hours for discussion and compilation of information
VOCABULARY:	Adaptation, food chain, food pyramid, food web, habitat, needs, niche
PRE-ACTIVITIES:	Activity 2 (chapter 8) on food webs

LESSON DESIGN

Study the plants and animals on and near the school grounds, in vacant lots, in a woods, in a grassland, and at a pond. Observe and record information about how the plants and animals in each area live: where their homes are located, what their food sources seem to be, other animals with which they come into contact, if any of the organisms seem out of place in that particular area, numbers of organisms observed, niche each fills within the system, and any other distinguishing features about the area and the organisms. Once each area has been carefully observed, have the students in groups of three or four discuss and list similarities and differences between each area, what physical characteristics each organism possesses, any observable changes in the areas brought about by people, adaptations necessary to live in the area, and the food cycles within each area. Draw food chains, food webs, and food pyramids of each area. Prepare a chart listing characteristics of each environment, characteristics of each organism, and adaptations required for each organism to survive in each area.

Supplementary Activities

Select a plant and an animal found on the school grounds. Observe them for several weeks and determine what they need for survival and how the environment meets their needs.

Questions

1. How did the plants and animals in one area differ from those in another area? How are they similar?

2. How have people changed these different areas? Have these changes been good, bad, or both, and in what ways?

3. How have plants and animals adapted to living in these areas?

4. Do you think there are any plants and animals that did not adapt to living in these areas?

5. Would an animal living on the school grounds have its needs fulfilled as well as the same species of animal living in a more natural setting? If so, how and to what extent?

6. What are the main characteristics of the different areas studied? How are they similar, and how are they different?

7. How have people learned to adapt to different situations and different climates?

8. What enables some animals to live in several different environments, whereas other animals can live in only one environment?

9. What are some of the physical characteristics of plants and animals that have enabled them to adapt to different environments?

10. What determines the kind of life that will be supported by a certain climatic area?

11. How is your environment different from the environment in which a polar bear, cactus, monkey, or protozoa live?

12. If a drought, flood, or fire occurred in one of the areas studied, how would the plant and animal life be affected? Would they be able to adapt? If so, how?

13. How do people use science and technology in adapting to their respective environments? Have scientific discoveries changed the environment? If so, in what ways? Has agriculture or industry changed the environment? How?

14. How are living things changed as their environment changes? What are some historical examples of living things that could not adapt to their changing environment? In what ways did people bring about these changes?

 Activity 9: Solar Energy 1

OBJECTIVE:	To determine the most efficient way of collecting and using solar energy
MATERIALS:	2 #10 cans, black paint, water, 4 thermometers, 2 pie pans, glass or plastic wrap to cover one can, shoe box, 4 jars of equal size, soil, sand, gravel, aluminum foil, coat hanger or wire, hot dogs, gallon jar, tea bags
LEVEL:	Lower to upper
SETTING:	Classroom and school grounds
TIME:	20–30 minutes for each activity
VOCABULARY:	Conductor, insulator

LESSON PLAN

Collect solar energy in several different ways. Paint one can black, inside and out. Leave the other can alone. Fill both cans with the same amount of room-temperature water. Put both cans in direct sunlight for several hours. Record the temperature in both cans before placing them in the sun and after several hours of sitting in the sun. Which can is hotter? Why?

Paint two pie pans black on both sides. Fill both with water from the faucet. Record the temperature of the water in both pans. Cover one of the pans with a piece of glass or plastic wrap. Place both pans in direct sunlight. Take and record temperature readings in both pans every hour from about 10 a.m. until 3 p.m. The water in the covered pan should get quite hot very quickly. Some of the heat in the water in the uncovered pan escapes, whereas some of the heat in the covered pan is prevented from escaping because of the glass. Since glass or plastic wrap is an insulator and water is a conductor, the covered pan got warmer quicker.

Solar collectors store solar energy in the form of heat. To make a solar collector, paint the inside of a shoebox black. Inside the box place a jar of water, a jar of soil, a jar of gravel, and a jar of sand. Place a thermometer in each jar. Cover the box with clear plastic. Record the temperature of each jar every hour for four or five hours. Place the box in the shade. One hour later take another temperature reading. Which jar was the best collector and retainer of heat? Why?

To build a simple solar cooker, cut a 2-inch square out of the side of a pop can. Line the inside of the can with aluminum foil. Skewer a hot dog using a wire inserted through one end of the can, through the hot dog and out the other end of the can. Set the can in the sun. Every so often turn your hot dog to ensure even cooking. The cooker collects reflected sunlight and produces enough heat to cook the hot dog. Make some sun tea to go with your hot dog by placing water in a gallon jar with eight or ten tea bags. Set the jar in the sun and leave it for several hours. Heat from the sun will make tea.

Paint nine bottles the following colors: black, red, orange, yellow, blue, green, indigo, violet, and white. Place a thermometer inside each bottle and seal the tops with clay. Place all bottles in a sunny area for approximately two hours, then record the temperatures. Then arrange the bottles according to temperature, from the coolest to the warmest, or vice versa. Repeat the experiment, but put water in the bottles. Compare any differences and similarities between the two experiments.

Supplementary Activities

Spray the inside of a 1-pound coffee can black. Drill a hole about midway down the side of the can big enough to slide a thermometer in. Cover the open end of the coffee can with plastic wrap and secure with a rubber band. Slide the thermometer in the hole. Place the can, thermometer side up, in a sunny location outside. Place rocks on both sides of the can so that it doesn't move and a small rock under the front to tip the plastic toward the sun. Record the temperature of the room, then every two minutes record the temperature inside the can until the temperature stabilizes itself. What other ways could solar heat be trapped and be just as effective? Experiment with different materials instead of the plastic wrap, the black paint, and the can.

To see if slope has anything to do with collecting solar energy, conduct the following simple experiment: fold a large piece of poster board or cardboard in two to form a shape like a house roof. Tape a thermometer on both sides of the roof and place the device outside so that one side faces straight south into the sun, and the other side faces directly north away from the sun. Record the temperatures of both thermometers in the classroom, then every five minutes after placement outside.

Questions

1. Was this an effective way to collect solar energy?

2. Would a larger model be more effective, just as effective, or less effective?

3. Which side had the highest temperature reading, the south or the north?

4. Would it matter which direction your house and windows faced if you wanted to take advantage of the maximum benefits of the sun?

 ## *Activity 10: Solar Energy 2*

OBJECTIVE:	To demonstrate the effect of solar energy in evaporating salt water to produce fresh water
MATERIALS:	Small shallow pan, larger shallow pan, salt, water, plastic wrap
LEVEL:	Lower to upper
SETTING:	Classroom
TIME:	30 minutes to set up and several days to a week for observation

LESSON DESIGN

Create a saltwater solution by mixing several tablespoons of salt with 1 quart of water. Set this pan in a larger pan and cover with a piece of clear plastic wrap. Set both pans in the sun, where they should remain for several days. Observe daily and record what is happening. Is there less water? Is water collecting in the larger pan? Taste the water in the smaller pan, then the larger pan. What differences do you observe? When all of the water has evaporated, salt should remain on the bottom of the smaller pan.

Another method for removing salt from ocean water is the following:

Add a tablespoon of salt to a beaker of water. Place a 1-hole stopper in the beaker. Put a piece of glass tubing, bent into two right angles, in the one-hole stopper and such that one right angle sets above another beaker so that water can drip into the second beaker. Heat the solution in the beaker over a hot plate or Bunsen burner until it boils. Taste the water that has collected in the second beaker.

Questions

1. Is it economically feasible to desalt ocean water in either of the above ways? Why or why not?

2. Why would it be important to be able to desalt ocean water in an economical and quick fashion?

 ## Activity 11: Solar Energy 3

OBJECTIVE:	To build a model solar hot water heater to see how it works and what benefits can be derived from it
MATERIALS:	Shallow box about 12-by-18 inches, 10 feet of flexible black tubing, black paint, glass to cover the box, wooden clothespin, tape, 2 coffee cans
LEVEL:	Upper
SETTING:	Classroom and outdoors
TIME:	1 hour to build, several hours outside (depending on your location)
PRE-ACTIVITIES:	Activity 9 (chapter 8) on solar energy; Activity 10 (chapter 8) on solar energy.

LESSON DESIGN

Spray paint the inside of the box black. Drill two holes in one end of the box approximately an inch from each side. Stick one end of the black tubing in one of the holes and start coiling it lengthwise from top to bottom inside the box, ending with the other end of the tubing coming out the other hole. Both ends of the tubing should extend over the edge of the box about 6–8 inches. Tape the glass over the box. Set the box up on a table outside aimed south. Place a can of water next to the box and put one piece of tubing in the water. Set up a siphon by sucking on the free end of the tubing. After the water starts to run through the tube, pinch it partially closed with the clothespin so that the water slowly drips into the second can. Measure the temperature of the water that drips into the can. After several hours of sitting in the sun, again measure the temperature of the water in the can.

Perform the same experiment with a different liquid in the tubes or with clear tubes instead of black ones.

Questions

1. Why was the water that dripped into the can after it had sat in the sun for a while warmer?

2. Would the water be as warm if it were allowed to flow quickly through the tube? Why?

3. Would clear tubes have the same effect as black tubes? Why or why not?

4. If you used oil instead of water in the tubes, what results could you expect?

 ## *Activity 12: Quadrat Studies*

OBJECTIVE:	To create a study plot of a small area called a quadrat
MATERIALS:	Ball of string; 12 stakes; yardsticks; compasses; hand lenses; shovel; hammer; paper; pencils; identification books on trees, flowers, insects, fungi, birds, and the like; weather instruments made in chapter 5; plant press made out of cardboard; newspapers to be weighed later; pH paper; and an optional soil testing kit and soil thermometer
LEVEL:	Upper
SETTING:	Natural setting of your choice; a more varied setting, such as a forest, is more interesting to study, but an open field is easier to study
TIME:	2 hours to measure and set up the boundaries, and 2–3 hours at different times to study the area
VOCABULARY:	Vocabulary from chapters on soil (chapter 1), plants (chapter 2), ecosystems (chapter 8), and weather (chapter 5)
PRE-ACTIVITIES:	Quadrats use knowledge from all other activities in this book, so it is wise to do quadrat studies after completing most of the other activities.

LESSON DESIGN

A method of sampling a small area is to create study plots, called quadrats, within the boundaries of this area. Quadrats may vary in size, depending upon the area being studied, and they may vary in shape. A quadrat study is made in an organized way to find out what kinds of flora and fauna can live together in a small community.

A typical quadrat is 9 yards on a side, or 81 square yards. Divide the class into groups of three to four students and choose four different areas to study and compare. This way, each group will make a quadrat of a different area.

Select an area of study and stake out four corners, each 9 yards apart. Run string from corner to corner along the ground. Divide this large quadrat into nine equal squares with the string and stakes. The finished, measured, and strung product should look somewhat like Figure 8.2. Assign numbers or letters to each square within the quadrat.

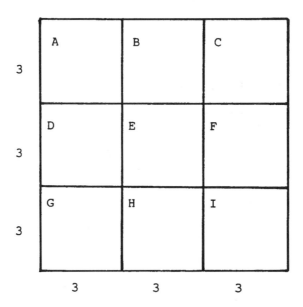

Fig. 8.2.

After the quadrat has been laid out, make a diagram and record of the kinds of plants in the different layers contained in the quadrat, including the understory, the canopy, and the ground cover. The canopy is the uppermost layer, which includes the tallest trees; the understory is the middle section, which contains the smaller trees, shrubs, and saplings; and the ground cover includes plant material, such as mosses, grasses, and other small plants. On the record sheet labeled Figure 8.3, record the number of plants in each layer. Name the plants once and put a tally mark next to the name each time you want to record another one of the same species. Record the number and kinds of animals seen and fill in the information at the bottom of the chart. Using the weather instruments made in the section on weather, record the readings from the instruments on the chart labeled Figure 8.4. Finally, analyze the soil by removing a sample of soil approximately 1 foot deep with a shovel. Diagram the layers in the soil and measure each one's depth. Find the pH of the soil, sketch a soil profile, and write a description of the things that are found in the topsoil and in the subsoil. Do the same thing for each section. In the end, you will have nine samples recorded and diagrammed.

RECORD OF LAYERS IN A QUADRAT

	SPECIES	NUMBER	COMMENTS
Canopy			
Understory			
Groundcover			
Animals			

1. Air Temperature _____ degrees F

2. Soil Temperature _____ degrees F (optional)

3. Light (intense/weak) _____

4. Greatest Number of plants _____

   Found in the _____ layer

5. Greatest Number of animals _____

   Found in the _____ layer

6. pH of the soil _____

7. Kind of soil _____

Quadrat Number: _____   Group Members: _____

_____

_____

_____

Fig. 8.3.

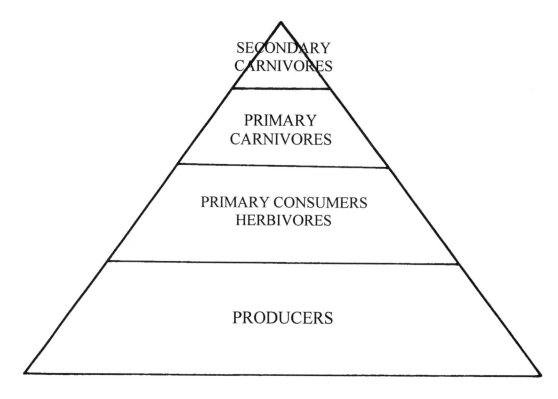

Fig. 8.4.

Supplementary Activities

An *ecostrip* is a long, narrow strip 1-by-100 yards. This strip identifies a greater variation in topography and types of plants and animals in a certain area. To make such a survey:

1. Mark out several strips in different locations.

2. Make a topographic map of the area.

3. Make a topographic profile from the map.

4. Survey the plant life. Record the types and their locations. Record the condition of the plants, such as whether they are growing, dead, or fruiting.

5. Are there any economically valuable plants? If so, what are their values?

6. Is there evidence of erosion? If so, what is the evidence, what could have been its possible cause, and what could help stop it?

7. Make a soil profile from different soil tests.

8. Record any evidence of animal life, such as scat, homes, tracks.

9. Record what changes can be observed from one end of the ecostrip to the other.

Questions

1. What does soil acidity tell us about an area?

2. What is the area of a quadrat? What is the area of a section of a quadrat?

3. Is temperature a determining factor as to numbers and kinds of life in a quadrat? If so, how and to what extent?

4. Are moisture content and light intensity determining factors as to the number and kinds of life in a quadrat?

5. Does vegetation type change with soil type? Why or why not? Is there a correlation between soil types and plant life?

6. Do other factors change as soil types change? If so, which factors?

7. Does wind affect soil, vegetation, and animal types in the quadrat?

8. What kind of a relationship can be established among wind, surface temperature, and moisture?

9. Why are there different amounts of moisture in different parts of the quadrat as well as in different layers of the soil in the quadrat?

10. What kind of correlation is there between moisture and light intensity?

11. What kind of correlation is there between moisture and temperature?

12. Are there any relationships between plants and animals in the quadrat? If so, what are the organisms, and what are the relationships?

 Activity 13: Carbon Cycle

OBJECTIVE:	To show that livings need carbon to live
MATERIALS:	2 healthy plants, 2 large jars, water, soda-lime crystals, shallow dish
LEVEL:	Lower to upper
SETTING:	Classroom
TIME:	15 minutes to set up, 3–4 weeks of observation

LESSON DESIGN

After watering two potted plants that are approximately the same size and the same species, place them in a sunny location. Invert a glass jar over one plant and label it Plant A. Spoon 2 tablespoons of soda-lime crystals in a shallow dish and place it next to the second plant. Cover the second plant and dish with a glass jar and label it Plant B. Keep a record of your observations over a three to four week period.

Questions

1. What was the difference between the two plants after one week, two weeks, three weeks, four weeks, and so on?

2. Why did Plant A continue to grow and prosper, and Plant B not do so well?

3. What was plant B not able to do? Why?

VOCABULARY DEFINITIONS

Adaptation—The ability to adjust to environmental conditions.

Amensalism—Relationship between two organisms in which one partner is harmful to the other but is not affected itself.

Aquarium—A tank filled with water in which aquatic plants and animals are kept.

Biome—A large geographic area named for the general type of climax vegetation that has maintained itself for a long period of time.

Biosphere—That part of the world in which life can exist, such as the surface area of the Earth (atmosphere, waters, lands, and living things inhabiting this area). It is the sum total of all the ecosystems of the Earth.

Carnivore—Any animal that eats only other animals, a predatory organism.

Carrying Capacity—The ability of a habitat to supply food, water, cover, and space for wildlife species. Population is dependent upon rainfall, climatic conditions, and competition.

Circumference—The distance around a circle.

Climax Community—The end of a succession, characterized by a state of dynamic stability.

Commensalism—Relationship between two organisms that is essential for one and neutral for the other.

Community—An association of plants and animals occupying a certain niche, inhabiting a certain environment, and affecting one another.

Consumer—Organisms that get their food energy from plants or other animals.

Decomposer—Organisms that break down and decompose or rot other organisms.

Diameter—A straight line segment that passes through the center of a circle.

Dominant Species—The species that is most characteristic of a habitat and is largely in control of the environmental conditions upon which plant growth depends.

Dystrophic—A lake that supports a limited variety of slow-growing species because of a lack of oxygen and a great amount of decayed humic matter.

Ecosystem—An ecological community with interacting biotic (living) factors and abiotic (non-living) factors.

Epilimnion—Warm, top layer of a lake.

Estuary—An arm of the sea that extends inland to meet the mouth of the river.

Eutrophic—A body of water in which the increase in organic matter has reduced the dissolved oxygen, producing an environment that favors plant life rather than animal life.

Evapotranspiration—A combination of evaporation and transpiration. For example, water transpiring from a tree next to a lake evaporating water.

Food Chain—The energy fixed in photosynthesis that flows through the biotic portion of an ecosystem (e.g., what organisms eat).

Food Pyramid—Demonstrates the general trophic levels in a system and the available energy to be used by life processes. The bottom of the pyramid is composed of the producers; the next level is composed of the herbivores; the level after that is the primary consumers, followed by the secondary consumers.

Food Web—The totality of interconnecting energy or food relationships within a community.

Habitat—The type of environment in which an organism lives.

Herbivore—Any animal that eats only plants.

Hypolimnion—Lowest layer of a lake not heated by the sun.

Interdependent—Organisms or components of an ecosystem that depend upon one another for survival.

Limiting Factors—Factors such as temperature, water, light, and food that limit the growth and development of plant and animal species within a certain area.

Mutualism—Relationship between two organisms in which each is dependent on the other.

Niche—The set of functional relationships of an organism to the environment it occupies.

Ogliotrophic—A deep lake lacking in oxygen with few organisms and a high concentration of cold bottom water.

Omnivore—Any animal that eats both plants and animals.

Parasitism—The characteristic behavior of an organism that grows, feeds, or is sheltered on or in another organism but which contributes nothing to its host.

Pioneer Stage—The first plants to become established in any succession.

Primary Succession—Earliest life of an area, such as bare rock, open water, or sand, not previously occupied by plants.

Producer—Green plants that produce their own food and are the beginning of any food chain, food web, or food pyramid.

Secondary Succession—Succession that begins whenever existing vegetation is replaced by a next stage of plants as the result of activity, such as lumbering or burning.

Symbiosis—The relationship of two or more organisms in a close association that may be, but not necessarily, beneficial to both.

Terrarium—A closed container in which plants are grown.

Thermocline—Transition zone separating surface water or epilimnion from the bottom water or hypolimnion.

Trophic Levels—Pertaining to the nutritive process; the different parts of a food chain or food process. For instance, green plants are the first trophic level, herbivorous animals the second level, and so on.

Vivarium—An enclosed container for raising animals.

BIBLIOGRAPHIC INFORMATION

RESOURCES FOR TEACHERS

Allaby, Michael. *Dictionary of the Environment*. New York: New York University Press, 1991.
    A great reference tool for studying the environment. It includes such topics as legislation, radiation protection, and acid rain.

———. *How the Weather Works*. Pleasantville, NY: Reader's Digest Association, 1995.
    Superb book of weather-related activities for students and teachers. Very workable activities that help children understand the basic principles of weather—air pressure, the water cycle, clouds, fronts, tornadoes, precipitation, and so on.

Caplan, Ruth. *Our Earth, Ourselves*. New York: Bantam Books, 1990.
    Covers nuclear energy, waste, ozone, and global warming.

Dashefsky, H. Steven. *Environmental Science: High School Science Fair Experiments*. New York: TAB Books, 1994.
    Great collection of in-depth experiments on environmental topics, such as acid rain, solar energy, soil ecosystems, and oil spills.

De Vito, Alfred, and Gerald H. Krockover. *Creative Sciencing*. New York: HarperCollins, 1991.
    Activities for teachers and children on biology, chemistry, earth sciences, and environmental sciences, with games, worksheets, and other activities.

Fleisher, Paul. *Ecology A to Z*. New York: Dillon Press, 1994.
    Detailed dictionary-like book with good descriptions of terms related to the environment, such as acid rain, DDT, extinction, niche, old growth forest, precycle, toxins, and zoo plankton.

Franck, Irene, and David Brownstone. *The Green Encyclopedia*, Englewood Cliffs, NJ: Prentice-Hall General Reference and Travel, 1992.
    Information on such environmental problems as endangered species, ecosystems, harmful substances, laws, and sources of information.

Gralla, Preston. *How the Environment Works*. Eneryvalle, CA: Ziff-Davis Press, 1994.
    Great color graphics of different aspects of the environment. How a sewage treatment plants works, for instance.

Gutnik, Martin J. *Experiments That Explore Oil Spills*. Brookfield, CT: Millbrook Press, 1991.
Excellent source of useful, in-depth experiments on oil spills. Some are highly technical.

Hilston, Paul, and Christine Rohn Hilston *A Field Guide to Planet Earth*. Chicago: Chicago Review Press, 1993.
Good coverage of various facets of earth science—maps, soil, minerals, drainage basins, rocks, and so on.

Hunken, Jorie. *Ecology for All Ages: Discovering Nature Through Activities for Children and Adults*. Old Saybrook, CT: Globe Pequot Press, 1994.
Collection of activities covering five common habitats: backyards, water systems, fields, woods, and dry zones. Activities range from simple discoveries, such as collecting plant specimens in your backyard, to more complex investigations on testing water and measuring acidity. Pretty basic. More nature study than scientific investigation.

Ingram, Mrill. *Bottle Biology*. Dubuque, IA: Kendall Hunt, 1993.
Great book on loads of different things you can explore using plastic soft drink bottles—decomposition and worm composting, fermentation chambers, sedimentation bottles, fruit fly breeders, terrariums, and ecocolumns.

Jeffords, Michael R., Audrey S. Hodgins, and Stephen P. Havera. *Wetland Wonders*. Champaign, IL: Illinois Natural History Survey, 1992.
Interesting step-by-step program to follow to study a wetlands environment. Contains background information, 12 activities with a materials list, and a set of slides to complement the study.

Johnson, Rebecca L. *The Greenhouse Effect: Life on a Warmer Planet*. New York: Discovery Books, 1990.
Discusses the Greenhouse Effect, what it is, consequences of it, and possible solutions.

Levin, Michael. *The Environmental Address Book*. New York: Putnam Publishing Group, 1991.
Great listing of environmentally related topics.

Mendell, Muriel. *Simple Weather Experiments with Everyday Materials*. New York: Sterling, 1990.
Basic weather experiments.

Roa, Michael L. *Environmental Science Activities Kit*. West Nyack, NY: Center for Applied Research in Education, 1993.
Prescriptive set of lesson plans for grades 7–12 covering a wide range of topics on environmental education—wildlife, recycling, oil spills, water conservation, air pollution, and so on. Very well organized and well-designed activities. Some reproducible worksheets.

Sarquis, Jerry L., Mickey Sarquis, and John P. Williams. *Teaching Chemistry with Toys: Activities for Grades K–9*. Middletown OH: Learning Triangle Press, 1995.

> Wonderful compilation of activities that use toys as the basis of learning, with cross-curricular activities and assessment options. Topics include detecting humidity in the air, density, surface tension, temperature, and salt solutions, to demonstrate principles of chemistry.

Sumich, James L. *An Introduction to the Biology of Marine Life*. Dubuque, IA: William C. Brown, 1996.

> An in-depth textbook on oceans, with chapters on plants, animals, coral reefs, estuaries, and pollution. Superb diagrams and wonderful color photographs enhance the concepts.

Symons, James M. *Drinking Water: Refreshing Answers to All Your Questions*. College Station, TX: Texas A&M University Press, 1995.

> Informational and fun facts about water—categories include health (do hazardous wastes contaminate drinking water?), aesthetics (why does my drinking water taste or smell funny?), home facts (what is hard water?), conservation (what activity in my home uses the most water?), sources, suppliers, distribution, regulation, and fantastic facts (why are fire hydrants sometimes called fire plugs?).

Wagner, Travis. *In Our Backyard: A Guide to Understanding Pollution and Its Effects*. New York: Van Nostrand Reinhold, 1994.

> Great resource on pollution—water (surface and groundwater), air, household, pesticide, and waste. In-depth analysis and discussion of each.

Williams, Jack. *The Weather Book*. New York: Vintage Books/Random House, 1992.

> An excellent book on weather by a weather editor for *USA Today's* weather page. Full-page color graphics help explain weather concepts—how clouds create lightning and thunder, a cross-section of a squall line, how dew and frost form—in a simplified manner. Each chapter also includes biographical sketches of atmospheric scientists.

Wingate, Philippa, Clive Gifford, and Rebecca Treays. *Usborne Essential Guides: Essential Science*. Tulsa, OK: EDC, 1992.

> This volume contains information on physics, biology, and chemistry. Invaluable book packed with a lot of practical information.

Zimmerman, Michael. *Science, Nonscience, and Nonsense Approaching Environmental Literacy*. Baltimore, MD: Johns Hopkins University Press, 1995.

> A fascinating look at some pressing problems facing the world today—from land use to food safety. Discusses the distinction between science and technology and how to evaluate everyday environmental issues.

RESOURCES FOR STUDENTS

Bleifeld, Maurice. *Botany Projects for Young Scientists*. New York: Franklin Watts, 1992.
Good projects for upper-level students.

Bonnet, Robert L., and G. Daniel Keen. *Environmental Science: Forty-Nine Science Fair Projects*. New York: McGraw Hill, 1990.
Covers the effects of pollution and chemical waste, landfills, recycling, and pests in an organized manner with an overview, a materials list, a procedure, and a follow-up section.

Darling, David. *From Glasses to Gases: The Science of Matter*. New York: Dillon Press, 1992.
Simple book but fun experiments with the three states of matter.

Earthworks Group. *50 Simple Things Kids Can Do to Recycle*. Berkeley, CA: Earthworks Press, Berkeley, CA, 1994.
At home, at school, in your backyard, fun projects that get kids involved in recycling.

Gartrell, Jack, ed. *Earth: The Water Planet*. Washington, DC: National Science Teachers Association, 1992.
Explores the importance of water in our lives with hands-on experiments that help students examine problems as a result of limited water supplies.

Harlow, Rosie, and Gareth Morgan. *175 Amazing Nature Experiments*. New York Random House Books for Young Readers, 1992.
Hands-on activities, games, and experiments.

Hessler, Edward W., and Harriet S. Stubbs. *Acid Rain Science Projects*. St. Paul, MN: Acid Rain Foundation, 1987.
Great projects that teach about the effects of acid rain on plants, fish, buildings, and so forth.

Hickman, Pamela M. *Birdwise: Forty Fun Feats for Finding Out About Our Feathered Friends*. New York: Addison Wesley, 1989.
Activities and projects to learn about birds, how to build bird houses, how to make bird food, and fun facts about birds.

Hilston, Paul, and Christine Hilston. *Field Guide to Planet Earth*. Chicago: Chicago Review, 1993.
Thirty-nine projects that examine rocks and materials from corn fields to backyards and discovering how the Earth was formed. Fun and different.

Levine, Shar, and Allison Grafton. *Projects for a Healthy Planet: Simple Environmental Experiments for Kids*. New York: John Wiley, 1992.
Simplified explanations and activities on pollution, acid rain, recycling, and wind power.

O'Neill, Mary. *Nature in Danger*. Mahwah, NJ: Troll Associates, 1991.
  Brief descriptions and coverage of basic tenants of planet Earth—food webs and chains, cycles in nature, and how habitats are threatened as people create changes.

Patent, Dorothy Hinshaw. *Children Save the Rainforest*. Dutton, NY: Cobblehill Books, 1996.
  Great photographs and good coverage of a special rainforest in Costa Rica: what a rain forest is, what lives in one, and why they are important.

Porritt, Jonathan. *Save the Earth*. Atlanta, GA: Turner, 1991.
  Great pictures and good coverage of the Earth's ecosystems—mountains, grasslands, oceans, rain forests, and lakes, as well as an overview of forces affecting these fragile ecosystems. Leading scientists and environmental experts share their opinions/concerns about overpopulation, disappearing rainforests, global warming, air pollution, and many other problems affecting the Earth.

Pringle, Laurence. *Global Warming: Assessing the Greenhouse Threat*. New York: Little, Brown, 1990.
  Easy-to-understand book on global warming.

———. *Vanishing Ozone: Protecting Earth from Ultraviolet Radiation*. New York: Morrow Junior Books, 1995.
  Straightforward account of the Earth's ozone and what needs to be done to protect it.

Prochnow, Dave, and Kathy Prochnow. *HOW? More Experiments for the Young Scientist*. Blue Ridge Summit, PA: TAB Books, 1993.
  Both this book and the next one include experiments on engineering, astronomy, chemistry, meteorology, biology, and physics. Organized with a materials list, procedure, results, and further studies. Simple and straightforward.

———. *WHY? Experiments for the Young Scientist*. Blue Ridge Summit, PA: TAB Books, 1993.
  Similar content and layout as their book *HOW?*.

Quayle, Louise. *Weather*. New York: Crescent Books, 1990.
  Super pictures. Covers storms (wind, lightning, monsoons, hurricanes); weather forecasting; light (auroras, rainbows, halos); weather cycles (Greenhouse Effect, droughts, ozone); and concerns for the future.

The Student Environmental Action Coalition. *The Student Environmental Action Guide*. Berkeley, CA: Earth Works Press, 1991.
  Great resource lists.

Van Cleave, Janice. *Biology for Every Kid*. New York: John Wiley, 1990.

———. *Chemistry for Every Kid*. New York: John Wiley, 1989.
  Easy to use; descriptive experiments that work.

————. *Earth Science for Every Kid*. New York: John Wiley, 1991.

————. *Earthquakes: Mind-Boggling Experiments You Can Turn into Science Fair Projects*. New York: John Wiley, 1993.

————. *Ecology for Every Kid*. New York: John Wiley, 1996.

————. *Oceans for Every Kid*. New York: John Wiley, 1996.

Vecchione, Glen. *100 Amazing Make-It-Yourself Science Fair Projects*. New York: Sterling, 1994.
> Great, simple, easy-to-do-and-follow experiments. Covers electricity, clouds, ecology, and chemistry.

Vorderman, Carol. *How Math Works*. Pleasantville, NY: Readers Digest, 1996.
> Great book on how to explain mathematical concepts in a straightforward way. Divided into sections on algebra, statistics, measurement, proportions, and shapes.

Wells, Susan. *Illustrated World of Oceans*. New York: Simon & Schuster Books for Young Readers/Simon & Schuster Children's Press, 1993.
> Designed for grades 3–8, this book covers geography, creation and topography of oceans, the water cycle, currents, waves, and plant and animal life. Along with the text, it includes relevant facts, maps, and illustrations.

White, Jack R. *The Hidden World of Forces*. New York: G. P. Putnam's Sons, 1987.
> Great experiments on matter, air pressure, electromagnetism, and surface tension.

Wong, Ovid K. *Hands-On Ecology*. Chicago: Childrens Press, 1991.
> Fun group of simple activities dealing with clean air, water, land and recycling and energy conservation. Practical—uses a minimum of materials—basic concepts.

Wood, Robert W. *Science for Kids. 39 Easy Chemistry Experiments*. Blue Ridge Summit, PA: TAB Books, 1991.

————. *Science for Kids: 39 Easy Plant Biology Experiments*. Blue Ridge Summit, PA: TAB Books, 1991.
> Simplified experiments without much detail or depth.

Woodburn, Judith. *The Toxic Waste Time Bomb*. Milwaukee, WI: Gareth Stevens, 1992.
> Lower level, nice picture book—simple format on toxic waste. Describes toxic wastes, how they get into the water and soil, examples of toxic waste accidents/disasters, and how they are cleaned up.

GOVERNMENT AGENCIES AND
PRIVATE ORGANIZATIONS

Acid Precipitation Awareness, 1037 Bidwell St. East, St. Paul, MN 55118

Acid Rain Foundation, 1630 Blackhawk Hill Rd., St. Paul, MN 55122

Acid Rain Information Clearinghouse, 33 S. Washington St., Rochester, NY 14608

Air Quality Division, Michigan Dept. Natural Resources, Box 30028, Lansing, MI 48909

Alliance for Environmental Education, 10751 Ambassador Dr., Manassas, VA 22110

American Forest Institute, 1619 Massachusetts Ave. N.W., Washington, DC 20036

Center for Children's Environmental Literature SERC, Box 28, Edgewater, MD 21037

Center for Environmental Education, 624 9th St. N.W., Washington, DC 20001

Conservation Foundation, 1250 24th St. N.W., Washington, DC 20037

Conservation International, 1015 18th St. N.W., Suite 1002, Washington, DC 20036

Defenders of Wildlife, 1244 19th St. N.W., Washington, DC 20036

Earth Force, 1501 Wilson Blvd., 12th Floor, Arlington, VA 22209

Environmental Action Coalition, 235 E. 49th St., New York, NY 10017

Environmental Defense Fund, 1616 P St. N.W., Suite 150, Washington, DC 20036

Environmental Protection Agency, 401 M St. S.W., Washington, DC 20460

Friends of the Earth, 218 D St. S.E., Washington, DC 20003

Global Tomorrow Coalition, 1325 G St. S.W., Suite 915, Washington, DC 20005

Greenpeace, 1436 U St. N.W., Washington, DC 20009

Lawrence Hall of Science Discovery Corner, University of California, Berkeley, CA 94720

Minnesota Sea Grant Education Project, 159 Pillsbury Dr. S.E., Minneapolis, MN 55455

National Audubon Society, 950 Third Ave., New York, NY 10022

National Parks & Conservation Association, 1015 31st St. N.W., Washington, DC 20007

National Wildlife Federation, 1400 16th St. N.W., Washington, DC 20036

Natural Resources Defense Council, 40 W. 20th St., New York, NY 10011

Nature Conservancy, 1800 North Kent St., Arlington, VA 22209

New York Sea Grant Institute, 37 Elk St., New York, NY 12246

Project WILD, P.O. Box 18060, Dept. B, Boulder, CO 80308

Rainforest Action Network, 301 Broadway, Suite A, San Francisco, CA 94133

Rainforest Alliance, 270 Lafayette St., Suite 512, New York, NY 10012

Rainforest Foundation, Inc., 1776 Broadway, 14th Floor, New York, NY 10019

Schoolyard Ecology for Elementary School Teachers, Institute of Ecosystem Studies, P.O. Box R, Millbrook, NY 12545

Sierra Club, 730 Polk St., San Francisco, CA 94109

Soil Conservation Service, P.O. Box 2890, Washington, DC 20013

U.S. Department of Agriculture, Forest Service, P.O. Box 2417, Washington, DC 20013

U. S. Department of Agriculture, Natural Resources & Environment Division, 14th Street and Independence Ave. S.W., Washington, DC 20250

U.S. Department of the Interior, National Park Service, Interior Building, P.O. Box 37127, Washington, DC 20013

Wilderness Society, 900 17th St. N.W., Washington, DC 20006

World Resources Institute, 1709 New York Ave. N.W., Washington, DC 20006

World Wildlife Fund, 1250 24th St. N.W., Washington, DC 20037

Worldwatch Institute, 1776 Massachusetts Ave N.W., Washington, DC 20036

Zero Population Growth, Inc., 1400 10th St. N.W., Suite 320, Washington, DC 20036

PERIODICALS OF INTEREST

American Biology Teacher—The National Association of Biology Teachers, 1420 North St., Washington, DC 20036

Audubon—The Audubon Society, 1130 Fifth Ave., New York, NY, 10023

Nature Study Magazine—Nature Study Society, 5881 Cold Brook Rd., Homer, NY, 13077

Ranger Rick—National Wildlife Federation, 1412 16th St. N.W., Washington, DC 20036

Science and Children—National Science Teacher's Association, 1201 16th St. N.W., Washington, DC, 20036

The Science Teacher—National Science Teacher's Association, 1201 16th St. N.W., Washington, DC, 20036

SCIENTIFIC SUPPLY COMPANIES

Carolina Biological Supply Company
2700 York Rd.
Burlington, NC 27215

CENCO
3300 Cenco Pkwy.
Franklin Park, IL 60131

Edmund Scientific Company
101 East Gloucester Pike
Barrington, NJ 08007

Fisher Scientific Company
4901 W. LeMoyne St.
Chicago, IL 60651

Frey Scientific Company
905 Hickory Ln.
Mansfield, OH 44905

Hubbard Scientific Company
P.O. Box 104
Northbrook, IL 60065

Lab-Aids, Inc.
249 Trade Zone Dr.
Ronkonkoma, NY 11779

Nasco
901 Janesville Ave.
Fort Atkinson, WI 53538

Sargent-Welch Scientific Company
7300 North Linder Ave.
P.O. Box 1026
Skokie, IL 60077

Schoolmasters Science
745 State Circle
Box 1941
Ann Arbor, MI 48106

Science Kit & Boreal Laboratories
777 E. Park Dr.
Tonawanda, NY 14150-6782

Ward's Natural Science
    Establishment, Inc.
5100 West Henrietta Rd.
P.O. Box 92912
Rochester, NY 14692-9012

La Motte Chemical Products
P.O. Box 329
Chestertown, MD 21620

INDEX

with **Teacher Ideas Press**

LEARNING FROM THE LAND
Teaching Ecology Through Stories and Activities
Brian "Fox" Ellis

Breathe life into the dry bones of geologic history! An integrative approach of hands-on science and creative writing lesson plans helps students explore ideas and hone a deeper understanding of ecological concepts. Step-by-step lesson plans give you the confidence and skills to take your classes outdoors. **All levels.**
xxviii, 145p. 8½x11 paper ISBN 1-56308-563-1

EXPLORATIONS IN BACKYARD BIOLOGY
Drawing on Nature in the Classroom, Grades 4–6
R. Gary Raham

Discover life science adventures in your own backyard (or school yard)! Exciting classroom and field activities give students the opportunity for hands-on exploration. Using drawing and writing skills, they record their experiences in a Naturalist's Notebook, which encourages further discoveries. **Grades 4–6.**
xix, 204p. 8½x11 paper ISBN 1-56308-254-3

INTERMEDIATE SCIENCE THROUGH CHILDREN'S LITERATURE
Over Land and Sea
Carol M. Butzow and John W. Butzow

These hands-on and discovery activities use scientific concepts and span all disciplines of the middle school curriculum. Focusing on earth and environmental science themes, topics such as oceans, rivers, mountains, air, weather, deserts, fossils, and plant and environmental quality are covered. **Grades 4–7.**
xxv, 193p. 8½x11 paper ISBN 0-87287-946-1

TEACHER'S WEATHER SOURCEBOOK
Information, Ideas, and Activities
Tom Konvicka

Help students understand why so much depends on the weather with this book of information on natural phenomena such as tornadoes, hurricanes, heat waves, floods, and droughts. Also useful for planning classes on hot topics such as global warming and air pollution. **Grades 4–8.**
xvi, 321p. 8½x11 paper ISBN 1-56308-488-0

THE INVENTIVE MIND IN SCIENCE
Creative Thinking Activities
Christine Ebert and Edward S. Ebert II

More than 50 mind-stretching activities integrate creativity and invention into the science curriculum. Help your students use their imaginations and problem-solving skills as they explore concepts articulated with word games, visual puzzles, and other reproducible projects. **Grades 4–8.**
xii, 241p. 8½x11 paper ISBN 1-56308-387-6

For a FREE catalog or to place an order, please contact:

Teacher Ideas Press
Dept. B9917 · P.O. Box 6633 · Englewood, CO 80155-6633
1-800-237-6124, ext. 1 · Fax: 303-220-8843 · E-mail: lu-books@lu.com

Check out the TIP Web site!
www.lu.com/tip